William Faulkner

and the

Rites of Passage

William Faulkner

and the

Rites of Passage

Christopher A. Lalonde

MERCER UNIVERSITY PRESS
MACON, GEORGIA 31210-3960

IBSN 0-86554-482-4

William Faulkner and the Rites of Passage
by Christopher A. LaLonde

Copyright © 1996
Mercer University Press, Macon GA 31210-3960
Printed in the United States of America

The paper used in this publication meets the minimum requirements
of American National Standard for Information Sciences—
Permanence of Paper for Printed Library Materials,
ANSI Z39.48–1984.

Library of Congress Cataloging-in-Publication Data

LaLonde, Christopher A.
    William Faulkner and the Rites of Passage / by Christopher A.
LaLonde.
        p. x + 178 6x9"
    Includes bibliographical references and index.
    ISBN 0-86554-482-4 (alk. paper)
    1. Faulkner, William, 1897–1962—Criticism and interpretation.
2. Anthropology and literature—Southern States—History—20th Century.
3. Identity (Psychology) in literature.   4. Rites and ceremonies in literature.   5. Narration (Rhetoric) 6. Youth in literature. 7. Aging in literature.   8. Bildungsroman.   I. Title.
PS3511.A86Z8737   1996
813'.52—dc20   95-38087
                                                                          CIP

Front cover photograph, *The Ruins of Windsor*, copyright © 1996
by Eyd Charles Kazery. Reproduced by arrangement
with Eyd Charles Kazery.

Contents

Publication acknowledgements

An earlier version of Chapter 1 appeared as " 'New Orleans' and an Aesthetics of Indeterminacy," *Faulkner Journal* 8/2 (Fall 1994): 13-29.

An earlier version of portions of Chapter 2 appeared as "Story, Myth, Rite of Passage, and *Mosquitoes*," *Faulkner Journal* 3/1 (Fall 1989): 26-38.

Earlier versions of portions of Chapter 4 appeared as "A Trap Most Magnificently Sprung: the Last Chapter of *light in August*" in *Faulkner and the Craft of Fiction*, edited by Doreen Fowler and Ann Abadie (Jackson: University of Mississippi Press, 1989): 92-104; and "Illuminating *Light in August*" in *Analecta Husserliana* 38, edited by A-T Tymieniecka, 149-61. Copyright © 1992 Kluwer Academic Publishers. Printed in the Netherlands.

I am grateful to the editors for their support of my work and their permission to reprint this material.

Author acknowledgements

I have incurred many debts, both professional and personal. I acknowledge with pleasure and humility those individuals whose help and support mean more than the following sentences can properly convey. Robert Daly, Robert Edwards, Bruce Jackson, Marcus Klein, and Neil Schmitz were there at the beginning. Neil Schmitz, in particular, was an unflagging source of reason, reasonable questions, and good cheer. Jack Matthews read an early version of the manuscript and offered valuable and valued commentary. I have benefitted from conversations with and correspondence from Donald Kartiganer, Noel Polk, and John Carlos Rowe, among other scholars, as I struggled to make sense of Faulkner and his work. I want to give special thanks to Walter A. Davis, who read the entire manuscript in two decidedly different drafts and helped keep me focused on the matters at hand. Still, any shortcomings in argument are mine and mine alone.

Steve Ferebee, Linda Flowers, and Michael Jackson were sources of strength and support. So too were Tim and Val Garry, particularly in the final stages of the work. Leverett Smith and his family could not have been kinder and more generous over the years. The same and more must be said for Jeff and Deb Schwiebert and their children Aaron and Allison: summer after summer they opened their home to me and thus gave me the freedom to work. Cornell College generously supported that work with office space and access to computer hardware and software. Stephen Lacey's generosity was and is boundless. Mentor and friend, he read and commented on much of the manuscript; moreover, he listened and responded as I time and again sat in his living room attempting to articulate my argument. The gifts of his eye and ear are surpassed only by his unfailing hospitality and encouragement.

Finally, especially given the focus on identity, I would be remiss if I failed to acknowledge the fundamental role played by my family in my struggles over identity. They know the particulars; it is enough here to say that their presence, and absence, shaped and shapes my life. This book is dedicated to them, with love.

Source abbreviations

The abbreviations of William Faulkner's works commonly cited in the text refer to the following editions:

AA   *Absalom, Absalom!*. New York: Vintage Books, 1936.

AILD   *As I Lay Dying*. The Corrected Text. New York: Vintage Books, 1987.

"Elmer" MQ.   "Elmer" edited by James B. Meriwether. *Mississippi Quarterly* 36 (Summer 1983): 342-447.

Flags   *Flags in the Dust*. New York: Vintage Books, 1974.

GDM   *Go Down, Moses*. New York: Vintage Books, 1973.

LIA   *Light in August*. The Corrected Text. New York: Vintage International Edition, 1990.

MOS   *Mosquitoes*. New York: Liverlight, 1927.

NO   *New Orleans Sketches*. Edited by Carvel Collins. New Brunswick NJ: Rutgers University Press, 1958.

REQ   *Requiem for a Nun*. New York: Vintage Books, 1975.

SF   *The Sound and the Fury*. The Corrected Text. New York: Vintage Books, 1987.

To Theodore and Barbara, father and mother,
and Cheryl, Stephen, and Jonathan, sister and brothers,
for lessons in love and life;
and to brother Michael, for lessons in love and loss

Introduction

Turning to

What follows is a study of both the relationship between rites of passage and identity in selected early and high modern works by William Faulkner and a consideration of the reader in and of Faulkner's texts. My examination of the early fiction traces the evolution of rites of passage as narrative strategy and as a thematic concern in Faulkner's work from the beginning of his career as a fiction writer through the time he finished *Light in August* (1932), put down his pen, and turned his attention to the various pursuits that prohibited the completion of a new novel for nearly three years. The examination of readers in *Flags in the Dust* (completed 1927; published 1973) and *Requiem for a Nun* (1951) comprise part of a speculation upon Faulkner's consideration of his audience and the intersection between rites and literature. My argument attempts to orchestrate Faulkner's work, his region, prevailing currents in Faulkner studies and contemporary anthropological thought and literary theory into, if not a symphony, something other than cacophony.

I write certain that there are those already fearful that I have little or nothing to offer save old wine. Perhaps the most felicitous way to alleviate those fears is to move directly to the body of this study and an argument built upon the careful interrogation of Faulkner's texts in light of an understanding of modern Southern culture, rites of passage theory, and the philosophical dimensions of the literary text. I wish to tarry, however, anxious to clear the field of *Go Down, Moses* (1942), a text that I choose not to examine in detail, and to articulate briefly the thinking about identity and culture I bring to bear.[1]

---

[1]The notion of articulation is central to this study. I am applying the term in both its primary senses: the act or process of speaking and the act of *jointing* together. Such is, for instance, the dual meaning of the word in British Cultural Studies (See George Lipsitz, "Listening to Learn and Learning to Listen: Popular Culture, Cultural Theory, and American Studies," *American Quarterly* 42/4 [December 1990]: 624 n19). Faulkner's novels are very much spoken texts, as critics have noted, and the concept of jointing is applicable to the tripartite structure of the rite of passage: its jointing liminal phase brings together the preliminal and the postliminal, the individual and the community. We might note here that the juxtaposition so prevalent in Faulkner's texts, specifically the contrapuntal qualities we will examine in detail in "New Orleans" and *Light in August*, is a telling feature of orality; see Walter J. Ong, *Interfaces of the Word: Studies in the Evolution of Consciousness and Culture* (Ithaca NY: Cornell University Press, 1977). On

My decision not to discuss *Go Down, Moses* at length is bound up in John T. Matthews's provocative and, I think, cogent reading of that text. It strikes me as pointless to recapitulate in toto either Matthews's argument or its grounding in Derridian deconstruction; more to the point, such a recapitulation is unnecessary. For our purposes it is enough to highlight what is most valuable in Matthews's argument, particularly one of the conclusions drawn, so that we may then most fruitfully turn to what are vital scenes in *Go Down, Moses*.

Matthews deftly discloses the importance of what he terms the ritual of mourning in *Go Down, Moses* as that text confronts the crises born of loss. In Matthews's reading of *Go Down, Moses* ritual is a language, and the "forms of articulation in *Go Down, Moses*—the rituals of the hunt, the initiation, marriage, the rehearsal of local legend—correspond to similar systems of discourse in the earlier novels."[2] The first three stories of the text function as a parodic prelude that "contaminates the rituals of the wilderness so as to demystify their content and emphasize their structure as statements."[3] This demystification prepares the reader for the statement of the "wilderness" trilogy—"The Old People," "The Bear," and "Delta Autumn"—which follows.[4] With the final story, "Go Down, Moses," the text "closes amid a sense that the agony of loss throughout the novel has finally been mastered by its ritualistic expression. All that remains is a repercussive sequence of gestures—gestures that have already ossified and which allow the reader to *turn away* as Gavin Stevens does."[5]

Gavin Stevens and the Editor most assuredly do turn away at the close of the story. Having successfully conspired to bring the body of Samuel Worsham Beauchamp back to Yoknapatawpha County and his grandmother Mollie Worsham Beauchamp, Stevens and the Editor follow

---

the spoken nature of Faulkner's texts see Warwick Wadlington, *Reading Faulknerian Tragedy* (Ithaca NY: Cornell University Press, 1987); on voice and sound in Faulkner see, for instance, Stephen M. Ross, "Rev. Shegog's Powerful Voice," *The Faulkner Journal* 1/1 (Fall 1985): 8-16; Wadlington, *Reading Faulknerian Tragedy*; and Karl F. Zender, "Faulkner and the Power of Sound," *PMLA* 99 (January 1984): 89-108.

   [2]John T. Matthews, *The Play of Faulkner's Language* (Ithaca NY: Cornell University Press, 1982) 215-16.

   [3]Ibid., 218-19.

   [4]Arthur F. Kinney, "Faulkner and the Possibilities of Heroism," *The Southern Review* 6 (Autumn 1970): 1110.

   [5]Matthews, *The Play of Faulkner's Language*, 269-70 (emphasis added).

the hired hearse up to and away from the train station, trail it through the center of town "in formal component complement to the Negro murderer's catafalque," and, after having "flashed past the metal sign which said Jefferson. Corporate Limit," first coast and then brake to a halt prior to clumsily turning their car back toward town while the hearse bearing the body and the car carrying Mollie Worsham Beauchamp and Miss Worsham pull "rapidly away . . . as though in flight" (*GDM*, 382-83). What Stevens and the Editor turn away from at the close of "Go Down, Moses" is ritual in general and rites of passage in particular. They participate in neither the funeral rite nor the rite of interment that will follow. Nor, for that matter, does Faulkner; he *inscribes* neither rite. As a consequence, the reader is left not only with Stevens's and the Editor's gestures and act of turning away: as *Go Down, Moses* closes we are left with the realization that Faulkner has turned away from ritual as well.

Faulkner's decision to turn away from inscribing rites of passage in "Go Down, Moses" is startling given the importance of rites of passage in much of his fiction, especially that written prior to 1933. *Go Down, Moses* concludes with the promise of funeral and interment rites vanishing with the rapidly receding hearse and car, a vanishing that undermines the important position held by rites in the wilderness trilogy and constitutes nothing short of a turning away from issues of identity and community as they had been articulated in Faulkner's earlier fiction; by comparison, the various rites of passage in *Mosquitoes* (1927), *As I Lay Dying* (1930), and *Light in August* (1932) enabled Faulkner to form his work successfully and hence enabled him to *turn to* issues of identity, community, change, and the nature of the fictional text.

Walter A. Davis, in *The Act of Interpretation*, develops a critique of the "radically organismic" definition of form held by some literary critics and theorists by first asking us to reconceive form in the traditional sense as "that principle of unity which determines the nature of a concrete whole."[6] For Davis the form of a literary work is realized when we "apprehend the purposive principle immanent in the structure of a work which determines the mutual interfunctioning of its component parts."[7] Form, then, is bound up in unity, and unity is in turn bound up in

---

[6]Walter A. Davis, *The Act of Interpretation: A Critique of Literary Reason* (Chicago: University of Chicago Press, 1978) 4, 1.

[7]Ibid, 2.

purpose. Identity in and of Faulkner's texts is also bound up in unity and purpose, and we shall see that my understanding of identity, conceived in the philosophical tradition of unity amid diversity rather than permanence amid change, as the purposive principle in and of the texts examined evolves from an interpretation that locates the rites of passage, a culture's device to confer identity as subjectivity for a purpose, as the texts' principle of unity.

Clifford Geertz offers a useful definition: culture is the "fabric of meaning in terms of which human beings interpret their experiences and guide their actions."[8] However, any definition of culture is compromised by what George E. Marcus and Michael M. J. Fischer have called the crisis of representation in the human sciences in general and anthropology in particular, for that crisis has revealed how problematic it is to get a definitive fix on culture. Culture is, as Stephen A. Tyler notes, a nonentity.[9] It is, in the words of James Clifford, "contested, temporal, and emergent."[10] From the perspective of postmodern anthropology and ethnography, culture "is always relational, an inscription of communicative processes that exist, historically, *between subjects* in relations of power."[11] Roy Wagner notes that the emergent and relational qualities of culture are what enable the field-worker to invent his or her culture through the act of observing another:

> before this [fieldwork, the field-worker] had no culture, as we might
> say, since the culture in which one grows up is never really "visible"—
> it is taken for granted, and its assumptions are felt to be self-evident. It
> is only through "invention" of this kind that the abstract significance of

---

[8]Clifford Geertz, *The Interpretation of Cultures* (New York: Basic Books, 1973) 145.

[9]Stephen A. Tyler, "Post-Modern Ethnography: From Document of the Occult to Occult Document," in *Writing Culture: The Poetics and Politics of Ethnography*, ed. Clifford and Marcus, 130.

[10]James Clifford, "Introduction: Partial Truths," in *Writing Culture*, 19.

[11]Ibid., 15. See also, Kevin Dwyer, *Moroccan Dialogues* (Baltimore: Johns Hopkins University Press, 1982) and "The Dialogic of Anthropology," *Dialectical Anthropology* 2 (1977): 143-51, and Dennis Tedlock, *The Spoken Word and the Work of Interpretation* (Philadelphia: University of Pennsylvania Press, 1983) and "The Analogical Tradition and the Emergence of Dialogical Anthropology," *Journal of Anthropological Research* 35 (1979): 387-400.

culture . . . Can be grasped and only through the experienced contrast that his [or her] own culture becomes "visible."[12]

We shall see that the culture of Yoknapatawpha that emerges in *As I Lay Dying* and *Light in August* is profoundly contested and that through the experience of reading the invention of culture that is Faulkner's inscription of Yoknapatawpha, we, like field-workers, are better able to see our own modern and postmodern culture and the problematic of identity.

In each of the novels examined, rites of passage and identity are bound together, as they are in life, for rites of passage are fundamental social constructs with which a culture attempts to confer identity. They are essential for the transformation of a physical, corporeal being into a person. Person, therefore, should be understood as a technical term that focuses on a human being's "roles in social relationships" rather than as a word that defines a human being by either its physical nature or some concept of self that transcends the corporeal in a union of body and spirit.[13] Borrowing a term from art, Michael Carrithers writes of person as personae, the "social and legal . . . conception of the individual in respect to society as a whole," and his phrasing makes it clear that the individual-qua-person is a construction born of and built by culture.[14] It is through the rites of passage, especially, that identity is constructed and that an individual becomes a person.

Arnold van Gennep, the pioneering rite of passage theorist, noted that

> transitions from group to group and from one social situation to the next are looked on as implicit to the very fact of existence, so that a man's life comes to be made up of a succession of stages with similar ends and beginnings: birth, social puberty, marriage, fatherhood, advancement to a higher class, occupational specialization, and death. For every one of these events there are ceremonies whose essential purpose is to

---

[12]Roy Wagner, *The Invention of Culture*, revised and expanded edition (Chicago: University of Chicago Press, 1981) 4.

[13]J. S. Lafontaine, "Person and Individual: Some Anthropological Reflections," in *The Category of the Person: Anthropology, Philosophy, History*, ed. Carrithers, 125.

[14]Michael Carrithers, ed., *The Category of the Person: Anthropology, Philosophy, History* (Cambridge: Cambridge University Press, 1985) 235.

enable the individual to pass from one defined position to another that is equally well defined.[15]

As a result of his fieldwork and research of similar recorded phenomena within many different communities of peoples, van Gennep was able to direct our attention to the primacy and repetition of rite of passage ceremonies and to articulate the rigid structure governing rites of passage. The paradigm of the rite of passage given to us by van Gennep and later substantiated by Victor Turner and others hinges upon the categories of preliminal, liminal, and postliminal.

In principle a rite of passage has three parts that correspond, variously, to the preliminal, the liminal, and the postliminal: rites of separation, rites of transition, and rites of incorporation. During the rites of separation, or preliminal rites, an individual or group is separated from the community. This separation is often physical and always psychological. During the rites of transition, or liminal rites, the individual or group loses its status as a part of the community. Participants in the rite are caught between states, what Turner labeled betwixt and between, and are not yet truly neophytes in the eyes of the community. The Okipa ceremony of the Mandan tribe of North America includes a graphic representation of the liminality of the participants in a rite of passage: initiates hang suspended in the air by thongs of leather drawn through their chest or shoulder muscles. The liminal quality of the rite of passage joins with the symbolic to separate each participant from the community.[16] During the rites of incorporation, or postliminal rites, the individual or group of individuals reenters the community. This signals the successful end of the rite of passage and the emergence of the individual or group into their new state and identity.

Lloyd Warner felt that rites of passage signalled

the movement of a man through his lifetime, from a fixed placental placement within his mother's womb to his death and final containment in his grave as a dead organism—punctuated by a number of critical moments of transition which all societies ritualize and publicly mark

---

[15]Arnold van Gennep, *The Rites of Passage*, trans. Monika Vizedom and Gabrielle Caffe (Chicago: University of Chicago Press, 1960) 3.

[16]See George Catlin, *O-Kee-pa* Centennial Edition, ed. John C. Ewers (New Haven: Yale University Press, 1967), esp. 62-66, and Alfred W. Bowers, *Mandan Social and Ceremonial Organization* (Chicago: University of Chicago Press, 1950), esp. 134-35.

with suitable observances to impress the significance of the individual and the group on living members of the community. These are the important times of birth, puberty, marriage, and death.[17]

Van Gennep and, later, Turner felt that rites of passage were not confined to Warner's "passage moments." Van Gennep stated that rites of passage are linked to "every change of place, state, social position, and age." Turner has written that "such rites [of passage] indicate and constitute transitions between states. By states I mean here a 'relatively fixed or stable position.'"[18] Both van Gennep and Turner make clear that those changes cannot occur without the indeterminacy of the transitional stage of the rite.

Indeterminacy, the crucial element of the rite of passage, is an "as-if" construction. Turner stresses that a rite's "indeterminacy is, so to speak, in the subjunctive mood, since it is that which is not yet settled, concluded, and known. It is all that may be, might be, could be, perhaps even should be."[19] The indeterminacy of the liminal phase constitutes the abyss of all that might be, the referential field against which the constructs of the rite as a whole and community, which may be defined as "declarations of form against indeterminacy," are played and examined even as those constructs are used in an attempt to insure that the individual is transformed into a person and that group and cultural identity are maintained.[20] In the rite, order is transformed by transgression; the destruction of boundaries, followed by a reconstruction of a new order *in light of* indeterminacy, is at the rite's heart. In Turner's words, "Ritual's liminal phase, then, approximates to the 'subjunctive' mood of socio-cultural action. It is, quintessentially, a time and place lodged between all times and spaces defined and governed in any specific biocultural ecosystem . . . by the rules of law, politics, and religion and by economic necessity. . . . For in liminality what is mundanely bound

---

[17]W. Lloyd Warner, *The Living and the Dead* (New Haven: Yale University Press, 1959) 313.

[18]Victor Turner, *The Forest of Symbols* (Ithaca NY: Cornell University Press, 1967) 93.

[19]Victor Turner, "Social Dramas and Stories About Them," in *On Narrative*, ed. W. J. T. Mitchell, 153.

[20]Sally Falk Moore and Barbara Myerhoff, eds., *Secular Ritual* (Leyden: Van Gorcum, 1977) 17.

in sociostructural form may be unbound and rebound."[21] The inter-
dependency between determinacy and indeterminacy, between structure
and anti-structure, which is played out through the rite of passage, then,
enables transformation to occur.

Wagner, Turner, Geertz, Knut Hanneborg, Rene Girard, and others
point out that the indeterminacy essential to the rites of passage prohibits
certain transmission of the traditional position(s) held by a culture.
Therefore, rites of passage serve to conserve and preserve communities
through their repetition, while at the same time allowing for the possibility of change through potential variation. Hanneborg, for instance,
writes that "the conservative stabilizing element [of the] cultural forms
constantly comes into conflict with the creative tendency to break the
established pattern and create new forms" that question, undercut, and
even do away with tradition's dominance.[22] Girard concludes that while
the rites seem to "assure the dominance of generations long gone over
generations yet to come . . . the mechanisms set in motion by the rite of
passage can never be fully anticipated"; as a result, the conclusion of the
rite, whether it be marked by movement through the postliminal or
recognition of fracture at the liminal or "redressive stage," may well undo
and redefine the traditional.[23]

One need only look to Native American cultures and literature for
evidence of the vitality inherent in ritual and rites of passage. In Leslie
Marmon Silko's *Ceremony* (1977), for instance, Betonie tells Tayo that
"there are balances and harmonies always shifting, always necessary to
maintain" and "the ceremonies have always been changing" in an effort
to maintain balance and harmony.[24] Betonie has made changes in the
rituals in order to keep the ceremonies vital, for he knows that "things
which don't shift and grow are dead things."[25] He knows, too, that if the
people "cling to the ceremonies the way they were," then witchery "will
triumph, and the people will be no more."[26] Betonie articulates a
commonplace of Native American cultures: rituals are "creative acts of

---

[21]Turner, "Social Dramas," 161.

[22]Knut Hanneborg, *Anthropological Circles: Observations on the Nature of views of
Man in Science, Philosophy and Religion* (New York: Humanities Press, 1962) 12-13.

[23]Rene Girard, *Violence and the Sacred* (Baltimore: Johns Hopkins University Press,
1972) 285. And Turner, "Social Dramas," 145.

[24]Leslie Marmon Silko, *Ceremony* (New York: Penguin, 1977) 130; 126.

[25]Silko, *Ceremony*, 126.

[26]Ibid.

the highest order" that help situate the participants in and with the world.[27]

In *Mosquitoes*, however, Faulkner has Dawson Fairchild inform us that modern society has ceased to reflect upon convention and consequently destroyed both ritual and life:

> "It's young people who put life into ritual by making conventions a living part of life: only old people destroy life by making it a ritual. And I wanted to get all I could out of college. The boy that belongs to a secret pirates' gang and who dreams of defending an abstraction with his blood, hasn't quite died out before twenty-one, you know. But I didn't have any money" (*MOS*, 117).[28]

Ideally, traditional cultural conventions come to life in the liminality of the rite, for it is there that they are subject to examination and redefinition. It is there as well that conflicts between opposing systems of order or between the individual and the community are played out. Fairchild, who will help guide us through Faulkner's second novel, tacitly suggests that what Wagner terms *invention* is lacking in an age where the whole of existence is reduced to fetishes. While it would be erroneous to identify Faulkner with Fairchild, for Fairchild eventually comes to lose faith in the efficacy of words, both share an awareness of and concern over what has become of ritual. Faulkner's inscription of the rites of passage as narrative strategy and thematic concern can be read as an attempt to supply the sort of reflection upon and interrogation of ritual that modern culture appears unwilling or unable to participate in.

Faulkner's concern with rites of passage in all likelihood stemmed from his awareness of the crucial role they and other forms of ritual and ritualized behavior played in his life. For instance, numerous biographical studies point out the importance of hunting to William Faulkner, both in his youth and his adulthood, and the biographical evidence, along with the evidence in his fictional texts, indicates an exposure to and an

---

[27]Sam Gill, "The Trees Stood Deep Rooted," in *I Become Part of It*, ed D. M. Dooling and Paul Jordan-Smith, 30.

[28]Fairchild's attempt at a rite of passage is fundamentally tainted by currency. We shall see in our examination of *Mosquitoes* how narrative can be tainted by a desire for money; our examination of *As I Lay Dying* will disclose how currency leads to a perversion of the rite of interment.

awareness and appreciation of the rites of the hunt. Biographical evidence also seems to me to suggest that Faulkner was aware of the rites of courtship and the ritualized behavior of the story-telling event, as well as of the importance of honor both within the family and the larger community. That his life was also shaped by death and rites of interment is equally clear.[29]

Furthermore, Faulkner's understanding of both the vitality of ritual and the need to reflect upon ritual and convention is evident in a hunting story told by Dr. Felix Linder. According to Linder, one of the rituals of the hunt entailed cutting off the shirttail of a hunter who shot at and missed a deer. Faulkner had sent Linder out to hunt squirrels because the group was running short of provisions. In the process of getting "a whole lot of squirrels" Linder "ran into one deer" which he shot at several times without, apparently, hitting it. When Linder returned to the cabin and recounted what had happened, many of the hunters were for cutting off the shirttail of his new wool shirt. Faulkner stopped them from doing so, however, by saying "'Gentlemen . . . the rest of us just been sitting around here taking a drink and Felix's been out shooting us something to eat . . . I don't think we ought to do that [cut off the shirttail].'"[30] Faulkner's words and actions suggest an ability and willingness to do more than simply blindly follow prescribed custom, rites, and ritualized behavior. In the case of the shirttail episode, Faulkner must have examined the rite in context in order to evaluate its appropriateness for the moment at hand. It is precisely that sort of evaluation of the rite in context that is at work in Faulkner's texts.

The context, broadly speaking, is the modern South and the ideologies that shaped it. Ideology, like culture, is a loaded term. For Marx and Engels, ideology has a pejorative meaning; it is that which produces false consciousness and prohibits a person from seeing the real conditions

---

[29]See, for instance, Joseph Blotner, *William Faulkner: A Biography* (New York: Random House, 1974); David Minter, *William Faulkner: His Life and Work* (Baltimore, Johns Hopkins University Press, 1980); Murray C. Falkner, *The Falkners of Mississippi: A Memoir* (Baton Rouge: Louisiana State University Press, 1967); John Faulkner, *My Brother Bill: An Affectionate Reminiscence* (New York, Trident Press 1963); James W. Webb and A. Wigfall Green, eds., *William Faulkner of Oxford* (Baton Rouge Louisiana State University Press, 1968); and Jim Faulkner, *Across the Creek: Faulkner Family Stories* (Jackson: University of Mississippi Press, 1986).

[30]James W. Webb and A. Wigfall Green, eds., *William Faulkner of Oxford* (Baton Rouge: Louisiana State University Press, 1965) 172.

of his existence. Later Marxists, particularly Louis Althusser, see ideology in a more neutral light. Ideologies are systems of ideas that enable the holder to maintain a particular worldview and relation to existence. Althusser adds that those ideologies—of education, of family, etcetera—are a product of, and are mastered by, the ideology of the ruling class. Fredric Jameson, following Althusser, "posits ideology in terms of strategies of containment, whether intellectual or (in the case of narratives) formal."[31] My use of the term is indebted to both Althusser and Jameson, for I see ideology as that which determines discourse, both verbal and written, and dictates action. Throughout the fictions examined, Faulkner discloses the ideologies that govern the words and deeds of his characters in such a fashion that the reader should read the texts as cultural critiques.[32]

Ritual and ritualized behavior played crucial roles in the culture Faulkner was critiquing, a culture still heavily imbued with the honor-shame ideology that had held sway in the antebellum South. For all that has been written about the South following the Civil War, there is nothing approaching consensus on the issues of the amount and type of change defeat brought and the pace with which change occurred. That some sort of change occurred there can be no doubt; nor can there be any doubt that the South, in Harold Woodman's words, attempted "to under-

---

[31]Fredric Jameson, *The Political Unconscious* (Ithaca NY: Cornell University Press, 1981) 52-53.

[32]For a reading of the relationship between, and within, ideology and the social sciences, with implicit connections to Althusser and Roland Barthes, see Geertz, *The Interpretation of Cultures*, 193-229. Geertz argues that "it is through the construction of ideologies, schematic images of social order, that man makes himself for better or worse a political animal" (218). For the effect of ideology on the anthropologist and the pursuit of culture see, for instance, Geertz, *Works and Lives: The Anthropologist as Author* (Stanford: Stanford University Press, 1988); George E. Marcus and Michael M. J. Fisher, *Anthropology as Cultural Critique* (Chicago, 1986); Clifford and Marcus, eds., *Writing Culture: The Poetics and Politics of Ethnography*; Jay Ruby, ed. *A Crack in the Mirror: Reflexive Perspectives in Anthropology* (Philadelphia: University of Pennsylvania Press, 1982); and Wagner, *The Invention of Culture*. For an extended attempt to understand culture in terms of symbols and symbolic actions see Wagner, *Symbols that Stand for Themselves* (Chicago: University of Chicago Press, 1986).

stand the changing new world by viewing through lenses that remained focused on the old."[33]

For every Southern leader who, like Henry Woodfin Grady, implored the South to embrace modernization and throw off the yoke of no longer viable attitudes and values, there was an opposite and equally if not more persuasive voice admonishing the South to vigorously hold to those attitudes and values that had conferred identity upon the region. Grady's late nineteenth-century voice was countered, for instance, by that of his contemporary Thomas Nelson Page, who wrote of the South: "Whilst it proudly boasted itself democratic, it was distinctly and avowedly anti-radical—holding fast to those things which were proved, and standing with its conservatism a steadfast bulwark against all novelties and aggression."[34]

The tendency to look back even while moving ahead continued to characterize the South after the turn of the century. Dewey Grantham makes clear that even Southern progressives were not interested in radical social change. Rather, "they accepted or accommodated themselves to a system whose major institutions were dominated by powerful economic and political interests. Representing the emerging professional and bourgeois elements of the South's social structure, they shared many of the assumptions and goals of Southern businessmen and entrepreneurs."[35]

Their "reformism was essentially 'preventive social work' designed to provide a stabilizing effect on society. In their eyes stability, tradition, and class structure were indispensable requirements for a strong social system."[36] This marriage of the old and the new in order to foster stability

---

[33]Harold D. Woodman, "Economic Reconstruction and the Rise of the New South, 1865-1900," in *Interpreting Southern History*, edited by Boles and Nolan, 303. I owe my understanding of the role rites of passage played in the "old" world of the antebellum South chiefly to Bertram Wyatt-Brown, *Southern Honor: Ethics and Behavior in the Old South*, (Oxford: Oxford University Press, 1982); Steven M. Stowe, *Intimacy and Power in the Old South: Ritual in the Lives of the Planters*, (Baltimore: Johns Hopkins University Press, 1987); and Drew Gilpin Faust, "The Rhetoric and Ritual of Agriculture in Antebellum South Carolina," *Journal of Southern History* 45 (1979): 541-68. And, for the ritual of dueling, Jack Kenny Williams, *Dueling in the Old South: Vignettes of Social History*, (College Station TX: Texas A&M Press, 1981).

[34]Quoted in Richard Beale Davis, C. Hugh Holman, and Louis D. Rubin, eds., *Southern Writing 1585-1920* (New York: Odyssey Press, 1970) 751.

[35]Dewey W. Grantham, *Southern Progressivism: The Reconciliation of Tradition and Progress* (Knoxville: University of Tennessee Press, 1983) 417.

[36]Ibid., 418.

and therefore insure economic gain meant that, like other groups in the South, the progressives were "cultural traditionalists, bent on maintaining [what they saw as] the best of their section's habits and values."[37]

That maintenance was becoming increasingly difficult following the conclusion of the First World War. As a consequence, "the compulsion to preserve cultural values, a basic characteristic of southern progressivism, became increasingly more defensive and negative in the 1920s" as both progressives and the region continued to find it difficult to reconcile the desire to embrace economic progress with the desire to hold on to tradition.[38] Even as the conflict deepened between the ideology at the heart of the "enthusiasm of southern businessmen and professional people for economic development" and the traditional ideology associated with agrarian values and paternalism, the rites, as Faulkner has Fairchild suggest, lost their critical and interrogative quality.[39]

The liminal phase of the rite that the traditionalists would have "maintain control over what threatens to become uncontrolled power and carry the world, or men's gardens, or society as a whole, to destruction" becomes in Faulkner's texts a creative space where certain conflicts are brought into "frightening prominence" in order that "fundamental aspects of society, normally overlaid by customs and habits of daily intercourse," might be illuminated.[40] The liminal phase of the rites of passage in and of Faulkner's texts "enfranchise[s] speculation" upon the relationship between the individual and the community as it is articulated in the

---

[37]See, e.g., ibid. Other works that helped to shape my sense of the region include C. Vann Woodward, *Origin of the New South 1877–1913* (Baton Rouge: Louisiana State University Press, 1951); George Brown Tindall, *The Emergence of the New South: 1913–1945* (Baton Rouge: Louisiana State University Press, 1967); John B. Boles and Evelyn Thomas Nolan, eds., *Interpreting Southern History* (Baton Rouge: Louisiana State University Press, 1964); Winifred B. Moore, Jr., ed., *Developing Dixie: Modernization in a Traditional Society* (New York: Greenwood Press, 1988); Robert L. Hall and Carol B. Stack, eds., *Holding on to the Land and the Lord: Kinship, Ritual, Land Tenure and Social Policy in the Rural South* (Athens GA: University of Georgia Press, 1982); and two informed personal histories, Gayle Graham Yates, *Mississippi Mind: A Personal Culture History of an American State* (Knoxville: University of Tennessee Press, 1990) and Linda Flowers, *Throwed Away: Failures of Progress in Eastern North Carolina* (Knoxville: University of Tennessee Press, 1990).

[38]Ibid., 415.

[39]Ibid., 416.

[40]Wagner, *Invention*, 122; Victor Turner, *Dramas, Fields, and Metaphors* (Ithaca NY: Cornell University Press, 1974) 35.

struggle over identity.[41] The articulations also illuminate for our speculation the role played by ideology in the construction of a person, a
community, and discourse.

The conflicts brought into "frightening prominence" in the two
Yoknapatawpha texts examined in greatest detail in the following
chapters, *As I Lay Dying* and *Light in August,* illuminate the role played
by ideology in determining rites, identity, and narrative. For instance, the
conflicts in the liminal phase of the rite of interment in *As I Lay Dying*
reveal the importance of an encroaching modern capitalist ideology to
individual narratives and the determination of identity. In that liminal
space, the Bundrens attempt to manage the indeterminacy of their state
by appropriating and narrating the rite of interment. However, their
narratives all too often disclose an allegiance to the modern ideology; that
allegiance effectively perverts the rite even as the ideology informing it
fuses with the rite to confer a disconcerting identity. Similarly, we shall
see that the rites central to characters in *Light in August* are rendered in
a fashion that reveals how they determine identity. Furthermore, the
rendering discloses and critiques the racist and sexist elements of the
traditional ideology governing the rites and narratives, an ideology still
vital in Yoknapatawpha and the South. That ideology necessitates Joe
Christmas's violent death and Lena Grove's entrapment within patriarchal
discourse; as such, it works to confer identities that are equally disconcerting.

Reading the dynamics of the rites of passage both in and as the text
will enable us to see the identities of Faulkner's characters and how they
are interpellated as subjects. We need, then, to move beyond a reading
that simply relies on "the taxonomic abstractness of structuralist
sociology," as it might be applied to the texts examined.[42] Indeed, I am
not interested in presenting a simple taxonomic study of the texts under
consideration. Rather, I wish to point out how the structure of the rites of
passage appears in selected Faulkner texts, how that structure relates to

---

[41]Victor Turner, *The Forest of Symbols* (Ithaca NY: Cornell University Press, 1967)
106.

[42]Walter A. Davis, *Inwardness and Existence: Subjectivity in/and Hegel, Heidegger,
Marx, and Freud* (Madison WI: University of Wisconsin Press, 1989) 210. For an
example of "the taxonomic abstractness of structuralist sociology" in the field of rites of
passage theory see Barney G. Glaser and Anselm L. Strauss, *Status Passage* (Chicago:
Aldine Atherton, Inc., 1971).

and informs issues of textual identity and the identity of Faulkner's characters, and the cultural forces that are at work in and through the rites. Such a reading enables us to see how the taxonomic structure of the rite of passage enables the texts to articulate a context in such a fashion that they can "be seen as negating that context."[43]

In order to articulate that context, however, Faulkner must find the proper phrase(s). He must find, that is, the rites of passage. In "Delta Autumn," the story that follows "The Bear" in *Go Down, Moses*, Ike achieves a rite of initiation after killing his first buck *despite* not having the words necessary to put into language the meaning of both the act of killing and the rite of initiation. Ike stands "trying not to tremble, humbly and with pride too though the boy of twelve had been unable to phrase it then: *I slew you; my bearing must not shame your quitting life*" as Sam Fathers marks his initiate's "face forever" with the blood of the slain deer (*GDM* 350-51). While as a boy of twelve Ike is able to achieve ritual passage without the appropriate language, Faulkner has, as Matthews suggests, little save the search for the correct phrases to commemorate the loss, or at the very least the radical endangerment, of a world informed by traditional passages such as that Ike experiences.

Jean-Francois Lyotard contends that "The differend is the unstable state and instant of language wherein something which must be put into phrases cannot yet be."[44] The differend, or conflict as we might construe it here, is not applicable to Ike McCaslin as a boy of twelve. It is unnecessary for young Ike to have the phrases in order to achieve passage. However, the differend is applicable to Faulkner, for in it "something 'asks' to be put into phrases, and suffers from the wrong of not being able to be put into phrases right away."[45] Such we are now ready to see is the case with identity in and of Faulkner's fictions, the differend that "'asks' to be put into phrases" and that must be, so that the Faulknerian text might reveal what has been concealed about identity.

---

[43]Fredric Jameson, *The Political Unconscious* (Ithaca NY: Cornell University Press, 1981) 38.

[44]Jean-Francois Lyotard, *The Differend: Phrases in Dispute*, trans. Georges Van Den Abbeele (Minneapolis: University of Minnesota Press, 1988) 13.

[45]See, e.g., ibid.

Chapter 1
"New Orleans" and
an Aesthetics of Indeterminacy

A. The Nature of "New Orleans"

If, to continue the conceit with which the introduction closes, we are to trace the organic development of the rites of passage as the appropriate phrase for the articulation of identity in and across a number of William Faulkner's texts, then it might well seem odd to begin with "New Orleans," Faulkner's first nationally published fiction, for it is concerned with rites of passage neither formally nor thematically. However, there are three reasons to begin with "New Orleans." First, the text helps us begin to see the identity of Faulkner's fictional constructs as he made what was for him the crucial move from writing poetry to writing fiction. This will help us to understand both the relationship between "New Orleans" and his later work and the philosophical underpinnings of Yoknapatawpha County when we approach that construct through *As I Lay Dying* in Chapter 3. Second, "New Orleans" articulates several of the major thematic concerns of the later works examined in this study. Third, the text is intertextually linked to *Mosquitoes*, where the rite of passage *is* of the utmost narrative and thematic importance, in a fashion that helps us see the development of Faulkner's understanding of fiction's power to disclose and determine identity even as it has the power to critique culture.

Faulkner's statement, made in a 1948 letter to Malcolm Cowley, that "even to a collection of short stories, form, integration, is as important as to a novel—an entity of its own, single, set for one pitch, contrapuntal in integration, toward one end, one finale" highlights the importance of unity to the identity of fictional constructs.[1] Form enables a collection of short stories, or a novel for that matter, to be "an entity of its own." That entity moves contrapuntally to its finale.[2] Such is the case with Faulkner's

---

[1]Malcolm Cowley, ed. *The Faulkner-Cowley File: Letters and Memories, 1944-1962* (New York: Viking Press, 1966) 115-16.

[2]This aesthetics can be seen microcosmically within individual texts and macrocosmically within the text that is Yoknapatawpha as it is delineated within and between those works concerned with that place. James G. Watson argues that Faulkner's fiction is dominated by short story structures existing as reflexive forms in counterpoint; hence,

"New Orleans." An analysis of the text's contrapuntal nature is essential to an understanding of a work that has been called "among the most curious, and the most enigmatic, of Faulkner's short fictions."[3] A focus on the way the pieces of "New Orleans" respond to each other, the intra-textuality of the text, enables us to better understand the process of making meaning in "New Orleans," the aesthetics implicit in that process, and the importance of both to a particular intertextual connection between "New Orleans" and *Mosquitoes*.

"New Orleans," a collection of eleven sections or vignettes published in the January-February 1925 volume of *The Double Dealer*, is "topo-graphically undifferentiated."[4] There is nothing in the sections which directly points to the city of New Orleans. The text's inability to be completely identified either with the objects of the external world of New

---

"Separate short stories are particularly suitable as units of structure in longer works because they are so often crafted in the same ways as the novels. . . . they depict worlds within worlds" ("Faulkner: Short Story Structures and Reflexive Forms," *Mosaic* 4 [1978] 134). Fruitful considerations of the formal qualities of Faulkner's work can be found in Kartiganer, *The Fragile Thread: the Meaning of Form in Faulkner's Novels* (Amherst: University of Massachusetts Press, 1979); Warwick Wadlington, *Reading Faulknerian Tragedy* (Ithaca NY: Cornell University Press, 1987); John T. Irwin, *Doubling and Incest/ Repetition and Revenge* (Baltimore: Johns Hopkins University Press, 1975); Doreen Fow-ler and Ann Abadie, eds., *William Faulkner and the Craft of Fiction* (Jackson: University of Mississippi Press, 1989); and George Toles, "The Space Between: A Study of Faulk-ner's *Sanctuary*," *Texas Studies in Literature and Language* 22/1 (Spring 1980) 22-47.

[3]James G. Watson, "New Orleans, *The Double Dealer*, and 'New Orleans'," *American Literature* 56/2 (May 1984): 215.

[4]Watson, "New Orleans," 217. Faulkner published "New Orleans" shortly after arriv-ing in New Orleans in January 1925; it is the point of origin for several sketches publish-ed in the Sunday section of the New Orleans *Time-Picayune* and several stories in the *Uncollected Stories of William Faulkner*, edited by Blotner. "The Cobbler," the fifth sec-tion of "New Orleans," was expanded and published with the same title in the 10 May 1925 *Times-Picayune*; "Frankie and Johnny," the third section, was substantially revised, expanded, and published in the 31 May 1925 *Times-Picayune* as "The Kid Learns"—the section appearing in "New Orleans" also exists with some revisions as the second section of an unpublished, untitled story that appears in Blotner's collection as "Frankie and John-ny." Critics find this process of repetition and revision to be one of the most interesting aspects of Faulkner's textual and narrative mastery, and a number of works have greatly advanced our understanding of his craft of composition and re-composition. See Irwin, *Doubling and Incest*; Matthews, *The Play of Faulkner's Language*; and Kartiganer, "Faulkner's Art of Repetition" and Moreland, "Compulsive and Revisionary Repetition: Faulkner's 'Barn Burning' and the Craft of Writing Difference," in *William Faulkner and the Craft of Fiction*.

Orleans or the internal world of the reader's experiences creates indeterminacy which must be managed through acts of interpretation. The lack of identification between New Orleans and "New Orleans" encourages the reader to see that the narrative of each section is primarily concerned not with representing the city but with desire and the production of meaning. The narrators' acts of production parallel ours as we attempt to fill the gaps created by indeterminacy so that we might satisfy our desire with the construction of meaning. "New Orleans," then, is at its core a metafictive text, as Faulkner employs his characters in order to confront how it is that fictions are meaningful and have value. We hear different voices: the affected tone of the wealthy Jew, the sorrowful and quiet cobbler, Frankie's speech with its dependency upon the idiom of the street, the syncopated rhythms of the longshoreman's language. Moreover, nearly every character in the piece struggles with language as a tool of description and definition. In "Frankie and Johnny," for instance, Johnny tells Frankie that "before I seen you it was like I was one of them ferry boats yonder crossing and crossing a dark river or something by myself; acrossing and acrossing and never getting nowheres and not knowing it and thinking I was all the time"; the priest, in the section bearing that title, describes the evening "like a nun shod with silence"; in "The Cobbler" the man says his life "is a house" and his wife is a "bush of golden roses" (*NO* 39-40, 38, 42-43). Throughout "New Orleans" characters move to the metaphoric quality of language in an attempt to articulate his or her life, his or her mind, his or her heart.[5]

"New Orleans" is ostensively a longing couched in language. That longing can be seen in the sections that frame "New Orleans." "Wealthy Jew," the first section of the piece, begins with a statement of desire: "'I love three things: gold, marble and purple; splendor, solidity, color'"; "The Tourist," the last section of "New Orleans," closes with a description of the city personified as an object of desire:

> New Orleans . . . a courtesan whose hold is strong upon the mature,
> to whose charm the young must respond. And all who leave her,

---

[5]Watson remarks on the importance of metaphor in "New Orleans" in "New Orleans," 219. Faulkner remained concerned with metaphor throughout his career, particularly in his high modern works. Metaphor and metaphorization are crucial, for instance, to *The Sound and the Fury*. Bleikasten examines Faulkner's use of metaphor in *Faulkner's As I Lay Dying* (Bloomington: Indiana University Press, 1973).

seeking the virgin's unbrown, ungold hair and her blanched and icy breast where no lover has died, return to her when she smiles across her languid fan. . . .

New Orleans. (*NO* 37, 49-50)

James G. Watson suggests that there is "continuity in the pattern of experience described from first to last in the body of work" that is "New Orleans."[6] As a consequence, Watson holds that "New Orleans" has "something of the contrapuntal unity of a single, extended narrative."[7] The desire to get something said, articulated by the narrator of each section and implicit in Faulkner's artistic enterprise, shapes the discourse that is this single, extended narrative. For Watson, "The Wealthy Jew is Faulkner's emblem in the collection of spiritual transcendence, and he serves as the norm against which all other, individual sufferings are judged."[8] However, an analysis of the sections in counterpoint shows that the structure and thematics of "New Orleans" work to deny the legitimacy of the wealthy Jew and his narrative as norms.

Christian Messenger argues that "the free exercise of the imagination in and through language is ultimately the category that links play and sport most closely to aesthetics."[9] Because of its indeterminacy "New Orleans" is a telling example of the exercise of the imagination. For Messenger and others, play is the mode that enables us to speak of or write about the largest contradictions, and the playful contrapuntal structure of "New Orleans" enables us to see the contradiction or conflict at the heart of that text. The text's focus on conflicting and conflicted values and norms makes the play of "New Orleans" agonistic in nature. The agonistic play of Faulkner's text can be read, then, as a "fight or contest" which "involves a decision to be made by the reader in relation to those opposing values, which are in collision with one another."[10] The agonistic nature of "New Orleans," the contest arising out of its contrapuntal nature, discloses that the wealthy Jew's narrative functions as

---

[6]Watson, "New Orleans," 223.

[7]Ibid., 224-25.

[8]Ibid., 223.

[9]Christian Messenger, *Sport and the Spirit of Play in Contemporary American Fiction* (New York: Columbia University Press, 1990) 2.

[10]Wolfgang Iser, *Prospecting: From Reader Response to Literary Anthropology* (Baltimore: Johns Hopkins University Press, 1989) 256.

a defense mechanism; it articulates the Jew's desire to achieve closure in a "world [fictional and otherwise] where open-endedness reigns."[11]

"I, too, am but a lump of moist dirt before the face of God" (*NO* 37). The Jew's admission of mortality and position before God is his response to the realization that "Suns rise and set; ages of man rise and joy and battle and weep, and pass away" (*NO* 37). The narrator's self- definition, intertextually invoking *Genesis*, signifies the conflation of birth and death, beginning and ending, at the same time that it specifies closure. *Genesis* informs us that "the Lord God formed man of the dust of the ground" after a mist had watered the whole face of the earth, and that following man's transgressions in the Garden, God decreed "In the sweat of thy face shalt thou eat bread, till thou return unto the ground; for out of it wast thou taken: for dust thou art and unto dust shalt thou return" (Genesis 3:19). Man is born from the earth and to the earth is Man bound to return. The Jew's line, when heard with *Genesis'* echo, is an articulation of the shape of man's life born of the Jew's desire to grasp his own identity.

The psychological desire to tell the shape of life that motivates the wealthy Jew is also crucially important to Frank Kermode's theory of fictional endings. Kermode has written,

"The artifice of eternity" is a striking periphrasis for "form," for the shapes which console the dying generations. In this respect it makes little difference—though it makes some—whether you believe the age of the world to be six thousand years or five thousand million years, whether you think time will have a stop or that the world is eternal; there is still a need to speak humanly of a life's importance to it—a need in the moment of existence to belong, to be related to a beginning and to an end.[12]

---

[11]See, e.g., ibid. Myra Jehlen also stresses the importance of "play," arguing that "Faulkner's South is homogeneous only in the sense of adding up to a coherent community; but that community itself is deeply rent and its parts in constant play. Characters define themselves out of stances and situations afforded by that play" (*Class and Character in Faulkner's South* [Secaucus: Citadel Press, 1978] 10-11). The reality of Faulkner's South, as well as the nature of the South inscribed in his fictions, makes a coherent community most difficult to achieve and maintain.

[12]Frank Kermode, *The Sense of an Ending: Studies in the Theory of Fiction* (New York: Oxford University Press, 1967) 3-4.

The Jew's narrative constitutes and articulates the attempted moment of belonging. His discourse is grounded in origin, "The wave of Destiny, foaming out of the East where was cradled the infancy of the race of man"; moves through history, invoking "Alexanders Caesars and Napoleons"; and plays out with his people cresting the seas of Destiny, "mayhap to be swept like blown trumpets among the cold stars." Like its pretext *Genesis*, the "Wealthy Jew" section attempts to be a history which is a "wholly concordant structure," and the attempt must necessarily project "[the narrator] past the End, so as to see the structure whole."[13] The inevitability of death, the end we must all face, propels the Jew's discourse and his attempted projection of self beyond the end. Like Dilsey, the Jew sees "de first en de last. . . . de beginnin en. . . . de endin" (*SF*, 371).[14]

The Jew's section expresses the twin desires for closure and the privileged position necessary to see it. In fact, what can be termed the section's intratextuality symbolizes a desire for closure that leads to overdetermination. I refer, of course, to the frame of the section: "'I love three things: gold; marble and purple; splendor, solidity, color'" (*NO* 37-38). Just as the fundamental allusion behind the Jew's description of himself as a lump of moist dirt conflates the beginning with the end, the close of the section sends us back to the beginning. The structure of the section is cyclical rather than rectilinear, and the circumlocution marks the section's collapse into itself.

The "Wealthy Jew" section uses a framing device in an attempt at achieving completed meaning. The next section, "The Priest," offers an alternative to the wealthy Jew's position on meaning. Let us consider the beginning of "The Priest" more closely: "Evening like a nun shod with silence, evening like a girl slipping along the wall to meet her lover. . . [the ellipsis is Faulkner's] The twilight is like the breath of contented kine" (*NO* 38-39). The section incorporates the process of the priest's

---

[13]Ibid., 6,8.

[14]*The Sound and the Fury* is itself concerned with completion. Faulkner stated that each section of that text was a revision of what had come before in an attempt to get it right. Reverend Shegog's Easter service articulates Christ's life from his birth to his death at Calvary, and the symbolism inside the church, the Christmas Bell present at Easter, directs the reader's attention to the issue of closure and a completely articulated statement. Faulkner also stated that he felt *The Sound and the Fury* to be a failure, which is in accord with what might be termed the aesthetics of indeterminacy which he was developing in and through "New Orleans."

attempt at definition. Apparently either unsatisfied or dissatisfied with his first attempt, he tries again. The second definition of the evening is diametrically opposed to the first as the priest moves away from the initial virginal, non-sexual vehicle and to a metaphor propelled by sexual activity. Finally, Faulkner puts an end to the process by inserting an ellipsis. The Greek root of ellipsis, *elleipein*, means a falling short or a defect. Like Genette's paralipsis, which "does not skip over a moment of time, as in an ellipsis, but. . . . sidesteps a given element," the ellipsis in "The Priest" signifies a defect or shortfall on the part of the narrator and, as a result, opens the text to the audience.[15] The ellipsis suggests that the priest's language and his ability to manipulate it are incapable of the act of descriptive definition or fixing which is being attempted. We see that the ellipsis both puts an end to the priest's attempt at metaphorization and re-opens the narrative to the endless play of signification that is necessarily the heart of language. That re-opening, in turn, raises the issue of fictionalizing. One might say that the questions implicitly posed are: *how* does the section mean? how does the section create meaning?[16]

"The Priest" is not the only section of "New Orleans" featuring the ellipsis: ellipses or elliptic-like structures occupy important positions in "The Cobbler," "The Longshoreman," "The Cop," "The Beggar," "Magdelen," and "The Tourist." "The Cobbler," for instance, responds directly to "Wealthy Jew." The Cobbler asks "Joy and sorrow—what mean these? Did I know once? But joy and sorrow are the birds which whirl screaming above the rushing flood" (*NO* 42). The cobbler closes by saying "I have known joy and sorrows, but now I do not remember. I am old: I have forgotten much" (*NO* 43). Similarly, the Jew articulates an intimate relationship with joy and sorrow: "But I am old, all the pain and passion and sorrows of the human race are in this breast: joys to fire, griefs to burn out the soul" (*NO* 37). The repetition—"I am old," joys and sorrows—inscribes a path joining the two sections. While the Jew's narrative responds to pain, passion, joy, sorrow, and grief by articulating an over-

---

[15]Gerard Genette, *Narrative Discourse*, trans. Jane E. Lewin (Ithaca NY: Cornell University Press, 1980) 52.

[16]Iser points out that traditional means of making meaning are called into question during the modern period. He is, of course, not alone in this observation. See Wolfgang Iser, *Prospecting: From Reader Response to Literary Anthropology*, 3-41 and 197-235. We shall see that the relationship among meaning, the rites of passage, and modern Southern culture is articulated in both *As I Lay Dying* and *Light in August*.

determination for closure, the cobbler's narrative succumbs to the ellipsis when he attempts to give voice to the role a woman played (and plays) in his joy and his sorrow: "But now that rose [his substitute for the missing woman] is old in a pot, and I am old and walled about with the smell of leather, and she. . . . and she . . ." (*NO* 43). The cobbler's narrative turns to elision, denies completion and closure, and in doing so escapes an articulation that would be painful. The ellipsis works in two ways. On the one hand, the silence interjected by the ellipsis discloses the cobbler's suppression, and in doing so it stands in telling contradistinction to the Jew's attempt to avoid the pain arising from the knowledge of death by creating a fully articulated structure. On the other hand, the silence opens the text to indeterminacy, and in doing so it stands as the text's response to the Jew's suppression of indeterminacy through narrative.

The repetition of the ellipsis throughout "New Orleans" serves to stress the text's intratextual dimension and contrapuntal quality. The continual falling short on the part of the narrators, the continual defect of the sections, is indicative of far more than an inability to master language. Both the ellipsis and the elliptic-like structure are narrative tools of admission, and their continued deployment helps unite the sections of "New Orleans" and "open" the text to uncertainty and indeterminacy. Perhaps the most graphic example of this process of opening the text occurs at the beginning of "The Longshoreman." There we read, "'She wouldn't do what I asked her to, so I socked her in the jaw . . .' Jesus, look down: see dat barrel ro-o-o-ll! White folks says and nigger does (*NO* 43). There is no connection between the first sentence of the section and what comes after, and the ellipsis both marks the gap and inscribes the space where the reader struggles with indeterminacy in order to develop an interpretation. If the first sentence of "The Longshoreman" has any intratextual connection to "New Orleans" it is to "Wealthy Jew." Both "The Longshoreman" and "Wealthy Jew" begin with direct quotations. However, whereas "Wealthy Jew" employs the direct quotation as a device to suppress indeterminacy and articulate closure, the quotation which opens "The Longshoreman" is immediately supplemented by the grammatical mark of indeterminacy and a tacit critique of closure.

The elliptic nature of "New Orleans" is the opening enabling the text to suggest that both the city of New Orleans and the fiction which is "New Orleans" can, paradoxically, only be fixed in indeterminacy. Neither single voice nor traditional narrative can fix or define the city. In this way at least, Faulkner's work articulates modernity in so far as "New Orleans" questions types of representations and "the link between language and representation."[17] The ellipses employed throughout "New Orleans" enable the text to respond to the representation in language of "Wealthy Jew" by supplementing indeterminacy for the overdetermination born of the Jew's desire for closure the possibility of achieving it. That is, "New Orleans" inscribes the enclosure of the first section and then turns to a paradigm of elision throughout the rest of the piece in order to deny closure.

Contrary to what James G. Watson argues, the original fictional design of the "Wealthy Jew" section is destroyed by the ellipsis, unbounded as it were, "in order to discover another rounding out than that one, another settling of the anxieties the text has aroused," anxieties inherent in both the necessary search for meaning and the meaning-making process which is fictionalizing.[18] "The ploy reforms itself in our minds and reforms our minds. Under such circumstances, ellipsis is a means by which we are made to surrender our attachment to one ploy proposed by fiction and then to seek an alternate."[19] In "New Orleans" the ellipses and what they represent *are* the alternatives and they help both text and reader move "toward one end, one finale." The uncertainty and indeterminacy which are transported into the text by the ellipses suggest that the meaning of "New Orleans" resides in the interstices where reader, author, and text come together. Given this, the reader must adopt the role of the tourist and end his or her search for closure and the production of meaning through acts of interpretation with a descriptive definition framed and governed by ellipses:

> New Orleans . . . a courtesan whose hold is strong upon the mature, to whose charm the young must respond. And all who leave her, seeking the virgin's unbrown, ungold hair and her blanched and icy breast where no lover has died, return to her when she smiles across her languid fan. . . .
> New Orleans (*NO* 49-50).

---

[17]Carolyn Burke, "Getting Spliced: Modernism and Sexual Difference," *American Quarterly* 39/1 (Spring 1987): 100.

[18]Millicent Bell, "Narrative Gaps/Narrative Meaning," *Raritan* 1 (Summer 1986): 89.

[19]See, e.g., ibid.

Grammatically, the ellipses deny the indicative mood in the above quotation, deny the possibility of objective fact, and deny any final fixing or figuration. Therefore, the ellipses here and elsewhere in "New Orleans" stress the necessary subjunctiveness at the heart of fiction and the process of fictionalizing.

The ellipsis, then, discloses each character's problems with and shortcomings using language, acts as the sign of the location for the production of meaning in "New Orleans," and in its final appearance in the text calls attention to the fiction-making process by denying the indicative in favor of the subjunctive. Michel Gresset writes that intertextuality is made possible by "an anastomosis which connects two texts and then itself (the connection) becomes one of the constituents of the later text."[20] The ellipses in "New Orleans" function as the anastomosis connecting the individual monologues of the text while at the same time serving as the metaphorization of the fictional text. In "White Mythology," Derrida argues that "that which seems to 'represent,' to figure, is also that which opens the wider space of a discourse on figuration," and such is the case with the ellipsis in "New Orleans."[21] The ellipsis is both the connection and, metafictively, the text. By means of the ellipsis, "New Orleans" "articulates its own situation and textualizes it."[22] As a result, "New Orleans"'s "discourse on figuration" illuminates the indeterminacy essential to Faulknerian narrative.[23]

---

[20]Michel Gresset, "Introduction: Faulkner Between the Texts," in *Intertextuality in Faulkner*, edited by Gresset and Noel Polk (Jackson: University Press of Mississippi, 1985) 4.

[21]Jacques Derrida, "White Mythology: Metaphor in the Text of Philosophy," in *Margins of Philosophy*, trans. Alan Bass (Chicago: University of Chicago Press, 1982) 216.

[22]Jameson, *The Political Unconscious*, 82.

[23]Faulkner uses the ellipsis or an elliptic structure to silence characters and halt or break the narrative in much of his major work. I am referring especially to instances in *Sanctuary*, *Light in August*, and *Flags in the Dust*. We might recall the scene of Temple Drake's rape, the murder of Joanna Burden, and Narcissa's avowal to avoid marriage. Bell argues that "Art conceals what it 'omits' by establishing an unanticipated coherence and sense of completeness which we recognize as meaning—and so expresses our mind's ineluctable compulsion to gestalt," but Faulkner's greatest art reveals as much as it conceals ("Narrative Gaps/ Narrative Meaning," 89). Those acts of disclosure, like the ellipsis in Faulkner, tend to deny closure and completion. See Matthews, "The Elliptical Nature of *Sanctuary*," *Novel* 17/3 (1984): 246-65, for a detailed analysis of the function of the ellipsis in one of Faulkner's novels.

B. Constraints . . .

The wealthy Jew's framing statement of desire disclosing his narrative's self-involvement is necessitated by the privileging of conquest and commerce that motivates his discourse and lurks behind the attempt at closure. The narrator immediately associates himself with his "ancient Phoenician ancestors" traveling the seas in "trading barques, seeking those things which I, too, love" (*NO* 37). The connection stresses the importance of imperialism in the name of commerce and the acquisition of material wealth. Indeed, the Jew's section revolves around commerce and currency. He may well lament that mixed races have tarnished dreams and do not know what they desire, but his frame and narrative make it clear that he desires wealth.

The section suggests that conquest and mastery are necessary if one is to acquire and keep wealth. Furthermore, conquest and mastery are arrived at in one of two ways: either by force or through language. On the one hand, land and peoples can be conquered by the application of an empire's might. The Jew invokes Alexander, Caesar, and Napoleon as representative of the sort of men who achieve their wealth by force: "Your Alexanders and Caesars and Napoleons rise in blood and gold" (*NO* 38). The rise in blood, that spilled in their conquests, leads to the rise in gold, the plunder from the expansion of their empires. The plundered gold then participates in an economy that further strengthens the empire. If this participation involves its transformation into a coin in order to facilitate the system of exchange, a transformation tacitly invoked by the Jew when we read "I flung you a golden coin, and you purchased martyrdom of Death in Ahenobarbus' gardens," then the gold comes to naturalize political authority in cultures that economize their leaders by placing their representations on the coin (*NO* 38). The iconography created means that the gold coin bears the double burden of a naturalized economy and a naturalized political authority.

The Jew's narrative, however, calls into question the legitimacy of political authority, naturalized or otherwise. While the leaders rise in blood and gold, and in "shrieking briefly of home" call to mind community and culture, they ultimately "are gone as waves hiss curling on the beach, and die" (*NO* 38). The Jew is well aware that reigns must come to an end and conquerors are themselves conquered by time. Faulkner's invocation of the strand is telling: the repetitive act of covering and uncovering parallels the repetitive process of inscription and reinscription which constitutes the Jew's vision of an economic history. The waves spend themselves on the shore, bounding and unbounding the strand, and the action constitutes both a definition of the shoreline and its slow erasure. As is the case with *exergue* and *usure* as Derrida appropriates them in "White Mythology," the waves both build and wear away.[24] The inscription on the coin fixes it at a certain moment in history, and at the same time the function of the coin in an economic system wears the object—coin, icon, inscription—away. The section's invocation of political leaders and their authority stresses this process of wearing away and suggests that conquest by force, with its attendant accumulation of wealth—of currency in the form of the coin, is constrained by time and the necessary erasure of arbitrarily naturalized political authority.

The Jew, having undercut the lasting legitimacy of conquest by force or political power and clearly not interested in purchasing the "martyrdom of Death" with his wealth, turns to the transmission of stories as a way to achieve mastery and conquest. He says, "No soil is foreign to my people, for have we not conquered all lands with the story of your Nativity?" (*NO* 38). Language is power, and the language forming the stories grounding a culture is most powerful. The story of the Nativity, the text that governs the functioning ideology of salvation grounding Western Christian culture, makes all soils home to the Jew and his people. Consequently, the Jew is able to seek and acquire the wealth he desires. What is more, he is able to use the story that is his narrative to avoid the martyrdom of death.

We must be careful how we take the Jew's discourse, however, for he simply substitutes religion for military conquest and political force in his attempt to validate a particular economic ideology. It is entirely appropriate that the Jew links religion and capitalism. As Walter Davis succinctly discloses, "Capitalism and Christianity . . . make perfect bedfellows because our heavenly father put us on earth to have all good

---

[24]*Usure*, that is, is both "erasure by rubbing, exhaustion, crumbling away. . . . [and] the supplementary product of a capital, the exchange which far from losing the original investment would fructify its initial wealth, would increase its return in the form of revenue, additional interest" ("White Mythology" 210). Mallarme, Lacan reminds us, links the common use of language to the exchange of a "coin whose obverse and reverse no longer bear any but effaced figures, and which people pass from hand to hand 'in silence'" (*Ecrits*, trans. Alan Sheridan [New York: Norton, 1977] 43).

things before getting even richer rewards in heaven. A less acquisitive response to life involves lack of respect for Creation."[25] The Jew links his pursuit of material wealth with religion, a conflation Faulkner discloses as early as the title of the section, in order to elevate both himself and his people. The "empty circularity" of accumulating money and property so that the "Good" is "always to have [and] never to be. . . . creates the need to make reflection the stilling of any questions or activities that might challenge the harmony of the whole exercise."[26] The wealthy Jew's narrative frame stylistically articulates that belief in harmony, and the "reflection" that is his story attempts to answer all questions and justify all activities.

The Jew takes comfort in the knowledge that the story of the Nativity makes him at home in all lands. Consequently, the pain of the knowledge of mortality is mitigated by an understanding that his people will endure. What is more, their endurance insures the continued transmission of the story of the Nativity, conquest by means of that transmission, and material gain as a result of the conquest. "Magdelen" offers a counterpoint to the "Wealthy Jew" by articulating a subtly different position on material gain. The immediate irony of "Magdelen" is that the narrator is not a reformed prostitute. The fact that she continues to work is made clear when she says "I can remember when I found days gold, but now the gold of day hurts my head. 'Tis night only is gold now, and that not often" (*NO* 48). The rich, bright, full promise of each day has been lost, both the gold and the dream of its acquisition have been tarnished, and in their place is the system of exchange whereby she receives money in return for sexual favors. We learn, however, that "Men aint what they used to be, or money aint or something. Or maybe its I that aint like I was once" (*NO* 48). "Magdelen" suggests that every element of this particular sexual economy—the woman, the man, and the coin—is different from what it once was, is tarnished, and one can argue that the difference is the result of the wearing away or erasure inherent to any economy. The narrator herself suggests as much when she says that her body "has died a hundred times" and that she has "died a thousand deaths" to wear the silk gowns she owns. In "Magdelen" the desire for property, "I saw women who had the bright things I wanted," is satiated and realized by an arbitrary assignation of value to the body (*NO* 48).

---

[25]Davis, *Inwardness and Existence*, 216.
[26]See, e.g., ibid.

(We will return to the body and value in chapters 3 and 4). In "Wealthy Jew" the desire for property is satiated and realized by the arbitrariness of language and story. These two economies of desire stand in tacit juxtaposition in "New Orleans," and the text depotentiates each by disclosing that both are subject to a wearing away or erasure.

Be that as it may, for the Jew story, language, religion, and the desire for wealth are all conjoined, and his narrative appropriates all of them in his attempt to deal with life and death. The artist admits his mortality with much the same language as the wealthy Jew uses: "I, too, am but a shapeless lump of moist earth risen from pain, to laugh and strive and weep, knowing no peace until the moisture has gone out of it, and it is once more of the original and eternal dust" (*NO* 47-48). The repetition of the phrase, "I, too, am but a shapeless lump of moist [either dirt or earth]" encourages the reader to see the two sections in light of each other. The repetition transports "Wealthy Jew" into a highlighted background position in relation to "The Artist." There are other shared points of reference. For instance, the Jew inherits the history of his race, and that inheritance motivates his life and his discourse. Similarly, the artist inherits "A dream and a fire" that he cannot control. Faulkner gives us repetition, but it is repetition with a difference. While the Jew's inheritance moves him to love solidity, the artist's fire moves him to be "without those comfortable smooth paths of solidity and sleep which nature has decreed for man" (*NO* 47). The difference is indicative of the difference between the Jew's position and the artist's.

The Jew's frame bespeaks a desire for closure and enclosure, for an inviolate whole, for, in other words, a complete and finished statement. "The Artist" both formally and thematically denies the possibility of satiating such a desire. The section ends with the artist exclaiming "But to create! Which among ye who have not this fire, can know this joy, let it be ever so fleet?", and the fact that the end is presented as a question transports the possibility of an answer into the text and leaves the section open (*NO* 48). Just as the enjambment of "Wealthy Jew" and "The Priest" calls attention to the first section's overdetermined attempt at enclosure, the intertextual connection between "Wealthy Jew" and "The Artist" calls the earlier narrative into question as well. What is more, as is true with the ellipses in the text, the artist's question actively engages the reader's response to the agonistic nature of the text.

"New Orleans" contains the fictionalization of two distinct and diametrically opposed aesthetics. The fact that the aesthetics implicit in the wealthy Jew's discourse is undercut suggests Faulkner's increasing realization of both the nature of fictional constructs and the inability to either achieve closure or find and fix truth. The metadiscourse that is "New Orleans" concludes that fiction is subjunctive and that readers would therefore do well to pay attention to the ideological constraints upon it *and* them. "New Orleans" discloses that the wealthy Jew's narrative is tainted because it suppresses indeterminacy and is the victim of ideological constraints. The narrative marker of this is the frame supplemented contrapuntally by the subsequent sections of "New Orleans."

I am not suggesting that the sections of "New Orleans" that follow "Wealthy Jew" are free of ideological constraints. Nor am I suggesting that their narrators are immune from the subjectivity ideology confers on us all. The narrator of "The Priest," for instance, attempts to avoid the troubling reality of bodily passions by turning to the comfort of his religious ideology. He laments the coming of night, saying "Ah God, ah God, that night should come so soon," because those hours are his darkest (*NO* 39). It is then that he thinks of lovers, both real and mythological, and physical desire. Even his vision of the Virgin Mary and Jesus has a sensual element: "Ave, Maria! a little silver virgin, hurt and sad and pitiful, remembering Jesus' mouth upon her breast" (*NO* 39). It is then, too, that he turns to a Christian ideology. Four times he resorts to the opening of the "Hail Mary" in an attempt to divert his attention away from physical desire and to an ideology that validates mortification. Furthermore, he pleads, "Ah God, ah God, ah God, that day should be soon!" so that he might be done with his troubling night (*NO* 39). His narrative, however, unlike the wealthy Jew's, is clearly the site of struggle over identity, between his socially constructed personhood as a priest and his physical human self, rather than an attempt to deny or repress that struggle. What is more, the questionable efficacy of the ideology for the priest is articulated both by a narrative that inscribes his struggles with desire and ideology and by ellipses. Nowhere is this clearer than the end of the section. There the priest attempts to suppress physical desire and end his struggle over identity by invoking religion, the Virgin, and grace. And there Faulkner inscribes ellipses in order to tacitly question the ideology governing prayer and the concept of grace while also denying the closure that would "mark" the cessation of the struggle.

C . . . Liberation

The danger inherent in the aesthetics that emerges in "New Orleans" is that because of its very nature fiction might be seen as powerless and ineffectual. The intertextual connection between "New Orleans" and *Mosquitoes* addresses this concern through the "operative repetition" and revision of the wealthy Jew's frame.[27] An analysis of that repetition and revision will help us begin to make the turn in our discussion from Faulkner's first nationally published fiction to his second novel.

It is important to note that the wealthy Jew's statement is a nearly exact quotation from *Mademoiselle de Maupin* by Theophile Gautier. Midway through that epistolary novel D'Albert writes to his friend Silvio "I deem the earth as fair as heaven, and I think that correctness of form is a virtue. Spirituality does not suit me, I prefer a statue to a phantom, and noon to twilight. Three things please me: gold, marble and purple, splendour, solidity and color. My dreams are composed of them, and all my chimerical palaces are constructed with these materials."[28] D'Albert is a poet and painter obsessed with ideal beauty. That obsession carries over into his romantic life; he searches for the ideal woman so that, in finding her, his desires will be satisfied. By invoking D'Albert's statement Faulkner lets the careful reader know that both "New Orleans" and *Mosquitoes* are concerned with the relationship(s) between form, desire, art, and artistic creation. The revision of the statement in *Mosquitoes* discloses the limitations of D'Albert's position while giving the reader a clear sense of literature's value.

While weaving drunkenly through the French Quarter with Dawson Fairchild and Gordon in the "Epilogue" to *Mosquitoes*, Julius Wiseman repeats portions of "I love three things: gold; marble and purple; splendor, solidity, color" (*NO* 37). However, the quotation, either from *Mademoiselle De Maupin* or from "Wealthy Jew," is never completely transported into *Mosquitoes*. Twice he says "I love three things," and between those two utterances he says "I love three things: gold, marble and purple" (*MOS* 335, 339, 338). At the end of the section he again begins the statement, only to have it broken by a chilling vision of reality:

---

[27]Gresset, "Introduction," 4.

[28]Theophile Gautier, *Mademoiselle de Maupin*, trans. Paul Selver (London: H. Hamilton, 1948) 130.

"I love three things: gold, marble and purple—")
The priests cross themselves while the nuns of silence blend anew their breath, and pass on: soon the high windowless walls have hushed away their thin celibate despair. The rats are arrogant as cigarettes. After a while they steal forth again climbing over the beggar, dragging their hot bellies over him, exploring unreproved his private parts. Somewhere above the dark street, above the windcarved hills, beyond the silence; thin pipes unheard, wild and passionate and sad. ("—form solidity color," he said to his own dark and passionate heart and to Fairchild beside him, leaning against the dark wall, vomiting.) (*MOS* 340).

By effectively fracturing d'Albert's aesthetics with a sobering depiction of poverty and death, the narrative undercuts its legitimacy and suggests that a more "correct" application of form and art will consider both the seemly and the unseemly. The narrative fracture, then, suggests that fiction must be grounded in extratextual "worlds" different from those d'Albert privileges. Faulkner's decision to place the last invocation of "I love three things: gold; marble and purple; splendor, solidity, color" within quotation marks also compels us to read the revision against the wealthy Jew's appropriation of the line as his framing device. Replacing "splendor" with "form" illuminates Faulkner's concern with the latter while also working to unbound the aesthetics of overdetermination underlying the wealthy Jew's use of the quotation.

Faulkner's return in *Mosquitoes* to a critique of the wealthy Jew's aesthetics also enables him to break the framing statement in order to articulate an awareness of fiction's nature and power. Gordon, after first asking for and receiving money from Julius, leaves the men to purchase the sexual favors of a prostitute. Julius and Dawson Fairchild go on and a portion of the framing statement is repeated. Here, however, the frame is broken with the first of two ellipses to be found in Section 9 of the "Epilogue," two ellipses that constitute a frame standing in juxtaposition to the wealthy Jew's frame, and in so doing transports the mark of indeterminacy into the text so that Faulkner might effectively supplement the wealthy Jew's narrative and aesthetics with a statement on the nature of literary art: "I love three things. . . . Dante invented Beatrice, creating himself a maid that life had not had time to create, and laid upon her frail and unbowed shoulders the whole burden of man's history of his impossible heart's desire" (*MOS* 339). Dante created Beatrice because "life had not had time to create" her, and he was able to do so because of fiction's nature. The play of intratextual and extratextual fields necessary for creation is only possible because of the subjunctive nature of fiction.[29] Indeterminacy, then, is liberating; just as the indeterminate nature of the ellipsis liberates Faulkner from the wealthy Jew's aesthetics, so too does the indeterminate nature of fictions liberate the artist from the "real" world so that he or she might create.

Thomas Pavel, in his examination of the connection between fiction and ritual, remarks that "periods of transition and conflict tend to maximize the incompleteness of fictional worlds, which supposedly mirrors corresponding features outside fiction."[30] While Pavel argues that the subsequent temptation is "to lift gradually all constraints on determinacy and to let incompleteness erode the very texture of fictional worlds," a temptation he considers dangerous, it is my contention that incompleteness and indeterminacy are both essential to Faulkner's fictions and vital components of the texture of Faulkner's fictional construct.[31] Such is in keeping with both the nature of language and that of social life. Regarding the latter, Sally Falk Moore has written, "the underlying quality of social life should be considered to be one of theoretical absolute indeterminacy."[32] Furthermore, while Pavel wants contemporary writers to "acknowledge gracefully the difficulty of making firm sense of the world, and to still risk the invention of a completeness/ determinacy myth" based upon ritual emotion, we shall see that Faulkner, in many ways our contemporary, invents no such myth.[33] Rather, Faulkner acknowledges the liberating quality inherent in indeterminacy in *Mosquitoes* and stresses it formally and thematically throughout the texts we have yet to examine even as his characters wrestle with it in their lives. Using the rite of passage as thematic and narrative concern enables Faulkner to point out the indeterminacy of his age, use the very qualities inherent in the indeterminacy of writing to undermine, subvert, and destroy overly determined historical and literary conventions, and create formed, balanced, ordered works of art.

---

[29]See Iser, "Feigning in Fiction," in *Identity of the Literary Text*, 204-228.

[30]Thomas Pavel, "Incomplete Worlds, Ritual Emotions," *Philosophy and Literature* 7 (1983) 52.

[31]See, e.g., ibid.

[32]Sally Falk Moore and Barbara Myerhoff, eds., *Secular Ritual* (Leyden: Van Gorcum, 1977) 48.

[33]Pavel, "Incomplete Worlds," 57.

"New Orleans" contrapuntal form hews to the aesthetics Faulkner articulated in 1948 and enables him to articulate the nature of fictions and the process of making meaning; the invocation of "New Orleans" in *Mosquitoes* creates an intertextual connection of contrapuntal integration enabling Faulkner to disclose his reading of fiction's value. Early on Sherwood Anderson told Faulkner to write about what he knew best, but "New Orleans" suggests that in 1925 Faulkner was already writing as he would in his major works. Like Dante, Faulkner would create, and his creations would articulate both his characters' desires and his own as he confronted the human condition as it was manifested in his region and his time. What remained left to discover in order to answer Anderson's admonition was the proper vehicle, the proper phrase, with which to confront the human condition in his fiction. That vehicle, and phrase, is the social structure of the rites of passage, which enables Faulkner to achieve his particularly modern "correctness of form" because its liminal stage, governed by indeterminacy, corresponds to the indeterminate and subjunctive nature of fiction. To see how the rites of passage begin to be successfully employed as narrative strategy and thematic concern we must turn to *Mosquitoes*.

Chapter 2

Mosquitoes *and the Rites of Passage: Making Space and Time*

A. From "Elmer" to *Mosquitoes*

Turning to *Mosquitoes* necessitates moving into and through "Elmer." Faulkner began both "Elmer" and *Mosquitoes* within a year of writing "New Orleans." Biographical evidence suggests that he turned away from work on the former to start what would become his second novel. In a letter written to his mother dated 22 September 1925 from Paris, Faulkner commented that "This [is] part of 'Elmer.' [Faulkner was referring to the writing on the reverse of a page upon which he had drawn his self-portrait.] I have him half done, and I have put him away temporarily to begin a new one."[1] The "new one" Faulkner began was most likely *Mosquitoes*, and, although he would return to "Elmer" a number of times over the next ten years, Faulkner never completed the work. Faulkner's aborted novel is instructive for our purposes because it is linked to both "New Orleans" and *Mosquitoes* in a fashion that enables us to see the increasing importance rites of passage had to Faulkner's fiction and the identity of his characters. Indeed, Faulkner's inability to successfully integrate rites of passage in "Elmer" may well be at least partially responsible for his inability to complete the work.

The artist in "New Orleans" laments the fact that he "can never give to the world that which is crying in [him] to be freed" and as a result cannot realize his desire (*NO*, 47). Similarly, Elmer Hodge is a failed artist because he too cannot realize his desire. When we first meet Elmer he is a young man sailing for Europe; he goes to his cabin and draws

> forth his new unstained box of paints. To finger lasciviously smooth dull silver tubes virgin yet at the same time pregnant, comfortably heavy to the palm—such an immaculate mating of bulk and weight that it were a shame to violate them, innocent clean brushes slender and bristled to all sizes and interesting chubby bodies of oil . . . Elmer

---

[1]William Faulkner, *Selected Letters of William Faulkner*, ed. Joseph Blotner (New York: Random House, 1978) 24-25.

hovered over them with a brooding maternity, taking up one at a time those fat portentous tubes in which was yet wombed his heart's desire, the world itself—thick-bodied and female and at the same time phallic: hermaphroditic. He closed his eyes the better to savoir its feel.[2]

Unlike Dante, however, who in creating Beatrice is able to articulate "his impossible heart's desire," Elmer is unable to bear "his heart's desire" wombed within the tubes of paint (*MOS* 339).

The overdetermined nature of the passage from the beginning of "Elmer" is indicative of the overdetermined psychological nature of the text as a whole. Yet it is precisely that overdetermination that proves so instructive. At the risk of belaboring the obvious, "Elmer" makes it all too clear that Elmer turns to painting in an attempt to manage his incestuous desires. Ultimately, however, the act of painting is a violation analogous to the act of violating the feminine, and in particular the mother, which Elmer is psychologically compelled to at once desire and repress. The narrative implies that his sister Jo-Addie sends Elmer crayons immediately after leaving the family for good, but because the crayons are Elmer's substitute for Jo-Addie, who is in turn a substitute for the mother, "for a long time he would not use them, would not deface their pointed symmetrical purity" ("Elmer" *MQ* 356). Like the tubes of paint Elmer fondles aboard ship, the crayons must remain undefiled if Elmer is to symbolically control his incestuous desires; however, the fact that he eventually uses the crayons suggests the depths of those desires and their pull upon the protagonist. Elmer is also fated to lose Myrtle, who is "clean and young and unattainable" and therefore like "that shape, that image within him [that] had become quite definitely alive: a Diana-like girl with an impregnable integrity" ("Elmer" *MQ* 359;378). The image of an impregnable woman is at some level precisely what Elmer must create if he is to manage his desire and avoid confronting the reality of loss, but the very act of creating that or any other image in art serves as an invocation of violation and loss inasmuch as the artistic object can only stand as the substitute for what it represents. Consequently, Elmer remains troubled by art, women, and the relation of both to his desire.

The text remains troubling as well, both because of its overly overt Freudian rendering of Elmer and because that rendering fails to provide

---

[2]William Faulkner, "Elmer," ed. James B. Meriwether, *Mississippi Quarterly* 36 (Summer 1983), 345.

Faulkner with the necessary vehicle for an articulation of identity. As a consequence, "Elmer" disintegrates and cannot be finished. The text breaks off at the point Elmer goes to the home of his former lover and meets his five-year-old "bastard" son. The child's ball rolls under Elmer's chair, and when Elmer does not retrieve it the child "scream[s], tearless above its gaping mouth, watching him with the blankness of a carven idol" ("Elmer" *MQ* 447). The image is fitting: Elmer is no more able to confront his child than Faulkner is able to confront the reality of his "offspring," the fictive text. The text must break there. The inarticulateness of the scream, pure unmediated despair and pain beyond the capability of words to express, voices Faulkner's failure to find and successfully use the right words or phrase to bring the text to life. Faulkner is unable to satisfactorily employ his understanding of the Freudian interpretation of the psyche to his character, and "Elmer" remains a projection of the issue of identity rather than a text whose structure, whose form, enables the writer to confront and articulate the problematic of identity.

Nevertheless rites of passage creep into "Elmer" in a fashion that suggests some awareness of their importance to identity, the individual, and culture. At one point in the manuscript the narrator tells us that Elmer "was through with women. He would never get married. He'd just be Elmer and paint pictures. Even his mother . . . ." ("Elmer" *MQ* 370). The narrative trails off into the silence of the ellipsis here in order to avoid putting into words the relationship between Elmer, his mother, and all the other women he might know. It is also interesting that when Elmer decides to be through with women it means that he will never marry. The statement discloses the intimate relationship between relationships, rites of passage, and community in a fashion similar to that later articulated by Narcissa Benbow in *Flags in the Dust*. (I shall plumb the depths of Narcissa's articulation in the afterword as part of the examination of the reader in and of Faulkner's texts.) Elmer cannot so easily be through with women, however, and years later, while in Paris, he thinks

> of that complete and virgin box of paints which he had brought five thousand miles with him. Tomorrow he would join a class, see pictures. Myrtle would wait: time enough for Myrtle. He would not even try to find her until he had done something, had something to show her. Elmer Hodge the painter; and the bodies of girls soon to be old and wrinkled but now troubling and sweet as music articulate beneath the

year turning reluctant as a young bride to the old lean body of death
("Elmer" *MQ* 432).

The troubling bodies of women are linked by two identifications
which are, respectively, either the product of a rite of passage, "young
bride," or occasion funeral and interment rites, "death." One is social; the
other is natural. Marriage is a rite by law, by collective consent rather
than natural, biological order, and hence is "not a material thing in the
same sense as biogenetic heredity is. It is not a 'natural thing' in the
sense of a material object found in nature."[3] Nevertheless, marriage
produces identity insofar as it transforms the individual woman into the
social constructs bride and, then, wife. The passage articulates a startling
nexus of the individual, the person as construed in subject positions
determined by the community, gender, and death. However, neither the
passage nor "Elmer" as a whole explores the implications of the
intersection.

Nor does "Elmer" successfully explore the implications of the rites
of passage as they relate to the protagonist. However, the text does
illuminate both *Mosquitoes* and Faulkner's concern with ritual, nature,
and culture by including a rite of passage that serves as an intertextual
connection to his second novel. Like the intertextual connection between
"New Orleans" and *Mosquitoes*, that between "Elmer" and *Mosquitoes*
appears in the troubling ninth section of the "Epilogue" of the latter text.
Again, it is in that section that Gordon, Dawson Fairchild, and Julius
weave drunkenly through the streets of New Orleans. What makes the
section so problematic for the reader are the portions surrounding or
framing the parenthetical passages narrating the three men's actions.
Those framing portions are revisions of material concerning funeral and
interment rites originally found in "Elmer."

While in Venice, Elmer and two companions eat, drink, and spend a
night on the town. The companions, a prostitute and one of Elmer's
recent shipmates, remain relatively sober, but Elmer passes from consciousness to a state where he has a hallucinatory, surrealistic vision of
what appears to be a carnival or celebration. Elmer sees heralds with
trumpets, torchbearers, a "young naked boy whose skin has been daubed
with vermillion," and "the naked headless body of a black woman" with

---

[3]David M. Schneider, *American Kinship: A Cultural Account* (Chicago: University of
Chicago Press, 1970) 36.

slaves bearing "her head on an ivory litter" ("Elmer" *MQ* 420). The spectacle seems at times celebratory, at times ceremonial, and at times macabre. Two groups of priests appear to weave along with the procession, and throughout the vision there is an attendant air of despair. The priests encounter a beggar—accosted by rats for the crust of bread he holds—they think is sleeping but eventually discover is dead. All of these elements are also present in *Mosquitoes*, are in roughly the same sequence as in "Elmer," and show minimal revision. However, in "Elmer" we also learn that,

> . . . . in the midst of women white and sorrowful, clad briefly in skins and chained one to another among which flame-clad pages neither boy nor girl and pages in blue and green leap like salamanders, there passes a white ass on which in a glass coffin lies a young man. He is still as pale amethyst marble, beautiful and cold in the light of torches; ("Elmer" *MQ* 421).

Elmer envisions, at least in part, a funeral procession; hence, the surrealistic ceremonial procession designates a rite of passage. The liminality of the scene is accentuated by the symbolic import of the "flame-clad pages neither boy nor girl" which Elmer sees, for androgynies "as symbols expressive of ambiguous identity" are often found in the liminal stage of rites of passage ceremonies, where their presence accentuates the ambiguous identity of initiates immersed in the liminal and betwixt and between states and subject positions.[4] The crucial scene disclosing that a rite of passage ceremony has been transported from "Elmer" to *Mosquitoes* is left out of the latter text. Consequently, readers unfamiliar with "Elmer" are unable to see that the framing material in section nine of *Mosquitoes* is at least partially governed by a rite of passage ceremony.

The ceremony in "Elmer" is clearly linked to the protagonist. As "the procession passes windows open like eyes in the blind walls and young girls leaning their soft breasts on the window-sills cast violets" upon the young man as he is borne away; earlier, Elmer had seen "seemingly motionless walls tapering upward to a strip of low soft intimate sky in which were huge stars like cast roses above an open coffin" immediately prior to passing out and having his vision ("Elmer" *MQ* 421; 419). The

---

[4]Victor Turner, *On the Edge of the Bush: Anthropology as Experience*, ed. Edith Turner (Tucson: University of Arizona Press, 1985) 295.

fact that the ceremony and Elmer's psychological connection to it are buried in the manuscript rather than integrated with the work suggests that the rite of passage does not play a significant role as either organizing principle or direct thematic concern. Hence, the inscribed rite remains as disintegrated as the unfinished manuscript. Elmer's vision suggests a romantic and almost ludicrous desire to be mourned by scores of women. The revised vision, on the other hand, is directly related to Gordon's sculpted feminine ideal and consequently suggestive of the novel's meditations on rites *and* art. While in "Elmer" "shadows and echoes and perfumes swirling upward slow as smoke gain form changing, becoming a woman slender as a taper with raised joined hands, taunt and proud, fierce and young and sorrowful; and a young rosy child is also in the cloud ere the shadows and echoes and perfumes whirl away," in *Mosquitoes* the shadows and echoes change into an image of Gordon's female and aesthetic ideal: "voices and sounds, shadows and echoes change form swirling, becoming the headless, armless, legless torso of a girl, motionless and virginal and passionately eternal before the shadows and echoes whirl away" (*MOS* 421; 339).

The revisions of material from "Elmer" found in *Mosquitoes* suggest that the latter text—with its preoccupation with the rite of passage, art, and the artist—is the supplement to and re-invention of the "excluded" rite of passage ceremony. Just as the repetition and revision of the wealthy Jew's framing statement from "New Orleans" enables Faulkner to disclose his awareness of fiction's power and value, the repetition and revision of the section from "Elmer," which is linked with the repeated and revised framing passages in section nine of the "Epilogue," discloses that rites of passage are integrated within the text of *Mosquitoes* as narrative strategy and thematic concern. While "The oblique eroticism of his early poetry [and fiction], in addition to reflecting his fondness for Swinburne, suggests that direct expression remained so difficult as to be almost impossible," the appropriation of the rites of passage as thematic concern and unifying principle enables Faulkner to create an expression of identity and community that is meaningful and fundamental.[5] It is the proper phrase. And while "Elmer" suffers from overly overt Freudianism, an insufficiently examined sexual fetishism, and what David Minter has described as Faulkner's own fictionalized "process of direct self-examina-

---

[5]Minter, *William Faulkner*, 28.

tion," the appropriation of the rites of passage in later texts enables Faulkner to examine art and male/female relationships more adequately and, for him, safely.[6] That examination—vital to the application of an aesthetics of indeterminacy to issues of identity, the individual, and community—takes place in *Mosquitoes*.

B. Mosquitoes and the Rite of Passage

Critics have not been kind to *Mosquitoes*: dismissals along the order of Cleanth Brooks's characterization of the work as Faulkner's "least respected novel" are common. The criticism of *Mosquitoes* falls into two general categories. Some critics take issue with what they perceive to be the novel's overwhelming preoccupation with talk, language, and words. These critics find the book to be too much talk and not enough action.[7] Other critics rightly stress the importance of *Mosquitoes* to Faulkner's maturing poetic.[8] In either case, what is missing is an appreciation of the formal aspects of the novel, as well as an understanding of how the form, the principle of unity, empowers the sexual/romantic issues and the metafictive concerns so fundamental to the novel. A careful look at the talk in the novel will enable us to see that the talk, what it is and what it is about, is fundamentally important to the novel's form and structure rather than a liability. *Mosquitoes* is a better and more carefully formed work than critics have previously noted. In addition, *Mosquitoes* is central to Faulkner's development as a writer, because one can see in the novel a group of characters immersed in liminal situations. *Mosquitoes* is the first true instance of Faulkner's work appropriating rites of passage as organizing principle, as narrative strategy, and as a specific and important

---

[6]Ibid., 55.

[7]See, for instance, Cleanth Brooks, *Toward Yoknapatawpha and Beyond* (New Haven CT: Yale University Press, 1978); William O'Connor, *The Tangled Fire of William Faulkner* (Minneapolis: University of Minnesota Press, 1954); Olga Vickery, *The Novels of William Faulkner* (Baton Rouge: Louisiana State University Press, 1964); and, to a significantly lesser extent, Judith Wittenberg, *William Faulkner: The Transfiguration of Biography* (Lincoln: University of Nebraska Press, 1979).

[8]See, for instance, Irwin, *Doubling and Incest*; Kenneth Hepburn, "Faulkner's *Mosquitoes*: A Poetic Turning Point," *Twentieth Century Literature* 17/1 (1971): 19-28; and, again, Wittenberg, *William Faulkner: The Transfiguration of Biography*.

theme. In addition, the novel has an important metaliterary aspect, as Faulkner also seems to be attempting to write out his own specific consideration of the rites of passage of the artist—perhaps so that he might in some sense define himself and the artistic space he was to inhabit.

Mosquitoes is separated into six sections: the "Prologue," "The First Day," "The Second Day," "The Third Day," "The Fourth Day," and the "Epilogue." It is possible to read the structure of the text as consistent with the structure of a complete rite of passage.[9] According to van Gennep, a rite of passage is separated into three parts: rites of separation, rites of transition, and rites of incorporation. During the rites of separation, or preliminal phase, the individual or group is separated from the community psychologically and, often, physically. During the rites of transition, or liminal phase, the individual or group exists "betwixt and between" states, to use Victor Turner's phrasing, and is subject to the loss and re-invention of identity. During the rites of incorporation, or postliminal phase, the individual or group reenters the community, and the successful closure of the rite marks the emergence of the individual or group into the new state. One can view the "Prologue" of *Mosquitoes* as the preliminal stage of a rite of passage. It is then that the ship's company is gathered and we begin to learn something about these characters. The four days aboard ship constitute the liminal stage, and the "Epilogue" marks the postliminal. The text focuses on the characters who make or attempt a rite of passage while aboard the *Nausikaa*: in particular Gordon, David West, Patricia Robyn, and Mr. Talliaferro. Examining these characters and Dawson Fairchild, what they say and where in the narrative they say it, and the mythic figures alluded to in the text enables the reader to see how important *Mosquitoes* is to Faulkner's developing concerns with the identity of his characters and his texts.

Dawson Fairchild and Julius Wiseman are topside talking after supper on the evening of the third day aboard the yacht. They begin talking about Gordon, who has been missing since the abortive attempt to pull

---

[9]Kenneth Hepburn writes that, "The somewhat tired suggestion of *Mosquitoes* is that all the characters have been removed from time, have had meaningful experiences in a timeless state, and, subtly altered, have been returned to a time sequence which will expect them all to be unchanged" ("Faulkner's *Mosquitoes*, 19-20). What Hepburn unknowingly glosses in this sentence is the rudimentary form and function of the rite of passage. That is, one typically emerges from the liminal period of the rite of passage changed.

the *Nausikaa* off the sandbar where she is aground. Soon, however, the men start discussing sin and youth and sex and death. According to Fairchild, when he was twelve he spent the summer at his Grandfather's home in the country. There are other children present, but Fairchild remains apart from them because he "didn't know how to go about getting acquainted with them" (*MOS* 232). Acting haughty and aloof, while all the time scared inside, Fairchild watches a young girl of about his own age become the leader of the group of children. Fairchild is down by the outhouse late in the summer when he sees the young girl coming down the path to go to the toilet. Afraid to pass the girl along the path, Fairchild goes into the men's side of the outhouse. He intends to wait there until the girl leaves, but curiosity overcomes him and he sticks his head through the seat in an attempt to spy on the girl.

> I remember how hot it was in there, and that feeling places like that give you—a kind of letting down of the bars of pretense, you know; a kind of submerging of civilized structures before the grand implacability of nature and the physical body. And I stood there, feeling this feeling and the heat, and hearing the drone of those big flies, holding my breath and listening for a sound from beyond the partition. But there wasn't any sound from beyond it, so I put my head through the seat (*MOS* 234).

To his surprise, Fairchild sees the inverted head of the young girl looking at him, and now, thirty years later, he and Julius sit in silence, "remembering youth and love, and time and death" (*MOS* 234).

In his essay on *Mosquitoes*, Brooks traces the source of the story to an incident that happened to William Spratling. According to Brooks, "In *File on Spratling* (pp 14-15), Spratling tells how, as a little boy, on his way to the outside privy, he noticed a little girl of about his age who was evidently bound for the same place. He entered as he thought unobserved and kept very quietly on his side of the partition. But overcome by curiosity, he puts his head through the privy hole to see what he could see. To his complete surprise he found himself looking into the face of the little girl."[10] Brooks speculates that Spratling, a sculptor, served as a model for Gordon in *Mosquitoes*. Spratling himself apparently believed that to be the case. While arguing that it is more fitting that Fairchild tell

[10]Brooks, *Toward Yoknapatawpha*, 139-140.

the story than Gordon, citing as evidence the fact that Faulkner is writing
fiction rather than biography, Brooks neglects the substance of the story
itself.[11]

A sentence describing the night sky appears midway through
Fairchild's story and illuminates his tale. The narrator tells us that,
"Arcturus, Orion swinging head downward by his knees, in the southern
sky an electric lobster fading as the moon rose" (*MOS* 234). The arch
language and shifting tense call immediate attention to a sentence which
disrupts reality, fractures sense, by placing an electric lobster in the sky.
To borrow from Riffaterre, both the "strangeness" of electric as a
modifier for lobster and the strangeness of a lobster in the sky suggest
that the sentence is constructed in order that the reader take notice.[12] The
lack of a concrete metonymic referent encourages the reader to linger
over the sentence and, as a consequence, see the implicit connection
between Orion and Fairchild. That is, Orion is situated with its head
down by its knees; Fairchild assumes the same position in order to look
through the privy hole. One is left wondering why Faulkner chooses to
make such a comparison between Orion and Fairchild.

Orion is one of the mightiest hunters in Greek mythology. He is also,
according to the tales Robert Graves compiled in *The Greek Mythologies*,
the handsomest man alive. Although Fairchild assumes the role of the
hunter, a role made clear by the similarity between the position Fairchild
assumed and the position of the constellation above Fairchild's head years
later, the role assumption is laced with irony. Fairchild is *not* a mighty
hunter; he is not, so far as we know, the handsomest man in the world;
he does not have a significant number of amorous or sexual relationships
with women. When Fairchild sticks his head through the privy hole he
becomes a hunter, a hunter poised on the threshold into adolescence, but
his prey turns the tables by assuming the role of hunter instead of the
hunted. Despite the similarity in their respective positions, then, there is
an ironic distancing between Orion and Dawson Fairchild.

What is more, Orion is at once the extraordinary hero figure, the
great hunter, and, according to the fragments we have, a man who
perishes at the hands of a woman. In one group of fragments Artemis
kills Orion because he tried to rape her. In another group, Artemis kills

[11]Ibid., 140.

[12]See Micheal Riffaterre, "Generating Lautremont's Text," *Textual Strategies*, ed.
Josue V. Harari (Ithaca NY: Cornell University Press, 1979), 404-420.

Orion because he amorously chased the seven Pleiades. Artemis, in still another group of myths, sends a scorpion to sting Orion because he has been chasing the Pleiades. Finally, in one group of myths Apollo tricks Artemis into killing Orion. Artemis is the virgin goddess of both the heart and the moon. She is woman unsoiled, and Orion's attraction to her leads to his death. Quite simply, Orion cannot have her. That unattainability might very well explain the position of the constellation in *Mosquitoes*. Head down by his knees, Orion is at least bowed if not beaten.

In "Elmer," Elmer constructs and craves his image of a "Dianalike girl of impregnable integrity." In invoking Orion, and hence Artemis, Faulkner subtly distances himself from the root of Elmer's desires while at the same time incorporating a figure of great importance to his text. Orion is one of two governing masculine images in the text, and his image is two-sided. For some, there may be a certain attractiveness in this mythological figure who possesses great physical and sexual prowess and takes what he wants. Yet those very qualities lead to his death. Orion comes to represent, then, one aspect of the male condition in relation to women as defined in *Mosquitoes*. Fairchild is unlike Orion insofar as Fairchild is not a great hunter and seducer of women, and Fairchild is like Orion insofar as his identity is determined by women. For Fairchild this determinism exists beyond the act of sexual intercourse: it also includes women as the primary audience for literature and, finally, for all art. Fairchild says that he believes that "every word a writing man writes is put down with the ultimate intention of impressing some woman that don't probably care anything at all for literature, as is the nature of women" (*MOS* 250). Nevertheless, Fairchild's message is that the pursuit of women, cast here in terms of a hunt, is fundamental to a determination of male identity. *Mosquitoes* supports this position insofar as Gordon, David West, and Mr. Talliaferro each pursue amorous and sexual relations with women during the voyage, pursuits which help determine their identity.

Several of the stories Fairchild tells aboard the *Nausikaa* serve to disclose the importance of rites of passage to the text. For instance, Fairchild tells Gus Robyn a story about his attempt to join a fraternity. When Fairchild was a freshman in college a man in his boarding house said Fairchild could join a fraternity if he gave him twenty-five dollars. Fairchild, who "wanted to get all [he] could out of college," takes a job at the college power plant in order to earn the money. He makes the money, gives it to the man, and is told to wait behind the library the next night. The man does not show up, and Fairchild waits alone and in the cold of a late November snow while a party goes on at the women's dormitory.

> "So I walked back and forth, stomping my feet, and after a while I went around the corner of the library where it wasn't so cold, and I could stick my head out occasionally in case they came looking for me. From this side of the building I could see the hall where the girl students lived. It was all lighted up, as if for a party, and I could see shadows coming and going upon the drawn shades where they were dancing and fixing their hair and all; and pretty soon I heard a crowd coming across the campus and I thought, here they come at last. But they passed on, going toward the girl's hall, where the party was.
>
> I walked up and down some more, stomping my feet. Pretty soon I heard a clock striking nine. In half an hour I'd have to be back at the powerhouse. They were playing music at the party: I could hear it even in spite of the closed windows, and I thought maybe I'd go closer. But the wind was colder: there was a little snow in it, and besides I was afraid they might come for me and I wouldn't be there. So I stomped my feet, walking up and down.
>
> Pretty soon I knew it must be nine-thirty, but I stayed a while longer, and soon it was snowing harder—a blizzard." (*MOS* 119).

Cheated by a man he trusted, wronged by the violation of a social contract, Fairchild is unable to participate in the rite of passage he desires. He remains on the outside. Years later, he is able to laugh at himself while recounting the incident to Gus, and his honest introspection upon reflection, coupled with the image of himself he creates in the story, brings him closer to becoming a sympathetic character than he has been up to this point in the novel. In the story Fairchild abandons his position of words for words' sake, a position also taken by Quentin Compson in *The Sound and the Fury*, in order to use words for personal illumination. In so doing he reveals something about what makes Dawson Fairchild an artist. He is outside the college world here, and as an artist he is really outside the world as well. In college he can move close to the world represented by the woman's dormitory—that world of laughter, music, dance, women, and courtship—but he cannot leave the world represented by the library—that world of words, of books, of art. He is not allowed a chance at initiation into a fraternity, and, a shy, watchful eighteen-year-old, he is unable to enter the community of the dorm where he might one day participate in rites of courtship. So it snows on Dawson Fairchild, and his life becomes something cold and white. That first white, hard blizzard of winter symbolizes the purity and clarity of Fairchild's world; it symbolizes the chilling sterility as well.

If the college story tells us something about Fairchild and the importance of ritual, then the story Fairchild tells about Al and Claude Jackson refers to what happens as a result of participation in a rite of passage.[13] Claude, one may recall, metamorphoses into an alligator-like beast after spending too much time in the water chasing what has become of Al's sheep. Old man Jackson raises sheep in the Tchufuncta river swamp on the assumption that the wool of his sheep will grow as well as the vegetation which grows on the trees in the swamp. The sheep take to the water, learn to swim and dive, and eventually cannot be caught at shearing time. Claude has to go into the water, swim down the "sheep," and herd them into a corral Old Man Jackson has built for the roundup at shearing time. Claude finally becomes more fish than man: "[his] eyes . . . kind of shifted around to the side of his head and his mouth . . . spread back a good way, and his teeth . . . got longer" (*MOS* 280).

The Claude Jackson tale is about transformation and is therefore linked with rites of passage. In this tale, in the college story, and in the allusion to Orion we have transformation, passage rites of initiation and courtship, the pursuit of women, and—given that the stories are themselves constructs created by an artist—art. These are precisely what *Mosquitoes* examines.

When the reader sees the importance of both the stories Dawson Fairchild tells and the allusion to Orion in one of the stories, then he/she sees that Faulkner has greater formal and stylistic control of his novel than most critics have heretofore acknowledged. For instance, Dawson Fairchild's tale of his aborted attempt to join a college fraternity is followed by the first meeting between David West and Patricia. The contrapuntal nature of the text compels the reader to read the latter in light of the former and see the relationship between David and Patricia in light of a failed attempt at a rite of passage. David's relationship with Patricia suffers from a similar lack of success.

---

[13]William O'Connor notes that, "Faulkner puts into Fairchild's mouth the first tall tales that will appear in his fiction. He has Fairchild tell a story, for example, of a man and sheep turning into fish" (31). Brooks mentions the same story. He criticizes Faulkner's mastery of the use of tall tales in *Mosquitoes*, calling the Al and Claude tales "early and crude," but makes no attempt to come to terms with their substance.

David West, the ship's steward, is a semi-literate drifter working on Mrs. Maurier's yacht. Patricia is intrigued by David's stories of Mediterranean ports and a place in the Alps where, "you could lay on your back on the mountain . . . and watch eagles flying around way up above the water, until sunset" (*MOS* 124). She immediately makes plans to go there next summer with David as her guide. Although hesitant, David is also attracted to Pat. They go swimming at midnight and immediately afterward decide to run off together early that morning. Pat runs off to get to the romanticized vision of Europe which David has given her. David runs off because he is physically attracted to Pat.

Patricia is clearly in control of the journey through a swamp where "trees heavy and ancient with moss loomed" and the "mist might have been the first prehistoric morning of time itself; it might have been the very substance in which the seed of the beginning of things fecundated" (*MOS* 169). David and Patricia get lost in this prelapsarian world where "against the hidden flame of the west huge trees brooded bearded and ancient as prophets out of Genesis" (*MOS* 211). The "prophets out of Genesis" are necessary because of Adam and Eve's transgressions in the Garden. Like them, David and Pat transgress a boundary when they run off together, only to find a swamp, heat, and torture instead of a garden. The allusion to Adam and Eve is especially ironic, for David and Pat never gain sexual awareness and knowledge of each other. Instead, Pat admonishes David for looking at her "like a man," and David is left with a desire which he is unable to satisfy. Lost in the "timeless swamp," David is unable to achieve any rite of passage. Patricia will hug him in a way which is "hard and firm and sexless," but she will not let David kiss her on the lips.

Reduced to complete passivity, David goes back to the yacht with Patricia. Later that evening, immediately after Fairchild finishes his story about the twelve-year-old girl, Fairchild comes across David sitting on the deck; he holds Patricia's slipper, "cracked and stained with dried mud and disreputable, yet seeming still to hold in its mute shape something of that hard and sexless graveness of hers" (*MOS* 235). David, overcome by his longing for Patricia, is left with only the soiled slipper to serve as a fetish object, a talisman. It is at moments like this one in the narrative that the text incorporates the Freudian interpretation of the psyche managed either within or by the structure of the rite of passage. The text makes it clear that fetishism can result in a dangerous removal from reality. Unable to achieve passage, David is left with an act of symbolization to fend off the castration complex brought up by his failure. His "fetishistic reverence for a woman's foot and **shoe** appears to take the foot merely as a substitutive symbol for the woman's penis which was once revered and later missed."[14] At the same time, David sits on a "coiled rope," and his attachment to the symbolic umbilical cord discloses his regressed state and the fact that he is no longer truly in the world.[15] Silent and pathetic, his passage failed and his psyche fractured, David can only leave the yacht.

While David West pursues the sexless Patricia, Mr. Talliaferro pursues the sensual but ultimately inert Jenny. Her appeal stems from "an utterly mindless rifeness of young, pink flesh, a supine potential fecundity lovely to look upon," but Talliaferro is unsure how to approach her (*MOS* 104). Mr. Talliaferro claims that the "sex instinct" is his "dominating compulsion," but throughout the voyage he fails to deal successfully with it. His romantic pursuit is determined in no small measure by the difficulty he has dealing with desire. Mr. Talliaferro is presented as naive when it comes to amorous relationships with women. This is ironic because Mr. Talliaferro works in the women's clothing department of a major New Orleans department store. Around women all the time, Mr. Talliaferro nevertheless leads a romanceless life. He believes that his failure to attract a woman is due to a succession of incorrect approaches. He therefore constantly turns to Dawson Fairchild for advice concerning the validity of this or that approach. Fairchild's advice to Mr. Talliaferro concerning Jenny is for Mr. Talliaferro to be bold, but not to be bold with words.

With Fairchild's advice echoing in his ears, Mr. Talliaferro comes upon Jenny sleeping in a lounge chair on deck. Mr. Talliaferro becomes the hunter; he "prowls restlessly" about while deciding how to be bold without words. Mr. Talliaferro does not truly know what to do, but with "a harried despair of futility and an implacable passing of opportunity" he gets on his knees to kiss her. Even as Mr. Talliaferro prepares to kiss Jenny, however, it seems "as though he stood nearby yet aloof, watching

---

[14]Sigmund Freud, *The Standard Edition of the Complete Psychological Works of Sigmund Freud*, 24 vols., ed. by James Strachey (London: Hogarth Press, 1966-74) XI:96 emphasis added.
[15]For Freud on the fetish see, *The Standard Edition of the Complete Psychological Works of Sigmund Freud*, 7:153-155, 21:152-159, and 23:195-204. For Freud on the relationship between the fetish and the castration complex see 11:96 and 21:152-153.

his own antics" (*MOS* 128).[16] Faulkner uses an interior monologue to disclose Talliaferro's perspective as he nuzzles for Jenny's mouth and she comes awake beneath him: "Hard this floor his old knees yes yes Jenny her breath Yes yes her red soft mouth where little teeth but showed parted blondeness a golden pink swirl kaleidoscopic a single blue eye not come fully awake her breath yes yes" (*MOS* 128). The monologue seems to echo Molly Bloom's at the end of *Ulysses*, but whereas the latter interior monologue ends in affirmation and fulfillment Mr. Talliaferro's interior monologue only leads to denial and a lack of fulfillment. On his knees, in the same position Orion is in in the text, Mr. Talliaferro jabbers in a falsetto voice, "Wake sleeping princess Kiss," only to have Jenny awaken in time to turn her face from him. Close to madness, laughing a "thin hysterical laugh," Mr. Talliaferro feels obsessed to complete the gesture. He tries again to kiss Jenny, she swears and thrusts him away, and he flees.

Both Talliaferro's garbled line prior to Jenny's awakening and that which follows, "'Wake princess with kiss'," allude to the cycle of "Sleeping Beauty" fairy and folk tales. Those tales, of which Perrault's "La Belle au bois dormant" (1697) is only one version, often hinge upon a structure of male dominance, control, and violation of the female. Talliaferro's invocation of "Sleeping Beauty" suggests that his attempted romantic and sexual relations are governed by strategies of masculine control and dominance. Even the most sanitized version of the tale, in which the prince has the "power" to bring the woman to life, indicates that Talliaferro believes that he has the power to awaken women.

Such a belief explains why, unlike David West, Mr. Talliaferro continues his attempt to capture the object of his romantic pursuit. Jenny does little to deter Mr. Talliaferro's advances: she dances with him in order to make her boyfriend Pete jealous; she allows him to accompany her while she roams the deck in the afternoon heat. During their stroll,

---

[16]Mr. Talliaferro is linked to both Dawson Fairchild and Quentin Compson here. Fairchild also stood nearby yet aloof while the other children played on his grandfather's farm and Quentin stands outside himself during a crucial moment in *The Sound and the Fury*. Quentin's moment of "disintegration" comes when he meets with Dalton Ames to tell him to leave town. That meeting quite fittingly occurs on a bridge; the location discloses the liminal nature of Quentin's narrative, even as the scene, showing the reader Quentin's failure to succeed in what John T. Irwin has labeled the "brother-avenger" role, discloses why Quentin remains immersed in the liminal, betwixt and between. That immersion, of course, will lead to his final immersion in the Charles River.

Jenny encloses him in the "sweet cloudy fire of her thighs." At this moment, when Mr. Talliaferro feels that "a lightness was moving down his members, a lightness so exquisite as to be almost unbearable," he denies his sexual instinct and flees (*MOS* 189). When Jenny makes her pass at Mr. Talliaferro and the exquisite lightness moves down his members, Mr. Talliaferro listens to the "dry, interminable incoherence of his own voice" (*MOS* 188). Here, sexual desire, coupled with the close proximity of both the object of that desire and the realization of sexual fulfillment, leads to inarticulation and the diminishment of the voice's effectiveness. Voice is supremely important to Mr. Talliaferro; he feigns an accent, not very well we learn, in order to appear more worldly and consequently more desirable. Words, the product of voice, are absolutely crucial to Talliaferro; he considers language so central that he has the "key" when he finds "the Word" necessary to win/seduce Jenny (*MOS* 306). One might remark here that he turns to words prior to action, "Wake sleeping princess kiss," when he tries to arouse Jenny while she is asleep. The failed outcome of each of Mr. Talliaferro's attempts suggests, however, that he is misusing or wronging language.[17]

Mr. Talliaferro flees from Jenny because she has reversed the roles and become the hunter. Locked into a patriarchal value-system and a pattern of ritualized courtship behavior that privileges *his* voice and discourse, Mr. Talliaferro cannot tolerate such a role reversal. He has to be the hunter; when he is hunted he has to run. Beth L. Bailey notes that the literature of courtship in America up and into the twentieth-century projected the belief that "masculinity translated into 'dominance' and femininity into 'submission.' These traits were acted out in various rituals and customs of etiquette, through which the woman demonstrated her need for protection and the man his ability to protect her."[18] Talliaferro flees Jenny because her "performing a role properly masculine," becoming the sexual aggressor, threatens his "dominance and thus his very masculinity."[19] The difference in age between Mr. Talliaferro and Jenny also may have had something to do with his reaction, and her actions.

---

[17]Words also fail Mrs. Maurier, so much so that they become like "vain unmated birds in the air," and consequently it is fitting that she and Mr. Talliaferro, both misusers of language, end up together (*MOS* 261).

[18]Beth L. Bailey, *From Front Porch to Back Seat: Courtship in Twentieth-Century America* (Baltimore: Johns Hopkins University Press, 1988) 110.

[19]See, e.g., ibid.

The customs and rituals of courtship operating for Talliaferro's generation were not so liberal as those for Jenny's. The youth of Jenny's generation, according to Paula Fass, "elaborated two basic rituals of social interaction —dating and petting."[20] Hence, as Ellen K. Rothman writes, "By 1930 the terrain through which young Americans passed en route to marriage would be almost unrecognizable to their parents. . . . The men and women who courted circa 1900 and their children coming of age in the 1920s were separated by as wide a gulf [in terms of courtship rituals and in terms of an understanding of them] as that between any two American generations."[21]

Mr. Talliaferro, then, has trouble making love with Jenny both because she does not seem to want to make love and because he is locked into a particular pattern of ritualized courtship behavior. As such he cannot complete the romantic pursuit which represents, for him, a rite of passage. His only recourse is to turn to Dawson Fairchild for advice on how to proceed. Fairchild again tells Mr. Talliaferro to be bold; Mr. Talliaferro again takes Fairchild's advice to heart. As a result of his boldness, Mr. Talliaferro mistakenly sleeps with Mrs. Maurier and thereby feels compelled to become engaged. But while he is engaged to go through a rite of passage ceremony, his upcoming marriage to Mrs. Maurier, it is clear that he has not changed in any substantial way. Mr. Talliaferro still attempts to seduce Jenny, and he still believes that he has simply to get the system, the secret down right.

In the "Epilogue," Mr. Talliaferro tries a new approach on Jenny; she ends up going home with another man. Inwardly despairing but outwardly the same as ever, Mr. Talliaferro goes home wondering what went wrong. He finds it "unbearable to believe that he had never had the power to stir women," and, "seeing freedom and youth deserting him again, had known at first a clear, sharp regret, almost a despair, realizing that marriage this time would be a climacteric, that after his he would be definitely no longer young" (*MOS* 346). Talliaferro is ultimately left as helpless as David West; he too has been unable to achieve any success in his quest.

Gordon differs from the other male "hunters" in the text in two ways: he fights his desire and he is an artist. Gordon wavers between going and

---

[20]Paula Fass, *The Damned and the Beautiful: American Youth in the 1920s* (New York: Oxford University Press, 1977) 262.

[21]Ellen K. Rothman, *Hands and Hearts: A History of Courtship in America* (New York: Basic Books, 1984) 289.

not going on the cruise. We learn in the "Prologue" that Gordon is a man who does not have time for women, or cruises, or anything else which might distract him from his artistic work. And yet he is torn between following through on his attraction to Patricia or staying away from her and near the attraction of his sculpture. He considers the sculpture his "feminine ideal: a virgin with no legs to leave me, no arms to hold me, no head to talk to me" (*MOS* 26). Gordon eventually goes on the cruise he thinks will be his "autogethesemane," only to have it serve as a place of mental and spiritual suffering.

Gordon invokes the celestial figure Israfel. Indeed, if Orion serves as symbolic of one aspect of the male condition in relation to women, the figure or type around which David West and Mr. Talliaferro can be clustered, then Israfel is the other governing masculine figure in the novel, the one around which Gordon gravitates, and the one which enables the reader to come to terms with the relation between *Mosquitoes* and Faulkner's ideology of the artistic object and developing aesthetics. Before the voyage begins Gordon thinks of Israfel, and later, when the *Nausikaa* is aground and Patricia is off with David, Gordon thinks, "ay ay struggle your heart o israfel winged with loneliness feathered bitter with pride" (*MOS* 187). The text posits that acting toward women like the angel Israfel is the alternative to acting toward them like Orion the Hunter. Orion can chase the Pleiades, but he can never catch them. Israfel, at least Edgar Allan Poe's Israfel, can catch the Pleiades with song and music:

In Heaven a spirit doth dwell
"Whose heart-strings are a lute";
None sing so wildly well
As the angel Israfel,
And the giddy stars (so legends tell),
Ceasing their hymns, attend the spell
of his voice, all mute.

Tottering above
In her highest noon
The enamoured moon
Blushes with love,
While to listen, the red levin
(With the rapid Pleiads, even,
Which were seven,)

Pauses in Heaven.

And they say (the starry choir
And the other listening things)
That Israfel's fire
Is owing to that lyre
By which he sits and sings—
The trembling living wire
Of those unusual strings.
(ll. 1-22)

Mosquitoes comes full circle back to Dawson Fairchild's contention that every word a man writes is intended to impress a woman. What is more, the ante has been raised so that art is being created, if not to impress women, to at least act as a defense, a sanctuary, against women. Art becomes a privileged, marginalized space. Through art, you may hold women for a time, and, at the same time, create in your art that which is your feminine ideal. Furthermore, art, as it is defined by Mrs. Maurier, has an added quality: she says, "There is so much unhappiness in the world . . ." and adds, "To go through life, keeping yourself from becoming involved in it, to gather inspiration for your Work—ah, Mr. Gordon, how lucky you who create are" (*MOS* 153). Art is presented as a way by which to avoid the unpleasantness of life; by practicing art the artist removes himself from the world. As I explore in the afterword, Mrs. Maurier's phrasing of the relationship between the artist and his work is analogous to the relationship between the reader and the work that Narcissa Benbow champions and that Faulkner's fictions contrive to subvert.

Gordon surely embodies and realizes this questionable artistic position; he has created in his statue his, "feminine ideal: a virgin with no legs to leave me, no arms to hold me, no head to talk to me" (*MOS* 26). Patricia wants to buy the statue from Gordon, but he refuses to sell the sculpture to her: to do so would be to give up his created feminine ideal. That would mean, as John Irwin points out, giving up "the artist's fated substitute for the real sexual possession."[22] Patricia's name "is like a golden bell" hung on Gordon's heart, but Gordon denies the golden bell which he desires. What Patricia asks for, which in Gordon's view is

---

[22]John T. Irwin, *Doubling and Incest*, 160.

nothing less than the abdication of the artistic self, is more than Gordon can give.

Israfel may be a model to emulate and strive for, but the narrative makes clear that it is ultimately lacking. The poet in Poe's "Israfel" laments the fact that Israfel, the ideal poet, sings his verse in heaven while the narrator is confined to earth:

> Yes, Heaven is thine: but this
> Is a world of sweets and sours;
> Our flowers are merely flowers (ll. 40-42)

The poet/narrator ends by saying that he too might sing so well if he could dwell where Israfel dwells. But he does not; nor does Gordon; nor do we. Hence Israfel is ultimately an unsuitable model. Gordon is troubled and unhappy when he lets Patricia go on the evening of the fourth day aboard the *Nausikaa*. His psychological state suggests that taking Israfel as your model for relationships with women means self-castration at some psychic and emotional level; one is therefore to some extent back into the world represented by Dawson Fairchild's cold blizzard. Finally, the narrator's description of Gordon as "Sufficient unto himself in the city of his arrogance, in the marble tower of his loneliness and pride" also serves to suggest the undesirability of Gordon's position (*MOS* 153).

What is more, Gordon's actions in the "Epilogue" serve to completely undermine the validity of Israfel as a role-model. A bitter and angry Gordon takes money from Julius in order to purchase intercourse with a prostitute:

> (A door opened in the wall. Gordon entered and before the door closed again they saw him in a narrow passageway lift a woman from the shadow and raise her against the mad stars, smothering her squeal against his tall kiss) (*MOS* 338-39).

Gordon goes through a door in order to get what acting like Israfel cannot get him. The prostitute, moreover, does not pose the threat that Patricia does; the prostitute is interested only in physical desires and pleasures. As such, she is less threatening than Patricia, who is interested in more than physical desires and pleasures. Patricia comes into Gordon's life "like a star, like a flame," like a Pleiad threatening to make him

Orion, and Gordon must take a perverse refuge with the prostitute in order to secure his kinship with Israfel (*MOS* 153). Still, Gordon's actions undercut his position insofar as Israfel's capture of the Pleiades is an aesthetic one while Gordon's turn to the prostitute is physical, economic, and involves a commodification of the body. In "New Orleans" Faulkner articulates the necessary limitations of turning to a commodification of the body in order to deal with desire. Faulkner constructs Gordon's position in *Mosquitoes* so that the reader sees it is similarly tainted. Gordon makes love with the prostitute to at once satiate physical desire and negate his physical *and* emotional feelings for Patricia. After his brief tumble down into the world of the fallen poet Gordon will attempt to clamber back up to his position beside Israfel. If the voyage is Gordon's autogethesemane, than he has survived his time of suffering: it remains for the reader to see exactly how well off he is following the voyage.

The door Gordon goes through in order to have sexual intercourse with the prostitute is the antithesis of a door Fairchild mentions while aboard the *Nausikaa*. While in conversation with Julius and Mrs. Wiseman, Fairchild says,

> "Well—" Fairchild stared again at the page under his hand. He said slowly: "It's a kind of dark thing. It's kind of like somebody brings you to a dark door. Will you enter the room, or not?" "But the old fellows got you into the room first," the Semitic man said. "Then they asked you if you wanted to go or not. "I don't know. There are rooms, dark rooms, that they didn't know anything about. Freud and these others—" (*MOS* 248).

The dark door opens into the artist's world. It is dark both because what is on the other side is uncertain and because one must give up much in order to cross the threshold. Gordon knows this, as does Dawson Fairchild. The potential artist must believe in the efficacy of his or her artistic medium in order to make the passage. Fairchild has lost his "childlike faith in the efficacy of words," and it is precisely because of that loss that he is no longer able to produce fiction. Like Gordon, Dawson Fairchild ends up with a prostitute at the conclusion of the novel, but unlike Gordon, Fairchild does it more out of futility and resignation than out of anger spawned by helplessness in the face of the feminine. Dawson Fairchild makes love with the prostitute because he understands the untenable position Israfel offers.

Paul Ricoeur contends that the identity of a literary text exists as a result of the interchange of identification with and deviation from "sedimented paradigms."[23] For Ricoeur any text exists within the "range of solutions . . . widely deployed between the two poles of servile repetition and calculated deviance, passing through all the degrees of 'deformation reglee.'"[24] He holds that traditional narratives such as myths and folktales "stand close to the pole of repetition," but in *Mosquitoes* Faulkner distances those forms from the pole of servile repetition by first incorporating them into the text and then engaging in a process of interrogation and revision.[25] In *Mosquitoes* the myths of Orion and Israfel —one a classical myth and the other an American poetic re-invention of a classical "myth"—are used to make a point about both relationships and the artist and his art.[26]

The denial of the viability of either the Orion or the Israfel role model suggests a maturation on Faulkner's part, a willingness to see male/female relationships in a more complex, and consequently more truthful, light. More importantly, Faulkner's denial of both Orion and Israfel as sufficient models opens the way for a conflation of the two myths with regard to his fiction. Having been found lacking as a sanctuary from women, the American poetic myth of Israfel nevertheless articulates art's potential as a privileged though marginalized space. Although divorced of any overdetermining notion of sexual fetishism, that space still remains the domain of the artist. The Orion myth, when looked at as myth, serves to suggest the proper activity for the artist in this privileged space. Myth is procreative and transformative; myth is the story which joins with ritual to create and transform community. Both myth and ritual transform the individual encounter with liminality at the heart of the rite into a generalized account of social adaptation and/or critique. The conflation of the two myths, then, moves Faulkner away from a simplistic belief in art for woman's sake while still recognizing art's transformative powers. *Mosquitoes* suggests that, like myth and ritual, literature can be transformative. At the metaliterary level, then,

---

[23]Paul Ricoeur, "The Text as Dynamic Identity," in *Identity of the Literary Text*, eds. Mario J. Valdes and Owen Miller (Toronto: University of Toronto Press, 1985) 182.

[24]See, e.g., ibid.

[25]See, e.g., ibid.

[26]John Carlos Rowe first pointed out to me that Poe re-invents and reinscribes the classical myth.

what Faulkner works to in *Mosquitoes* is an understanding of both the procreative and transformative powers of art and the need for those powers to be directed at something more than male/female relationships and sexual fetishism.

The movement away from fetishism and toward more serious social examination begins to be born in *Mosquitoes*. Fairchild suggests that his and succeeding generations have outdone their forefathers by reducing "the whole of existence to fetiches" (*MOS* 37). *Mosquitoes* deflates and/or undercuts this notion of fetishism by denying the rites of passage which David and Mr. Talliaferro attempt. Gordon's fetishism, that "modern day fetich of virginity" and its relationship to artistic creation, is deflated and/or undercut as well (*MOS* 318). The text's vivid rendering of failed overly-stylized rites of romantic pursuit prefigures Faulkner's later, more mature explication and critique of the rites of passage and the ideological voices which govern them. That is, Faulkner uses his fiction to transform the individual's encounter with liminality at the heart of the rite into a narrative strategy so that he may disclose the ideologies governing social adaption and, hence, his culture. We need only look to *Light in August*, for instance, to see how Faulkner at once depotentiates, deconstructs if you will, both Joe Christmas's and Lena Grove's rite of passage, *and* illuminates the figuring patriarchal ideological voice of the community. The importance of the rites of passage to fiction engaging in cultural critique is suggested in *Mosquitoes*, because what is left after the deflation of fetishism and overly stylized romantic pursuits is an appreciation of and approach to the social. Mrs. Maurier keeps her yacht because it is "that island of security that was always waiting to transport her comfortably beyond the rumors of the world and its sorrows" (*MOS* 163). On that yacht, in the liminal, Faulkner begins to suggest that the word, and consequently his art, is important not so much as a device to be used to "get" women, or even for its own sake, but because, as Julius suggests, it is "'the word that overturns thrones and political parties and instigates vice crusades, not things'" (*MOS* 130).

C. Leaving the *Nausikaa*

The stories of transformation and failed rites of passage in *Mosquitoes* direct the reader to the text's inscription of the failed rites of passage of its main characters. The denial of the ideologies governing the attempted rites and their language directs the reader to the relationship between language and more meaningful, transformative social concerns. To some extent the value of that turn is articulated in the novel's curious inclusion of Mrs. Maurier's family history in the "Epilogue." Julius, the man who understands language's power as an instrument of social transformation, discloses that history in what is in many ways the most telling story in *Mosquitoes*.

Gordon sculpts a bust of Mrs. Maurier immediately after the *Nausikaa* lands in New Orleans. That bust, containing "somewhere within those empty sockets, behind [them], ... something else--something that exposed her face for the mask it was, and still more, a mask unaware," stops Fairchild cold because it contains the essence of Mrs. Maurier which he had always missed (*MOS* 322). Fairchild immediately attempts to ascertain the facts governing what is essential to the woman; he asks, "But it's the usual thing, aint it? Plantations and things? First family, and all that?", and Julius responds with his story *(MOS* 323).

According to Julius, Mrs. Maurier was forced by her family to relinquish her loved one and marry a man many years her senior. That man, although wealthy, was not accepted by the Southern noblesse. "'He had been overseer on a big place before the Civil War,'" had come back from the war riding a Union cavalry horse and bearing a great sum of money, had parlayed that money several-fold thanks to his participation in "'several rather raw land deals in which he was assisted by a Jew named Julius Kauffman,'" and eventually had set himself up as "'proprietor of that plantation on which he had once been a head servant'" (*MOS* 323-24). Maurier's career is nothing short of a gloss of Thomas Sutpen's later rise from obscurity to "landed gentry" in *Absalom, Absalom!*. Julius announces the trauma associated with that type of ascension when he remarks, "Well imagine for yourself a situation like that: a tradition of ease unassailable and unshakable gone to pieces right under you, and out of the wreckage rising a man who once held your stirrup while you mounted. . . . Thirty years is barely the adolescence of bitterness, you know" (*MOS* 326).

She was from the North. Her family, once in good social standing, was becoming dispossessed of their position, and consequently they came with the father to New Orleans on what was apparently a government appointment. In marrying Maurier, enacting "'the harlequinade of aristocracy'" decreed by her family for the sake of wealth at the expense of love, Mrs. Maurier dons the mask which she eventually ceases to realize she wears (*MOS* 326). Faulkner's choice of "harlequinade" is revealing, for it discloses the foolishness behind the aristocracy's actions forcing Mrs. Maurier to relinquish love or at least its possibility for money and status. Her social transformation from single woman to married woman is governed by economics and class.[27] This economization of the rite of marriage, traditional in many cultures and according to some historians not foreign to the antebellum South, prefigures Faulkner's later examination of the rite, money, and correct or natural action in *Go Down, Moses*. What is immediately clear in *Mosquitoes*, although not elaborated upon, is Mrs. Maurier's position as currency to be spent by her family under the aegis of social status. Faulkner would expand upon this notion of the individual as currency, not uncommon in a region where slaves were thought of as property and poor white tenant farmers where forced to act under the laws set up by the postbellum Southern aristocracy, in *As I Lay Dying*.[28] In that work, the Bundrens spend both the body of Addie and her rite of interment.

Julius's story of Mrs. Maurier's rite of marriage discloses both how that rite has determined her life and the cultural constraints, in this case class and economic in nature, necessitating the particular identity Mrs. Maurier is compelled to assume. At the same time, the narrative of *Mosquitoes* discloses the constraints upon Julius. His story is precisely that, a story: twice he begins "'The story is,'" and every instant of his tale is related conditionally (*MOS* 323, 324). No one knows the amount of money Maurier brought back from the war: "'Lord knows what the amount really was, or how he got it, but it was enough to establish him'" (*MOS* 323). Julius speculates that Maurier does not splurge with his

---

[27]In *Southern Honor*, for instance, Wyatt-Brown considers the class, kinship, and economic motivations governing marriage in the antebellum South (see chapter 4); however, Steven M. Stowe, in *Intimacy and Power in the Old South: Ritual in the Lives of the Planters* (Baltimore: Johns Hopkins University Press, 1987), argues that because the desires of courting couples began to "take precedence over parental judgment" in the nineteenth-century and at the same time "the means for distributing property between the generations in the planter class became more regular (partible inheritance among sons, and for daughters a trend toward giving slaves as dowry)" (50), economics and class had a diminishing effect on marriage. As a consequence, the rite of marriage became more and more a matter of personal satisfaction and happiness based on love and less a passage dictated by family and forces beyond the individual.

[28]William N. Parker, "The South in the National Economy, 1865-1970," *Southern Economic Journal* 46/4 (April 1980): 1022.

money immediately upon his return because "'Perhaps he'd got rid of his inhibitions during his sojourn at the war'" (*MOS* 323). Julius does not "'doubt that he [Maurier] had dug up some blueblood emigre ancestry,'" does not "'doubt that he sat at times in the halls of his newly adopted fathers, and laughed'" (*MOS* 324). Mrs. Maurier "probably" has "'a background of an exclusive school'" (*MOS* 324). Julius "'imagine[s] he— her father—was pretty near at the end of his rope'" (*MOS* 324).

Julius, we discover, received the story from his grandfather Julius Kauffman. Julius himself was not there, though he'd "'like to have seen her, coming out of the church afterward,'" and he closes his story with an admission of the distance between himself and it: "'I believe . . . But who knows? I don't. Anyway, that explains her, to me'" (*MOS* 326). The structure of the episode and its admitted fictiveness anticipates the concluding chapters of *Light in August* and Faulkner's later more complete readings of history as story which he in turn storied. In *Mosquitoes* the phenomenological aspect of Julius's story, its very fictionality, is extremely valuable. Julius, that is, *does not know*, can only announce that he believes and then have his narrative open into the indeterminacy of and signalled by the ellipsis disclosing both his story's fictiveness and an awareness of its fictional nature; however, his lack of knowledge does not curtail his story's explanatory power. The story ends "'Anyway, that explains her, to me'" (*MOS* 326). Again we see that the liminality of fictions, like the liminality of the rite of passage (in this case the liminality of Mrs. Maurier's rite of marriage bounded by the ideological determinacy of class), produces both ontology and cognition. We use fictions, as we use rites of passage, to invent others, ourselves, and our world.

A fetter on Julius's rendering of the story is disclosed when he says "But you can't ignore money, you know: you can only protest. And tremble. It took my people to teach the world that. . . ." (*MOS* 325). Here the ellipsis is the stylistic and grammatical marker of repression in the narrative. Julius, that is, represses a discussion of his people, money, and power in order that he can complete the story of Mrs. Maurier's family history. That story, however, is tainted by currency. Julius's suppositions, his subjectivity, the "as-if" of his fiction, always reveal a monetary ground. Earlier Julius had said that "You can't argue against money: you only protest," and the nearly exact repetition—"'But you can't ignore money, you know: you can only protest. And tremble'"; "'You can't argue against money: you can only protest'"—suggests Julius's awareness of and preoccupation with the value and power of money (*MOS* 323, 325). This in turn suggests that Julius's reading of Mrs. Maurier's history is governed more by the things he loves, "gold, marble and purple," than it is by anything else (*MOS* 340).

In both form and content the story Julius tells helps us understand *Mosquitoes* and directs us to an understanding and appreciation of Faulkner's later work. The story is about a rite of passage, about culture, and ultimately about itself. It lets us know that the word and stories are capable of acts of creation (or invention) and transformation, but they are always themselves constrained. Language is neither pure nor innocent, and Faulkner deftly discloses this fact in Julius's story even as he discloses the thematics of his works to come. Language and rites of passage are employed to transform individuals into subjects of particular ideologies. In *As I lay Dying* and *Light in August* we have the two finest examples of Faulkner's use of language and rites to disclose the identity as subjectivity of his characters in a fashion that should encourage his audience to reflect on their own identity as subjectivity.[29] In order to accomplish this disclosure he had to create the fictional construct that is Yoknapatawpha County. It is to those two texts in that place, then, that we turn in order to see how the best of Faulkner's Yoknapatawpha fiction turns us to the issues of identity and community, language and rite.

---

[29]For Faulkner's characters, *subjectivity* is often both being a subject, conscious or otherwise, to a particular ideology and articulating that in discourse. If subjectivity also means to be conscious of one's being, however, then reading Faulkner helps make us conscious of what Davis terms the situated subjectivity that is the reality of our existence. Thus awakened, we can come to realize that "our relationship to our subjectivity is not a matter of fitful and evanescent psychological states, but a question of taking determinate actions in specific situations that always find us already involved in the world" (Davis, *Inwardness and Existence*, 155-56).

Chapter 3

As I Lay Dying:
The Economization of Loss

A. *As I Lay Dying* and
the Subjunctive Nature of Yoknapatawpha

Faulkner called Yoknapatawpha "my apocryphal county" and it should be clear from our analysis of the disclosure of the nature of fiction in "New Orleans" and *Mosquitoes* that he did not mean the comment derisively.[1] The representation that is the literary text, possible because of the subjunctive and hence "counterfeit" or feigning nature of fictions in general and Yoknapatawpha in particular, enabled him to construct his apocryphal county and critique culture. But what do we make of this apocryphal county, this place of dubious authenticity that both is and isn't the "Word," both is and isn't a place? What is its identity? And how are the identities of the characters who people it determined? David Minter has uncharacteristically harsh words for those who focus on either the historical or sociological dimensions of Faulkner's Yoknapatawpha: "Since Faulkner's fiction is not informed by any set of ideas or theories about southern history or southern society, and since his methods are not those of a historian or a sociologist, it is clearly wrongheaded to regard his Yoknapatawpha fiction as history or sociology."[2] Althusser's description of the disappearance of ideas, however, offers us a way to respond to Minter's admonition and see Faulkner's Yoknapatawpha fiction ethnographically as we delve into the issue of identity.

According to Althusser, ideas as they are typically construed disappear as soon as we see that ideology is manifested in representations that attempt to perpetuate "the imaginary relationship of individuals to their real conditions of existence."[3] Understanding the nature of ideology enables us to see that "transcendent" ideas share with individual subjects the reality "that their existence is inscribed in the actions of practices

---

[1]Malcolm Cowley, ed., *The Faulkner-Cowley File*, 25.

[2]David Minter, *William Faulkner*, 86.

[3]Louis Althusser, *Lenin and Philosophy*, trans. Ben Brewster (London: Monthly Review Press, 1971) 162.

governed by rituals defined in the last instance by an ideological apparatus."[4] This means, on the one hand, that Minter is after a fashion correct when he writes that "Faulkner's fiction is not informed by any set of ideas," because there are no ideas in the transcendent sense. What appears when ideas disappear are the practices and rituals that function as the ideological apparatuses through which the ideology of a culture is made manifest. It is precisely those practices and rituals that Faulkner's fiction *is* informed by, for Faulkner grew up subjected to them, and it is with them that Yoknapatawpha is constructed and its culture, with as we shall see its competing ideologies, is evoked.

The relationship between construction and fiction is immanent in Faulkner's work and crystallized in a statement Faulkner made late in his career in response to a question about his apocryphal county. Turning there now will enable us to begin to see the connections between Faulkner's earlier fiction—"Elmer" and *Mosquitoes*—and the construction he came to call Yoknapatawpha. A student at the University of Virginia asked Faulkner if he considered his "fictitious county" a pageant, and Faulkner replied,

> "No, it was not my intention to write a pageant of a county, I simply was using the quickest tool to hand. I was using what I knew best, which was the locale where I was born and had lived most of my life. That was just like the carpenter building the fence—he uses the nearest hammer. Only I didn't realize that I was creating a pageantry of a particular part of the earth. That just simplified things for me."[5]

Faulkner likens Yoknapatawpha to a physical construction, to something built with tools and materials. Given this, it is fitting that Faulkner first names his fictional world Yoknapatawpha County in *As I Lay Dying*, because that text is fundamentally concerned with the raw materials necessary for the construction and representation of space, place, and time.[6] In addition, Faulkner's use of the word "locale" discloses his interest in the place *and* the events that are connected with it. In Faulk-

---

[4]Ibid., 170.

[5]*Faulkner in the University*, eds. Fredrick Gwynn and Joseph Blotner (Charlottesville: University of Virginia Press, 1959) 3.

[6]When the Bundrens get to Mottstown and stop to buy cement to use on Cash's broken leg Moseley says "They came from some place out in Yoknapatawpha county, trying to get to Jefferson with it."

ner's South the events and circumstances are grounded in rites of passage and highly stylized rituals that determine the identity of the person and the nature of the place. The fictional nature of *As I Lay Dying* is disclosed early in the work so that the reader's attention might be directed to the text's concern with the materials Faulkner uses to construct his fictional world: language and the rites of passage. *As I Lay Dying* makes it clear that both are used by the characters to determine value and by Faulkner to disclose that determination.

As I Lay Dying focuses on a family at a moment of crisis. The dominant action of the text concerns the attempts of the Bundren family to transport the body of Addie, recently deceased wife and mother, to her burial site in Jefferson. The narrative comes to the reader in the form of fifty-nine different interior monologues from fifteen different characters. As such, the narrative of *As I Lay Dying* is necessarily fragmentary, inherently unsettling for the reader, and thoroughly modern. The structure of the text is consistent with the modernist view of a fractured older order. As Bruce Kawin notes, the anxiety producing such a view was, paradoxically, liberating. In "acknowledging fragmentation and then butting the fragments up against each other" the modernists constructed, or acknowledged, a juxtaposition that "did not so much provide the longed for connective tissue. . . . as pointed beyond itself to a conceptual space in which the fragments might cohere."[7] In Faulkner's case, employing the rites of passage as the phrase to articulate the problematic of identity in and of his fiction binds together the individual, the individual-as-subject, community and culture, determinacy, and indeterminacy and enables the act of reading that articulation to reproduce in the reader's imagination the conceptual space where the fragments cohere. The phenomenological nature of the literary text is essential to the production and reproduction of the conceptual space where change is articulated and may be interrogated.

In *Ideas*, Edmund Husserl constructs a neo-Kantian metaphysics of consciousness that posits that fiction "is the source whence knowledge of 'eternal truths' draws its sustenance."[8] Husserl states that one can "draw extraordinary profit . . . from the gifts of art" because fiction gives us a

---

[7]Bruce Kawin, "The Montage Element in Faulkner's Fiction," in *Faulkner, Modernism, and Film*, eds. Harrington and Fowler, 106.

[8]Edmund Husserl, *Ideas*, trans. W. R. Boyce Gibson (New York: Colliers, 1962) 184.

pure apprehension of an objectification of a factor of mind.[9] That apprehension "has the actuality of the directing activity, but it is not 'real' apprehension, but mere apprehension in the modified form of the 'as-if' [the subjunctive]."[10] What we apprehend when we read a fiction is a represented object presented as a represented object. That object "is characterized not as being really present, but as being 'as though' it were present."[11] Hence, "With the glance turned towards the 'image' (not towards that of which it is the copy), we do not apprehend anything real as object, but an image, a fiction."[12] Fictions, then, indeed all works of art, are images of the representational quality of the mind. Fictionalizing is the construction of a shadow-consciousness whereby what Husserl terms the "fruits of the imagination," speaking of all artistic objects, "greatly excel the performances of our own fancy, and moreover, given the understanding grasp, pass through the suggestive power of the media of artistic presentation with quite special ease into perfectly clear fancies."[13] Hans Vaihinger extends Husserl's critique by arguing that "the essential element in a fiction is not the fact of its being a conscious deviation from reality, a mere piece of imagination—but we stress the useful nature of this deviation."[14] The deviation that is fiction is useful and valuable because it enables comparisons to be made between the represented object and the real world. This in turn allows for the possibility of forming new attitudes toward both. Fictions are useful precisely because they afford the reader this opportunity to change his or her mind.

The beginning of *As I Lay Dying* might at first glance seem to be completely free of deviation; we read a scene so meticulously rendered as to move beyond realism and suggest documentary. However, the opening narrative of *As I Lay Dying* discloses the relationship between fictions and the representational quality of the mind, and therefore highlights the devious nature of the text, through Darl's construction and representation of space and the body of his brother Jewel:

---

[9]See, e.g., ibid.

[10]Ibid., 291.

[11]Ibid., 290.

[12]Ibid., 291.

[13]Ibid., 184.

[14]Hans Vaihinger, *The Philosophy of 'As If'*, trans. C. K. Ogden (London: Lund Humphries, 1924) 99.

Jewel and I come up from the field, following the path in single file. Although I am fifteen feet ahead of him, anyone watching us from the cottonhouse can see Jewel's frayed and broken straw hat a full head above my own.

The path runs straight as a plumb-line, worn smooth by feet and baked brick-hard by July, between the green rows of laidby cotton, to the cottonhouse in the center of the field, where it turns and circles the cottonhouse at four soft right angles and goes on across the field again, worn so by feet in fading precision.

The cottonhouse is of rough logs, from between which the chinking has long fallen. Square, with a broken roof set at a single pitch, it leans in empty and shimmering dilapidation in the sunlight, a single broad window in two opposite walls giving onto the approaches of the path. When we reach it I turn and follow the path which circles the house. Jewel, fifteen feet behind me, looking straight ahead, steps in a single stride through the window. Still staring straight ahead, his pale eyes like wood set into his wooden face, he crosses the floor in four strides with the rigid gravity of a cigar store Indian dressed in patched overalls and endued with life from the hips down, and steps in a single stride through the opposite window and into the path again just as I come around the corner. In single file and five feet apart and Jewel now in front, we go on up the path toward the foot of the bluff (*AILD*, 3-4).

The emphasis on geometry in the second and third paragraphs suggests a careful observer using precise language to detail for the audience a particular scene. It also highlights what we will soon see is the text's preoccupation with the link between construction and representation. At the same time, Darl's desire to describe the scene, and hence control it and the reader, leads to a disclosure of the "lie" that is his narrative. When Darl reaches the cottonhouse Jewel is still "fifteen feet behind" him. Here things begin to get muddled. The narrative reads, "When we reach it I turn and follow the path which circles the house," but there can be no "we" reaching the cottonhouse, for Jewel and Darl are not walking together. Nor has Jewel caught up with Darl. Furthermore, the narrative never informs us that Darl looks back, yet he knows the exact spatial relationship between himself and his brother—"I am fifteen feet ahead of him"; "Jewel, fifteen feet behind me." Darl also knows without looking back that Jewel is "looking straight ahead." But Darl can no more know the direction of Jewel's gaze than he can know either how Jewel entered the cottonhouse or how he crossed its interior. Nevertheless, Darl remarks that Jewel "steps in a single stride through the window" and "crosses the floor in four strides with the rigid gravity of a cigar store Indian" while "still staring straight ahead." Far from being an instance of narrative sloppiness or imprecision on Faulkner's part, the rendering of Darl's representation of his brother as an imaginative "enduing" with life discloses the text's concern with construction, representation, and fiction. Darl's opening narrative, then, indicates that the process of fictionalizing is the construction of a subjunctive or 'as-if' phenomenological space which gives narrators and author the freedom to redefine the paradigmatic and syntagmatic. Darl uses that freedom to offer to the reader what can only be fanciful speculation.

Perhaps a more obvious example of the "as-if" or fictive is offered to the reader in Darl's second chapter. Darl's second narrative, the third chapter in the text, begins where the first leaves off: Anse and Vernon Tull are sitting outside on the porch when Darl arrives at the house from the cotton field. Jewel is not with him. In response to Anse's question concerning Jewel's whereabouts Darl says, "Down to the barn . . . Harnessing the team" (*AILD* 10). He then thinks,

> Down there fooling with that horse. He will go on through the barn, into the pasture. The horse will not be in sight: he is up there among the pine seedlings, in the cool. Jewel whistles, once and shrill. The horse snorts, then Jewel sees him, glinting for a gaudy instant among the blue shadows. Jewel whistles again; the horse comes dropping down the slope, stiff-legged, his ears cocking and flicking, his mismatched eyes rolling, and fetches up twenty feet away, broadside on, watching Jewel over his shoulder in an attitude kittenish and alert (*AILD* 10).

Again we have a meticulous rendering of scene, and again we have the disclosure of the fictionality of the rendering. The narrative's shift in tense and mood reveals what it attempts to gloss over: that Darl's vision is a fiction created in and by his imagination. Faulkner accentuates the fictiveness of Darl's representation by having his narrative in the next paragraph describe Jewel and the horse "like two figures carved for a tableau savage in the sun" (*AILD* 11). Jewel and the horse are precisely that: works of art that are carved in Darl's (and Faulkner's) imagination and disclosed by Faulkner (but not by Darl) as such.

The freedom of fiction is curtailed by the fact that it is built both with and in language. Words are the materials with which Faulkner constructs his texts. Faulkner conflates the coffin and the essential quality of language in order to disclose his awareness of the nature of both. The coffin, itself a symbol, symbolizes a signifier in *As I Lay Dying*, something built and then filled, and therefore serves as a metaphorization of the sign that is the word. The essential nature of language is disclosed with Vernon Tull's representation of the coffin:

> They laid her in it reversed. Cash made it clock-shape, like this ⬡
> with every joint and seam bevelled and scrubbed with the plane, tight
> as a drum and neat as a sewing basket, and they had laid her in it head
> to foot so it wouldn't crush her dress (*AILD* 77-78).

The coffin is meaningful only when it is filled with Addie's body. The construction of the coffin, then, together with Faulkner's playful representation of it as a figure and simultaneous disclosure of its nature, stresses the significance of how we build and fill both the rite of interment and language with meaning and, as a result, determine value.

The text's concern with textualization, with its nature as a fiction, is as evident in Faulkner's rendering of the construction of the coffin and the placement of Addie Bundren in it as it is in his narrative manipulations. Cash's construction of the coffin within the "shadow spaces," which are a metaphorization of the phenomenological space of fiction, is carefully represented by Faulkner through roughly the first third of the text in order to stress the text's preoccupation with the significant shapes that are the coffin and language as each is related to value (*AILD* 4). Darl describes the boards of the coffin as "yellow as gold, like soft gold"; Cash is a "good carpenter," and as a consequence, "Addie Bundren could not want a better one, a better box to lie in" (*AILD* 4). Cash's act of construction, paralleling each character's acts of narrative construction and Faulkner's act of construction and disclosure, creates a space for Addie that will, again according to Darl, "give her confidence and comfort" (*AILD* 4). It is from within that space that Addie discloses language's essential nature. As a result, Addie's sole chapter in the text enables the reader to see the importance of language's arbitrary nature to the construction and disclosure of the aesthetics of indeterminacy that is at work in *As I Lay Dying*.

Addie Bundren's life has been little more than a series of denials and frustrations. After experiencing the pain of childbirth, Addie comes to hate Anse for dressing pain and the pain of violation in a word: "He had a word, too. Love, he called it" (*AILD* 158). For Anse the word "love" matters because, according to David Schneider, it embodies and articulates "an explicit cultural symbol of American kinship. . . . Love in the sense of sexual intercourse is a natural act with natural consequences according to *its cultural definition*. And Love in the sense of sexual intercourse at the same time stands for unity."[15] Addie sees no difference between "love" and any other word. After giving birth to Cash she "knew that living was terrible" and "that words are no good; that words dont ever fit what they are trying to say at" (*AILD* 157). The word, Addie believes, is "just a shape to fill a lack" (*AILD* 158). There is unity in neither language nor human relations. What Addie says unbounds the cultural construct of family and American kinship structures while at the same time suggesting the lack of exact or natural correspondence between the object and the word, between idea and language.

Addie allows Anse to have his shapes, his fictions, until she becomes pregnant again. Then she realizes that "It was as though he had tricked me, hidden within a word like within a paper screen and struck me in the back through it" (*AILD* 158). Anse lets words envelop him, or lets himself be enveloped by words, and as a consequence language becomes his sanctuary. At the same time that sanctuary becomes a prison-house, because Anse is obligated to honor his promise to Addie to bury her with her family in Jefferson. Addie, then, discloses the shadowy figure of Anse enclosed by the thin and translucent skin of language. That disclosure in turn suggests the nature of fictional characters: they are themselves shadowy figures enclosed in language.

Faulkner constructs Addie's theory of language, a theory that denies logocentricism, in such a fashion that it is related to the rites of passage. She thinks,

> Why are you Anse. I would think about his name until after a while I could see the word as a shape, a vessel, and I would watch him liquefy and flow into it like cold molasses flowing out of the darkness into the vessel, until the jar stood full and motionless: a significant shape profoundly without life like an empty door frame; and then I would find that I had forgotten the name of the jar. I would think: the shape of my body where I used to be a virgin is in the shape of a   and I couldn't think *Anse* (*AILD* 159).

---

[15]Schneider, *American Kinship*, 38-39 emphasis added.

The acknowledgement and representation of the blank that is essential to language captures the reader's attention in the passage and helps us to understand the blanks that will occur in later chapters from Samson, Vardaman, and Darl. It is relevant to note here that although Addie leaves her discourse open she metaphorizes Anse. To metaphorize Anse is to "wrong" him: he is not cold molasses. At the same time, the metaphorization binds together Addie and the audience; the text is constructed to throw us into collusion with Addie. She talks to us, and we see how it is that Anse, slow to start and unhurried along the way, is quite a bit like cold molasses. Addie's metaphor is especially apt because it calls attention to the rites of passage in general and the rite of interment in particular. Liquefy necessarily implies a change of state and flow suggests the transportation to Jefferson necessary to Addie's rite of interment.

Addie's representation of language and the body also points to ritual and the rite of passage. The word becomes a shape for Addie, a vessel into which the body of Anse flows. Anse's body is transported into the vessel that is the word, and once full the vessel is "a significant shape profoundly without life like an empty door frame" (*AILD* 159). Throughout Faulkner's fiction door and window frames symbolize either the threshold into liminality or the liminal space itself. In either case, the threshold and liminal zone are intimately related to the rites of passage in which Faulkner places his characters. We might briefly consider where it is that Quentin fixes Caddy on the day of her wedding. Twice he remembers her "standing in the door" (*SF* 91, 141-42). It is an important image for Quentin. He sees Caddy poised on the threshold, ready to move through liminality to a new state. The image of Caddy at the threshold is really the last one that Quentin can remember. Van Gennep writes that "the rites of the threshold are . . . not union ceremonies properly speaking, but rites of preparation for the transitional stage."[16] While in the threshold Caddy is still Caddy, as it were, whereas in the rite of passage of the wedding ceremony she loses her former identity and after the rite she is no longer the Caddy Quentin knew and desires to hold on to. In *As I Lay Dying* Addie's conflation of language and ritual highlights their essential similarity. Both the word and the rite of passage are "significant [signifying] shapes." Both the word and the rite are "profoundly [at bottom] without life." Still, both language and ritual determine the individual

---

[16]Van Gennep, *Rites of Passage*, 20-21.

as a person. Born into culture, we are "always already subjects, and as such constantly practice the *rituals of ideological recognition,* which guarantee for us that we are indeed concrete, individual, distinguishable and (naturally) irreplaceable subjects."[17] Those rituals, be they secular or religious, along with language, are the thresholds through which we pass in our trajectory as subjects. As Addie's metaphorization makes clear, when you enter the liminal space symbolized by the empty door frame, by the coffin, and by the vessel or jar, you are not. The individual ceases to be what he/she once was and is not yet what he/she might be. The individual's identity and too often his or her value, indeed his or her person if he or she is a member of a community, are determined by the rites of passage which construct the individual as a person/subject in light of cultural values.

B. The Rite and Narrative

Vaihinger's theory of the subjunctive nature of philosophical, intellectual, and scientific inquiry holds that scientific and aesthetic fictions are similar insofar as both "serve the purpose of awakening within us certain uplifting or otherwise important feelings."[18] Vaihinger stresses that in "real fictions" (an admittedly odd phrase) violence is done to both reality and thought in order that we might be awakened.[19] Iser's theory of fictionalizing is predicated upon violent acts that transgress reality. In Iser's words, fictionalizing "brings to the fore the intentional object of the text, whose reality comes about through the loss of reality suffered by those empirical elements that have been *torn away* from their original function by being transposed into the text."[20] In *As I Lay Dying* the violence of fictionalizing leads to the reader's experience of what Wagner terms "culture shock" as the construct and the culture of Yoknapatawpha become visible and the problematic of identity moves to the foreground for scrutiny and interrogation.[21] Faulkner's inscription of Darl's arbitrary vision in the first chapter of the text discloses the nature of his construct and its inherent

---

[17]Althusser, *Lenin and Philosophy,* 172-73 emphasis added.
[18]Vaihinger, *The Philosophy of 'As If',* 82.
[19]Ibid., 98.
[20]Wolfgang Iser, "Feigning in Fiction," 208 emphasis added.
[21]Wagner, *The Invention of Culture,* 9.

violence. The chapter's inscription of audience in the second sentence serves as a tacit invitation to the reader to engage the text, experience the shock that comes with that engagement, and be awakened to the problematic of identity: "Although I am fifteen feet ahead of him, anyone watching us from the cottonhouse can see Jewel's frayed and broken hat a full head above my own" (*AILD* 3). The reader is the "anyone watching"; if we watch closely we see that *As I Lay Dying* asks for our active participation with its second sentence, for that sentence implicitly poses a question. That is, why does the narrative draw our attention to Jewel's hat while omitting, and one might say here eliding, Jewel's face? By directing our gaze upon the "frayed and broken hat" rather than upon Jewel's face, which we could but do not see, the narrative subtly turns our attention to class and economic station and immediately suggests that identity is determined by material manifestations of subjectivity and personhood. Jewel's face, an alternative location for at the very least either making an identification or for an articulation of identity, is more than submerged beneath the battered hat; it is erased.[22] We do not see Jewel's face because we do not need to in order to see Jewel in the subject position of poor, white tenant farmer in the Deep South during the first third of the twentieth century.

Narrative and rite come together in *As I Lay Dying* to commit the violence to thought necessary for the reader's awakening. Both the rites of passage and Faulknerian narrative share a characteristic indeterminacy that is employed in *As I Lay Dying* to "remake" and disclose "cultural sense" or nonsense.[23] Turner argues that "the narrative component in ritual and legal action attempts to rearticulate opposing values and goals in a meaningful structure, the plot of which makes cultural sense."[24] Such is the case at every level of the narrative component of *As I Lay Dying*. The Bundrens rearticulate opposing values and goals, the larger com-

---

[22]By way of comparison one might consider the practice of facial marking, especially on the forehead, by which identity is traditionally revealed in Indian culture. Napier points out that "throughout the history of India the forehead has played an important role in distinguishing members of various sects as well as designating the physiological locus of exceptional esoteric power" (*Foreign Bodies* 100). See Napier, *Foreign Bodies: Performance, Art, and Symbolic Anthropology* (Berkeley: University of California Press, 1992), esp. 89-105, and *Masks, Transformation, and Paradox* (Berkeley: University of California Press, 1986), esp. 145-55.

[23]Turner, "Social Dramas," 164.

[24]See, e.g., ibid.

munity rearticulates opposing values and goals, and Faulkner rearticulates opposing values and goals, all within the "plot" that is the narrative strategy of the rite of interment. Plot plays a number of ways in *As I Lay Dying*. It is the burial spot where the conflicts generated within the text should in theory be laid to rest, the action of the novel as the "human beings in conflict" work toward and through acts of narration that will enable them to resolve conflict, and the secret of the text. All of this quite fittingly occurs within the liminal stage of the rite where the conflicts between opposing systems of order and between the individual and the community are played out.

The extraordinary time and space of *As I Lay Dying* is a product of the rite of interment that determines the shape of the text. According to van Gennep, rites of interment enable the bereaved to define a space for their grief:

> mourning is a transitional period for the survivors, and they enter it through rites of separation and merge from it through rites of reintegration into society. In some cases, the transitional period of the living is a counterpart of the transitional period of the deceased, and the termination of the first sometimes coincides with the termination of the second.[25]

In funeral and interment rites, then, the focus is as much on the community of mourners as it is on the passage of the deceased. However, the mourners must make a commitment to a "process of binding oneself with minimum reservations to certain statuses, roles, attitudes, plans, activities, understanding and perceptions, and beliefs."[26] Such a commitment to the ritual process transforms mourners and deceased into "a special group, situated between the world of the living and the dead, and how soon [the living] individuals leave the group depends on the closeness of their relationship with the dead person."[27] In *As I Lay Dying* Peabody articulates the necessity of the rite of interment for the bereaved when he thinks,

---

[25]Van Gennep, *Rites of Passage*, 147.

[26] *Grief and Mourning in Cross Cultural Perspective*, eds. Paul C. Rosenblatt, R. P. Walsh, and D. Jackson (New Haven CT: HRAF Press, 1976) 87.

[27]Van Gennep, *Rites of Passage*, 147.

She has been dead these ten days. I suppose its having been a part of Anse for so long that she cannot even make that change, if change it be. I can remember how when I was young I believed death to be a phenomenon of the body; now I know it to be merely a function of the mind—and that of the minds of those who suffer the bereavement (*AILD* 39).

The space and time for the bereaved determined by the rite also defines "sorrow as a conventional social state."[28] Cora Tull succinctly discloses the role of the honor-shame ideology upon the conventional social state when she says it is her duty to return to the Bundren home after Addie dies.[29] For antebellum Southern whites the rite of interment enabled mourners to learn from the deceased.[30] In *As I Lay Dying* the rite of interment enables the reader to learn what determines the actions of the characters as they "participate" in the rite.

The Bundren's journey to Jefferson constitutes passage through a timeless liminal zone that inscribes the middle ground of indeterminacy where mourners and deceased move. That middle ground of indeterminacy should be where mourners engage in the process of reflection so necessary to the act of holding on to the deceased for a time so that we can then truly let go. In his determination of the psychoanalytic subject Davis writes that "not letting go can also be an insistence on facing something, on not being done with an experience until one has plumbed its depths, its quotient of necessary suffering."[31] For too many of the characters in *As I Lay Dying*, however, there is an insufficient amount of reflection and a concomitant lack of engagement in the rite; for the reader, holding onto the text means facing the story, "plumbing its depths," and suffering himself/herself.

The liminality of both the rite of passage and narrative energizes the transitional period in and of the text by incorporating the indeterminacy

---

[28]Wagner, *Invention*, 90.

[29]For the role of duty in the Southern honor-shame culture see Wyatt-Brown, *Southern Honor*, especially 25-116 and 327-61.

[30]Wyatt-Brown, *Southern Honor*, 45.

[31]Davis, *Inwardness and Existence*, 282.

necessary for each to function as vehicles for achieving meaning.[32] The importance of narrative to the rite of passage and hence to identity is made clear in Samson's chapter of *As I Lay Dying*. Samson meets the Bundrens three days after Addie's funeral as they continue their search for a bridge across the swollen river. He puts them up for the night and advises them that their best course of action is to bury Addie in New Hope. He has "got just as much respect for the dead as ere a man" and feels that the best way to respect Addie "is to get her into the ground as quick as you can" (*AILD* 102). What is most telling about Samson's narrative is his failure to remember and articulate MacCullum's first name. Samson's narrative begins

> It was just before sundown. We were sitting on the porch when the wagon came up the road with the five of them in it and the other one on the horse behind. One of them raised his hand, but they was going on past the store without stopping.
> "Who's that?" MacCullum says: I cant think of his name: Rafe's twin; that one it was (*AILD* 98).

Samson's inability to come up with MacCullum's first name haunts him throughout the rest of the chapter. His narrative tells us that MacCullum says "You better holler at them" to let them know the bridge is out and immediately adds "Durn it, the name is right on the tip of my tongue" (*AILD* 99). Finally, Samson closes his narrative with a return to the figure of the unnamed MacCullum:

> That MacCullum. He's been trading with me on and off for twelve years. I have known him from a boy up; know his name as well as I do my own. But be durn if I can say it (*AILD* 105).

---

[32]Iser states that "no one would deny that literary texts do contain a historical substratum; however, the manner in which literature takes it up and communicates it does not seem to be determined merely by historical circumstances, but by the specific aesthetic structure inherent in it" (*Prospecting* 5). The aesthetic structure of indeterminacy essential to Faulkner's fictions, what I have termed an aesthetics of indeterminacy, is precisely what enables the texts to take up and communicate the historical realities of modernity and modern Southern culture.

MacCullum's identity remains undetermined because of Samson's inability to say his name. That inability creates a blank in the narrative that Samson is compelled to return to again and again. The fact that the blank is connected to the name of a person nicely brings together the text's concerns with narrative and indeterminacy, identity, and community. Both narrative and the rite of passage are strategies of containment, and Samson's struggle to control and manage indeterminacy in and with his narrative is analogous to the Bundrens' attempt to control and manage indeterminacy by means of the rite of interment and their narration of it.

Samson's failure is indicative of the Bundrens' failure to successfully interpret the rite of interment and establish meaning. The rite fails because of the "secret unvoiced purposes" operating upon it.[33] The transitional period of the Bundrens might perhaps seem to coincide with Addie's rite of interment, but the liminal period of the rite reveals just how close the Bundrens are to the deceased and how committed they are to the rites of mourning. Anse's mourning is a sham. He starts thinking about how he can get his new teeth immediately after Addie dies. Even the minimal appearance of mourning his loss ends when Anse selects his new wife in Jefferson before Addie is buried. Dewey Dell keens when Addie passes away, but that cry of mourning is all too quickly replaced by her attempt to figure out a way to get an abortion while in either Mottstown or Jefferson. Darl goes "mad"; Vardaman nearly joins him, tottering on the brink of madness. It is really only Jewel's transitional period, I hesitate to call it a period of mourning, which ends when Addie is buried. Jewel, that is, does not want to mourn so much as he wants to be done with the rite of interment in order that Addie's body can be out of the sight of man. As Warwick Wadlington states, "since the family lacks a common perspective on her burial procession, it becomes, instead of the public transformation of shame, the increasingly public display of it."[34] That public display, what motivates it, and the text's disclosure of both are fundamental to *As I Lay Dying*. The family's actions are shameful both because Jewel does not reflect upon the rite of interment, and thus cannot determine the meaning of it or its relationship to him, and, most importantly, because Anse and Dewey Dell attempt to appropriate the rite for illegitimate ends.

---

[33]Wadlington, *Reading Faulknerian Tragedy*, 121.
[34]See, e.g., ibid.

Jewel's lack of reflection on the rite is indicated by and within his sole chapter. That chapter is primarily concerned with his desire that Addie be allowed to die in peace. He wishes only that "It would just be me and her on a high hill and me rolling the rocks down the hills at their faces, picking them up and throwing them down the hill faces and teeth and all by God until she was quiet and not that goddamn adze going One lick less," and his narrative offers no reflection on the meaning of her death or the necessary rites of funeral and interment (*AILD* 14).

Jewel's actions, as recounted by others, suggest that he is interested in seeing the rite of interment through to its conclusion. His is a single-minded pursuit: he refuses to let the elemental states of fire and water fundamental to various burial rites stop him from getting the coffin containing the body of Addie to Jefferson. Nor does he accept help from others. As a result, the rite becomes a crusade for Jewel, rather than a shared, communal effort. It is precisely Jewel's "selfish" single-mindedness that prohibits him from understanding the meaning of the rite. A rite of passage, we should recall, looks back to the state of being one has left and forward to the state of being one is trying to reach. Jewel neither reflects nor looks ahead to anything other than the *act* of interment. His paucity of narration in *As I Lay Dying* discloses his inability to seek the meaning of the rite and the role narrative plays in determining identity, even as his actions suggest a will to power and mastery without a desire for understanding.

Anse and Dewey Dell also wish to master rather than understand the rite. Their appropriation of it is bound up in notions of value rather than a search for meaning. The importance of value in *As I Lay Dying* is disclosed in Cora Tull's curious first chapter, the second in the text. That chapter points us back to Darl's first chapter—and hence to the nature, meaning, and value of fiction—and ahead to Anse and Dewey Dell's determination of the body of Addie Bundren. The chapter at first glance seems almost entirely out of place with the beginning if not the whole of the book. It is not until more than halfway through the short chapter that one realizes that Cora and several other women are in Addie's bedroom as she lies on her deathbed. The first half of the narrative is dominated by Cora's account of her labor to bake cakes for a woman from town. Cora's story is about the creation and determination of surplus value. She is concerned with baking the cakes so that they will not cost her anything. Toward that end she says that her chickens "laid so well [that week] that I not only saved out enough eggs above what we had engaged to sell, to bake the cakes with, I had saved enough so that the flour and sugar and the stove wood would not be costing anything" (*AILD* 5-6).

The town woman decides not to take the cakes, however, and Cora is left arguing to her friends that the cakes did not cost her anything except for the baking. The pride Cora takes in her production and determination of surplus value reveals the extent to which she is mastered by it. The self-alienation that is a product of that determination of value leaves Cora no option save to point out that the woman had no use for the cakes because there was no party. When she is pressed by a friend who keeps saying that the woman from town "ought to taken those cakes when she same as gave you her word," Cora attempts to justify her position in relation to the woman's actions by arguing that "The Lord can see into the heart. If it is His will that some folks has different ideas of honesty from other folks, it is not my place to question his decree" (*AILD* 6). Cora's decision to ignore the import of the woman's word discloses both a turn away from the traditional honor-shame ideology in favor of the capitalist ideology and a recourse to a religious ideology that denies her the possibility of the reflection necessary to achieve meaning and extraction from her reified state. Thus the text makes clear that Cora's narrative remains bound up by the notions of surplus value, use value, and exchange value.

Cora's first narrative prepares the reader for Anse's and Dewey Dell's arbitrary assignations of value to the rite of interment. As Turner states, following Dilthey, "Meaning is the only category which grasps the full relation of the part to the whole in life, for value, being dominantly affective, belongs essentially to an experience in a conscious present" that prohibits any determination or understanding of a coherent whole. Meaning and the rite *should* be bound together.[35] The rite of interment in *As I Lay Dying* exists so that the Bundrens might see Addie's body, the rite of interment itself, and their relationship to both. Only then can the Bundrens assign the body and the rite their proper *meaning*. In order to see Addie, the Bundrens must conceive her in the light of their individual beliefs and the circumstances that occasion their interpretations. Because they lack the necessary commitment to the rite, however, they misread. In order to complete their wronging acts of interpretation Addie's body

---

[35]Turner, "Social Dramas," 152.

and the rite are transformed into currency: Anse and Dewey Dell spend Addie's body and the rite in and through their attempts to narrate them.[36]

The commodification of the body and hence the rite is disclosed when, before Addie's funeral occurs and the journey is undertaken, Darl links together a discourse on identity, a discourse on economic exchange, and a discourse on Addie. The passage helps the reader see the text's concern with the relationship between the body, the rite, and value in an economic system. Darl thinks,

> I dont know what I am. I dont know if I am or not. Jewel knows he is, because he does not know that he does not know whether he is or not. He cannot empty himself for sleep because he is not what he is and he is what he is not. Beyond the unlamped wall I can hear the rain shaping the wagon that is ours, the load that is no longer theirs that felled and sawed it nor yet theirs that bought it and which is not ours either, lie on our wagon though it does, since only the wind and the rain shape it only to Jewel and me, that are not asleep. And since sleep is is-not and rain and wind are *was*, it is not. Yet the wagon *is*, because when the wagon is *was*, Addie Bundren will not be. And Jewel *is*, so Addie Bundren must be. And then I must be, or I could not empty myself for sleep in a strange room. And so if I am not emptied yet, I am *is* (*AILD* 72).

Darl, who we will see understands the economic taint perverting Addie Bundren's rite of interment, does not know what he is: human being or person; natural entity or social construct. Jewel, on the other hand, "knows he is" because, according to Darl's narrative, he does not reflect upon his subjectivity. Jewel "is not what he is," a person, and "he is what he is not," a human being. In Darl's idealistic formulation we are all first and foremost humans, or so he hopes. However, the power of ideology to shape or determine identity is made clear in the passage. Consider the load of wood: it is not the Bundrens', although it is on their wagon, "since only the wind and the rain shape it." Jewel and Darl cannot possess what is shaped by nature, literally and figuratively, because possession belongs to the order of culture, and therefore to the order of ideology. Within that order of culture the Bundrens do not possess the

---

[36]On the relationship between a commodification of the self, the body, and the "lack of connectedness" endemic in contemporary Western society in general and the United States in particular see Napier, *Foreign Bodies*, 139-76.

load of wood because they are neither producer nor consumer. Addie takes the place of the load of wood in the passage and on the wagon and, like the wood, is not the Bundrens' because they pervert the rite of interment with notions of possession and exchange. The root of that perversion is disclosed in the passage. Darl's articulation of commerce foreshadows the Bundrens' articulation of Addie as commodity and currency to be spent and serves as a metaphor for the failed rite. Addie's body is not truly theirs that transport it because they assign it a wrong and wronging value at the expense of determining meaning. This perversion makes Addie and the rite, like the coin, meaningless.

Addie is herself not immune to a telling assignation of value. Her adherence to a system of currency and exchange is made clear in her articulation of her children. Addie says that she "gave Anse Dewey Dell to negative Jewel. Than I gave him Vardaman to replace the child I had robbed him of"; the notions of erasure and recompense are both present here (*AILD* 162). In addition, the names of several of the children signify their objectification as arbitrary units of value: Cash, Jewel, and Darl[ing].

The notion of arbitrary value marks the intersection between language, the rite, and economy. Pierce and Saussure each showed us that the relationship between the signifier and the signified is always arbitrarily assigned. Therefore the very process in language of the formation of a signifier is already an economy, already the formation of a unity from disparate elements at the expense of what is left out. Derrida argues that if one accepts the "Saussurean distinction, we would say that. . . . the question of metaphor derives from a theory of value and not only from a theory of signification," and what is true of metaphor is true of all language and, as Faulkner makes clear as early as "New Orleans," all narrative.[37] What we value determines what we say. In *As I Lay Dying* the discourse of the characters discloses the intertwined relationship between language, narrative, and currency.

At no time is this more apparent then when Anse repeats, as much to himself as to anyone else, why he is taking Addie's body to Jefferson: "'I give her my word,' Anse says. 'It is sacred on me. I know you begrudge it, but she will bless you in heaven'" (*AILD* 126). Here Anse's word is equivalent to currency. What is more, while Anse may, as Addie

---

[37]Derrida, "White Mythology," 217.

suggests, fall prey to a misreading of the paradigmatic plane of language, he is quite aware of its syntagmatic plane. The spoken word, the word in action, is binding, is the word as action, here. At the same time, Anse's statement discloses its ideological subtext. To give his word is for Anse to place himself firmly within the Southern honor-shame matrix whereby his word becomes a contractual construct that must be fulfilled. Anse speaks in the present tense to accentuate the importance of his utterance and its continued immediacy: "'I give her my word.'" To speak in the present tense is to keep the contract firmly before addressor and addressee and make it less likely that Anse will fail. Failure would mean experiencing the "definitive *social* emotion" of shame.[38] In invoking the honor-shame ideology governing, however tenuously, the modern South, with its patterns of ritual and ritualized behavior, Anse is recruiting support for his actions even as those actions serve to subvert the traditional ideology by perverting the rite of interment. Anse is well aware that "At the heart of honor lies the evaluation of the public," and his declaration seeks public approval for what he has made of Addie's body and the rite of interment.[39] In addition, Anse's comment "It's sacred on me" at once brings to bear the religious ideology that Cora Tull, for instance, is so willing to wear, and suggests that ideology is indeed placed upon Anse. Ideologies are instruments of suppression and repression, both psychologically and socially, and Faulkner's choice of preposition enables him to illuminate them as such. Finally, the indefinite pronoun "it" could well be read as signifying both Anse's word and the honor-shame structure determining it. In *As I Lay Dying* Anse spends both structures in order to attempt to suppress and repress any awareness of his perverting transformation of the rite of interment from a structure of meaning to solely a structure of value.

Anse would have it both ways: he wants the larger community to see his actions as meaningful while employing those actions to get what he values. He will say "It's a deliberate flouting of her and of *me*" when Cash brings his tools along so he can begin to work on Tull's roof upon their return from Jefferson, when Dewey Dell brings "Mrs. Tull's cakes" to town (she is in fact bringing her nicest clothes and shoes), and when Jewel rides his horse rather than going in the wagon with the rest of the family (*AILD* 90 emphasis added). Anse thinks "It's bad that a fellow

---

[38]Wagner, *Symbols that Stand for Themselves*, 63 emphasis added.
[39]Wyatt-Brown, *Southern Honor*, 14.

must earn the reward of his right-doing by flouting hisself and his dead" (*AILD* 97). According to Anse, "Nowhere in this sinful world can a honest hard-working man profit. It takes them that runs the stores in the towns, doing no sweating, living off of them that sweats" (*AILD* 97). The irony is that Anse does not work hard. He is also dishonest, at least to "hisself." He defers to a religious ideology, proclaiming that he keeps working "because there is a reward for us above, where they cant taken their autos and such," but the end of this particular narrative discloses that he sees only the value of Addie's rite of interment to him: "But now I can get them teeth. That will be a comfort. It will" (*AILD* 97).

Addie's body exists as capital for Anse and Dewey Dell. Their perception of Addie's body is no different than the prevailing Southern notion that saw people, both black and white, as capital. The South's position both within a market economy and an economy based on what Fernand Braudel terms material life necessitated the expenditure of individuals in order that the prevailing, although often conflicting, capitalistic, kinship, and honor-shame ideologies be preserved. Because material life "denote[s] the repeated actions, empirical purposes, old methods and solutions handed down from time immemorial," one should consider ritual and rites of passage as active foundational constructions in the culture of material life.[40] If man has "throughout the course of his previous history" made material life "a part of his very being, has in some way absorbed [it] into his entrails," then it is through the rites of passage that this internalization and re-internalization has been achieved.[41] In *As I Lay Dying* the transformation of Addie into currency transforms and perverts the relationship between mourners and deceased that is fundamental to the rite of interment and suggests the "parasitic" role encroaching economic systems have on traditional systems of signification.[42] The larger framing community—the voices of Cora Tull and her husband, of Peabody, of Samson, et al—discloses the perversion by constantly reminding the reader that the Bundrens are only increasingly shaming themselves while seeming to do the honorable thing.

---

[40]Fernand Braudel, *Capitalism and Material Life*, trans. Miriam Kochan (New York: Harper and Row, 1973) xii.

[41]Fernand Braudel, *Afterthoughts on Material Civilization and Capitalism*, trans. Patricia M. Ranun (Baltimore: Johns Hopkins University Press, 1977) 8.

[42]Ibid., 69-70.

Anse's only recourse to the community's criticism is to continually disclose, to the reader if not the community, his real reason for taking the rotting body to Jefferson. Moseley's narrative informs the reader, for instance, that Anse says "It's a public street. . . . I reckon we can stop to buy something same as airy other man. We got the money to pay for hit, and hit aint airy law that says a man cant spend his money where he wants" (*AILD* 189). Faulkner's manipulation of language in Anse's discourse is striking. Both man and law are revealed as abstract constructs built and maintained by a culture. Both, that is, are airy: at some level without reality and lacking solid foundation. The use of airy in the sense of lacking a solid foundation is rich with ironic complexity, for its articulation by Anse—or one should say its revealing reinscription in Moseley's narrative as Anse's articulation—at once suggests the lack of solid foundation to Anse's actions (both word and deed) and points to the lack of solid foundation of all cultural constructions of persons and law. Furthermore, the transformation in Anse's discourse of the pronoun "it" to the verb (or noun) "hit," offered twice by Faulkner in this brief passage to draw our attention to the transformation, suggests both the violent nature of Anse's actions and how he breaks and abuses cultural codes linked to articulations of identity (pronouns become verbs; dishonorable acts are presented as honorable) in order to achieve his own selfish ends. In the passage Anse also turns to currency and the law, both mediating social devices that exist only because they bear the stamp of the state, in order to attempt to substantiate his abuse of the rite of interment. If Addie is "money," then Anse's statement is truly apt: he spends her where and as he wants.

Olga Vickery notes that Vardaman (unlike Jewel, Anse, or Dewey Dell) "attempts to define for himself the meaning of death."[43] His narratives, however, disclose that his attempt is undercut by an unwillingness or inability to confront the meaning of the rite of interment and his relationship to it. Instead, he arbitrarily decides that Addie is a fish in order to resolve the question of how his mother is to breathe in a sealed coffin. The act is both a gloss and a perversion of the transfiguration central to the rite of passage. While it is dictated by the liminality and the "change-of-state" aspect of the rite, it is employed by Vardaman in order

---

[43]Olga Vickery, *The Novels of William Faulkner*, 62.

that he might avoid his own necessary immersion in the liminal. His narrative does all it can to keep Addie from being dead. He labels Addie "it" in order to use the indefinite pronoun as a refuge. Because "it" is unfigurable, however, while the body, coffin, and rite must be read and interpreted in order that meaning be achieved, Vardaman has to move to his act of transfiguration. That act enables Vardaman to fish in a backwater for *the* fish that is his mother and bore holes in the coffin so that Addie/fish can breathe.

There is more to the act of boring holes in the coffin than letting air in or letting the spirit out. Metaphorically the act is Vardaman's attempt to deal with the wall of mystery of Addie's rite of interment. Vardaman's confused and confusing narratives ask the fundamental question motivating all rites of interment: what is being buried? Like Melville's Ahab, Vardaman attempts to pierce the veil so that he can see. He fails in his struggle to grasp the meaning of Addie's death and the rite of interment because the light of his interpretation is a wronging light; as a consequence his narratives suffer. Blank spaces appear and "meaning" is lost: "The moon is not dark too. Not very dark. *Darl he went to Jackson is my brother Darl is my brother*   Only it was over that way, shining on the track" (*AILD* 232). His narrative moves from an articulation of kinship and identity to the blank of indeterminacy. Like the cobbler's narrative in "New Orleans," which turns to the indeterminacy marked by the ellipsis to avoid a painful articulation, Vardaman's narrative turns to the blank of indeterminacy in order to avoid the painful articulation of what has become of his brother Darl. However, unlike the cobbler's narrative, which trails off into silence, Vardaman's returns here to an articulation of commodity fetishism that stands as the substitute for an articulation of identity. Faulkner's decision to link Darl, the blank, and the toy train is a brilliant one, for it points to the loss of meaning as a result of commodities and commodity fetishism. Just over one hundred years earlier Heine described the "surprisingly enchanted sparkle" of the store window.[44] The commodity "emerges as the new fetish of the bourgeois world" and in that world the store display window is a "pseudo- sacral space . . . in which commodities are celebrated like cult objects encourag[ing] amazed

---

[44]Quoted in Albrecht Betz, "Commodity and Modernity in Heine and Benjamin," *New German Critique* 33 (Fall 1984): 181.

devotion."[45] Like the people of Jefferson standing transfixed by the sound coming from radios and phonographs in Jefferson stores in *Sanctuary*, Vardaman becomes transfixed by a commodity that he transforms into a fetish.

And what of brother Darl? What do we make of his actions? He sets fire to Gillespie's barn in order to burn the coffin and the body because he realizes that the journey is a trip governed by "unvoiced purposes" rather than a rite of interment. Tired of the travesty, Darl attempts to put an end to it. As a result he achieves a rite of passage that leaves him disintegrated and insane. The text makes it clear that burning the barn was not the act of a madman, however, by depicting a rational and cool-headed Darl the next day. Then, Darl keeps Jewel from getting into a fight with a white man as the Bundrens enter Jefferson. His quick thinking saves Jewel from being knifed by the man. Darl explains that Jewel "dont mean nothing. He's sick; got burned in a fire last night, and he aint himself" (*AILD* 213). Clearly, then, Darl is still himself, still contemplative, but not insane.

Michel Foucault points out that "in its most general form, confinement is explained, or at least justified, by the desire to avoid scandal."[46] This is certainly true in Darl's case. Cash thinks, "It wasn't nothing else to do. It was either send him to Jackson, or have Gillespie sue us, because he knowed some way that Darl set fire to it" (*AILD* 215). Darl is committed by his family in order to avoid a lawsuit. As such, he becomes the final currency the Bundrens spend to get what they want.

Even so, one is still not sure why Darl goes mad. When Cash tries to come to terms with insanity he offers the reader the answer to the question of the cause of Darl's madness:

> Sometimes I aint so sho who's got ere a right to say when a man is crazy and when he aint. Sometimes I think it aint none of us pure crazy and aint none of us pure sane until the balance of us talks him that-a-way. It's like it aint so much what a fellow does, but it's the way the majority of folks is looking at him when he does it (*AILD* 215-16).

---

[45]See, e.g., ibid.

[46]Michel Foucault, *Madness and Civilization*, trans. Richard Howard (New York: Random House, 1965) 57.

Darl goes crazy because of the way the majority of folks, in this case most tellingly his family, looks at him and his actions. Indeed, Darl's final narrative makes it clear that the way his family looks at him and then stops looking at him is what drives him to insanity and mad laughter:

> The wagon stands on the square, hitched, the mules motionless, the reins wrapped about the seat-spring, the back of the wagon toward the courthouse. It looks no different from a hundred other wagons there; Jewel stands beside it and looking up the street like any other man in town that day, yet there is something different, distinctive. There is about it that unmistakable air of definite and imminent departure that trains have, perhaps due to the fact that Dewey Dell and Vardaman on the seat and Cash on a pallet in the wagon bed are eating bananas from a paper bag. "Is that why you are laughing, Darl?" (*AILD* 236).

Darl laughs, that is, because his family first turned on him and now his brothers and sister sit in the wagon calmly eating bananas, apparently oblivious of Darl's presence on the train taking him to Jackson and the state mental institution. He is all too aware, moreover, of the selfish reasons necessitating their actions.

Of equal importance to *As I Lay Dying*'s concern with identity, the rite of passage, and narrative is Cash's disclosure that one's state of mind and being are determined in and by narrative discourse. The *act* of discourse is crucial. Faulkner's text forcefully articulates the consideration of language as medium and as act, a consideration that Shlomith Rimmon-Kenan sees as central to the revitalization of the study of narrative. It is precisely language's and fiction's indeterminacy, as we have seen, that is liberating, and it is "language as act" that is constitutive.[47] Cash's comment stresses narrative as action rather than narrative as structure; it "aint none of us pure crazy" and "none of us pure sane until the balance of us *talks* him that way." Because "the balance of us talks" a person into

---

[47]Shlomith Rimmon-Kenan, "How the Model Neglects the Medium: Linguistics, Language, and the Crisis of Narratology," *Journal of Narrative Technique* 19/1 (Winter 1989): 160. See, also, Barbara Hernstein-Smith, "Narrative Versions, Narrative Theories," *Critical Inquiry* 7/1 (1980): 213-36. We will return to the constellation of narrative, identity, value, ideology, and community in our examination of *Light in August.*

his or her identity as a subject, both identity and narrative are bound up with value, ideology, and community.

Foucault's reading of classical madness helps us see the relationship between narrative, value, and ideology as it applies to Darl Bundren. According to Foucault,

> If there is, in classical madness, something which refers elsewhere, and to other things, it is no longer because the madman comes from the world of the irrational and bears its stigmata; rather it is because he crosses the frontiers of bourgeois order of his own accord, and alienates himself from the sacred limits of its ethic.[48]

Darl crosses the frontiers of bourgeois order when he acts to destroy the coffin and put an end to the sham. His family commits him because they disagree with his actions. Their disagreement stems from their inability or unwillingness to see the rite of interment for anything other than its exchange value. This is disclosed by Cash's narrative, which articulates Darl's actions in economic terms: "Of course it was Jewel's horse was traded to get her nigh to town, and in a sense it was the value of his horse Darl tried to burn up" (*AILD* 216). Later Cash adds, "But I don't reckon nothing excuses setting fire to a man's barn and endangering his stock and destroying his property" (*AILD* 216). According to Cash, perverting the economic system, no matter what the reason, is how he "reckon[s] a man is crazy" and what determines that "he [the insane individual] cant see eye to eye with other folks" (*AILD* 216).

Unable to end the travesty of Addie's rite of interment and unsanctioned by his family for his attempt, Darl can only slip into mad laughter. The laughter is two-edged: Darl laughs at himself for thinking that he could end the travesty to the satisfaction of his family; he also laughs at the world because of its apparent willingness to allow the travesty to continue while turning the individual into currency. Two law officers accompany Darl on the train to Jackson, and Darl thinks that one of them had to sit facing him, riding backward, "because the state's money has a face to each backside and a backside to each face, and they are riding on the state's money which is incest" (*AILD* 235). To ride on the state's money is to see its value even while being blinded to the fact that the value has been arbitrarily assigned. It is to miss the meaning and

---

[48]Foucault, *Madness*, 57.

nature of money. Money and taboo sexual desire are conflated because riding the state's money is incestuous: you are engaging in intercourse with that which you have created. Darl's madness discloses his understanding that money brings "incomprehensible relationships in which a man no longer recognize[s] either himself, his customs or his ancient values. His work [becomes] a commodity, himself a 'thing.'"[49] The economic taint upon the rite of interment shows how the modern system of exchange-value and use-value perverts the traditional (the narrative), the customs (the rite of interment), and the ancient values (inherent to the South's honor-shame ideology). While standing outside of and looking at himself in his final narrative Darl thinks, "Darl is our brother, our brother Darl" (*AILD* 236). Darl seems to fully understand the irony implicit in that statement. The Bundrens have stripped him of his identity and divorced him from his self. Passage complete, but a passage that puts him outside family and community, Darl is left madly laughing from within the "quiet interstices" of narrative.

Currency is emptied in *As I Lay Dying*, the efficacy of words is called into question, and the possibility of successful rites of passage in either the culture of Yoknapatawpha or the modern South is undercut. Hegel felt money an "abstraction of need and labor that makes for a 'monstrous system,' or 'life of the dead body' which requires 'continual dominance and taming like a beast.'"[50] *As I Lay Dying* discloses both how the Bundrens breathe life into Addie's dead body, as currency, and how their effort at valuation runs contrary to the traditional meaning encoded in rituals and rites of interment. The text, then, bears out Jameson's contention, following Nicos Poulantza, that "every social formation or historically existing society has in fact consisted in the overlay and structural coexistence of several modes of production all at once," for the social formation that is Addie Bundren's rite of interment in the historically existing society that is the modern South transposed into the apocryphal world of Yoknapatawpha through the act of fictionalizing

---

[49]Braudel, *Capitalism*, 325.
[50]Quoted in Marc Shell, *Money, Language, and Thought* (Berkeley: University of California Press, 1982) 154.

throws into relief the conflicting ideologies of Southern paternalism and high capitalism in their uneasy coexistence in Faulkner's time.[51]

At its most successful—in the eyes of the community at least—ritual in general and rites of passage in particular establish in the minds of the participants "a symbiotic interpenetration of individual and society" that fails to occur in *As I Lay Dying*.[52] *Communitas*, which Turner defines as anti-structure infused with "the egalitarian 'sentiment for humanity' . . . representing the desire for a total, unmediated relationship between person and person . . . [that] liberates" identities is lacking in *As I Lay Dying* because the Bundrens cannot or will not achieve an unmediated relationship between individuals or, at the very least, see the ways in which their interpersonal relationships are mediated.[53] Bounded and blinded by ideology, the Bundrens pervert the liminal phase and the rite by failing to achieve or even recognize the sense of *communitas* that "tends to characterize relationships" between those immersed in the liminality of the rite of passage.[54] Conversely, our immersion in *As I Lay Dying* enables us to see Faulkner's awareness of the importance of rites of passage to culture and community, the conflicting ideological systems of his culture, and the role fictions can play in unmasking culture's structures, their ideological underpinnings, and their perversions.

Jameson contends that a work of fiction "articulates its own situation and textualizes it."[55] The reader must "see" how this act of articulation and textualization occurs on three horizons of cultural revolution if he or she is to see the political unconscious of and manifested in the text. The first horizon, that of symbolic act, is understood through recourse to Kenneth Burke's "play of emphases, in which a symbolic act is on the one hand affirmed as a genuine act, albeit on the symbolic level, while on the other it is registered as an act [whose] resolutions [are] imaginary ones that leave the real untouched."[56] Given that this horizon is consistent with our understanding of the subjunctive nature of fictions, for the act of fictionalizing is both genuine and phenomenological, it is easy enough to see how, in the present instance, *As I Lay Dying* exists on Jameson's

---

[51]Jameson, *The Political Unconscious*, 95.
[52]Turner, *Dramas, Fields, Metaphors*, 56.
[53]Ibid., 274.
[54]See, e.g., ibid.
[55]Jameson, *The Political Unconscious*, 82.
[56]Ibid., 81.

first level. According to Jameson, moving to the second horizon, where one sees the literary text as an "ideologeme or dialogical organization of class discourse," demands that the reader "rewrite" or "refocus" the text away from its existence as parole, or individual utterance, and to the "vaster system, or langue, of class discourse."[57] No such rewriting or refocusing is necessary in the case of *As I Lay Dying*, however, for through the narrative stratagem of the rites of passage and narrative acts of disclosure the text already invites the reader to see it on this second horizon. There remains, then, the third or final horizon, within which the text is "restructured as a field of force in which the dynamics of sign systems of several distinct modes of production can be registered and apprehended."[58] Again, with *As I Lay Dying* there is no need for such a restructuring, because the narrative reveals the dynamic sign systems of the ideologies of Southern paternalism and capitalism. The strength of the text, and we will see that this is true of *Light in August* as well, resides in its ability to avoid the reductiveness of a recourse solely to class in its interrogation of the problematic of identity.

In the light of Gillespie's burning barn Darl thinks that Jewel, struggling to rescue the coffin,

> springs out like a flat figure cut leanly from tin against an abrupt and soundless explosion as the whole loft of the barn takes fire at once, as though it had been stuffed with powder. The front, the conical facade with the square orifice of the doorway broken only by the square squat shape of the coffin on the sawhorses like a cubistic bug, comes into relief (*AILD* 201).

Darl's representation is governed by images of construction. Jewel is a figure "cut leanly from tin." The coffin, seen within the doorway that symbolizes both the threshold and the liminal zone, squats "like a cubistic bug." Faulkner's allusion to the thoroughly modern practice of cubism discloses that the Bundren's way of seeing the coffin and hence the rite of interment is modern in the worst sense of the term. The allusion also suggests that Faulkner throws his apocryphal county into relief in *As I Lay Dying* by breaking a rite of passage that determines identity into its constitutive parts in order "to evolve a new awareness through a demon-

---

[57]Ibid., 98, 85.
[58]Ibid., 98.

stration of the inadequacy of received genres and forms to a historical understanding struggling to be."[59] The focus on the liminal period of the rite of interment in *As I Lay Dying* enables Faulkner to disclose and interrogate his culture's essential nature while maintaining the formal integrity necessary for the reader's suffering and awakening.

---

[59]Davis, *Inwardness and Existence*, 230.

Chapter 4
Light in August:
Identity, Ideology, and Interpretation

A. Reading Joe Christmas and Lena Grove

In the summer of 1933, which is to say sometime after the publication of *Light in August* in 1932 but well prior to the publication of *Pylon* in 1935, Faulkner worked on an introduction for a limited edition of *The Sound and the Fury* that Bennett Cerf hoped to publish. Cerf never brought out the planned edition and Faulkner's introduction, which survives in two distinctly different versions, was not published intact until the 1970s. Faulkner used the "Introduction" (the word in quotation marks designating the project as it has come to us in both its versions) to articulate both his sense of *The Sound and the Fury* and his career as a novelist to that time. In the "Introduction" Faulkner explicitly describes the sense of deliberateness that *As I Lay Dying* and *Light in August* share. Of the former he wrote that it was "a deliberate book. I set out deliberately to write a tour-de-force. Before I even put pen to paper and set down the first word, I knew what the last word would be and almost where the last period would fall."[1] Faulkner opted to forego the possibility of experiencing again the ecstasy he had during the composition of *The Sound and the Fury* so that he might "write a book by which, at a pinch, I can stand or fall if I never touched ink again."[2]

When he did "touch ink again" to compose *Light in August* he did so with the hope of repeating the writing experience of *The Sound and the Fury*. By the time he had nearly completed *Light in August*, however, Faulkner had acquiesced to the fact that "it [the ecstasy] would not recur."[3] And again the failure stemmed from consciousness and deliberation: "I was now aware before each word was written down just what the people would do, since now I was deliberately choosing among

---

[1] William Faulkner, "An Introduction to *The Sound and the Fury*," ed. James B. Meriwether, *Southern Review* 8 (Autumn 1972): 709. Subsequent references to this version of Faulkner's introduction to *The Sound and the Fury* will be cited as: "Introduction," *SR*.

[2] "Introduction," *SR, 709*.

[3] Ibid.

possibilities and probabilities of behavior and measuring each choice by the scale of the Jameses and Conrads and Balzacs."[4] The deliberate nature of both *As I Lay Dying* and *Light in August* is, I think, a direct result of Faulkner's awareness of the "possibilities and probabilities of behavior" scripted by the culture of Yoknapatawpha. When his apocryphal kingdom came alive in his imagination, a county was born populated by people subject to particular cultural codes that both create the rites of passage and discourse and are revealed in them.

That apocryphal kingdom and its cultural codes are, as we have seen, intimately connected with the modern South thanks to Faulkner's artistic vision and the process of fictionalizing. By 1933, if we are to believe the "Introduction," Faulkner despaired of his region. He wrote that "the South (I speak in the sense of the indigenous dream of any given collection of men having something in common, be it only geography and climate, which shape their economic and spiritual aspirations into cities, into a pattern of houses or behavior) is old since dead."[5] Faulkner contends in the "Introduction" that the Civil War killed the South and takes issue with those who hold that there is a "New South." He writes that "There is a thing known whimsically as the New South to be sure, but it is not the south."[6] *As I Lay Dying*, as we have seen, discloses that the encroachment of modern capitalist ideology upon his region leads to perversions that prohibit the "New South" from being, in Faulkner's mind at least, the "South."

In *As I Lay Dying* funeral and interment rites are placed in the foreground. The text discloses that the rite of interment in particular functions in a fashion analogous to the disrupted funeral rite Geertz observed while conducting fieldwork in Java. Geertz read the latter as "a microscopic example of the broader conflicts, structural dissolutions, and attempted reintegrations which, in one form or another, are characteristic of contemporary Indonesian society."[7] The essential conflicts in *As I Lay Dying*, especially the crucial one between meaning and value born of

---

[4]Ibid.

[5]William Faulkner, "An Introduction to *The Sound and the Fury*," ed. James B. Meriwether, *Mississippi Quarterly* 26 (Summer 1973): 411. Subsequent references to this version of Faulkner's introduction to *The Sound and the Fury* will be cited as: "Introduction," *MQ*.

[6]Ibid.

[7]Geertz, *Interpretation*, 146-47.

opposing ideologies, function to pervert the rite of interment. The text discloses that the conflicts and their "resolutions" are grounded in the competing ideologies of paternalism, with its fundamental honor-shame dialectic, and capitalism. Geertz concludes that the failed Javanese rite is dictated by the fact that "much of recent Javanese social change is perhaps most aptly characterized as a shift from a situation in which the primary integrative ties between individuals (or between families) are phrased in terms of geographical proximity to one in which they are phrased in terms of ideological like-mindedness."[8] Geertz's characterization of "phrased" to describe how individuals are recruited to a particular ideological (and hence political) position directly relates to *As I Lay Dying* because the rite of passage is the phrase, in Lyotard's sense of the term, which Faulkner uses as narrative construction and strategy in that text. Faulkner focuses on the rite in order to articulate and interrogate the relationship among ideology, ideological like-mindedness, the individual-as-subject, and identity.

This is not to say that Faulkner merely looked upon his region with nostalgia and created his apocryphal kingdom of Yoknapatawpha to stand as a monument to a culture already past. *Light in August*, the text Faulkner described as akin to *As I Lay Dying* in its deliberateness, inscribes the culture of Yoknapatawpha in general and Jefferson in particular in a fashion that illuminates the distinctly unpalatable ways in which the traditional honor-shame ideology remained at work in the South. To be aware of possibilities and probabilities of behavior is to be aware of their opposite; it is to be aware of exclusion and the creation of an other. In *Light in August* Faulkner discloses among other things how the community of Jefferson and its subjects create both Joe Christmas and Lena Grove as others in the service of the traditional Southern honor-shame ideology.

Rites of passage are fundamentally important to *Light in August*. The lives of Joe Christmas and Lena Grove are governed by their attempts to achieve ritual passage into the state of marriage. Christmas's life becomes a pattern of ritualized actions culminating in his death as a result of his failure to achieve the passage he had desired; Lena's attempt to achieve the social change of state from woman to wife in order to sanction her impending natural change of state from childless woman to mother

---

[8]Ibid., 148.

dictates both her actions and the actions of those she meets. As is the case with *Mosquitoes* and *As I Lay Dying, Light in August* discloses the importance of rites of passage and narrative as the locations of the determination of and resistance to subjectivity while positing the reader's engagement in the act of interpretation and the recovery of meaning. The importance of narrative and its relationship to identity and interpretation is made clear in a seemingly insignificant scene in the first chapter of the text.

Lena, pregnant and unmarried, treks the Deep South in search of her unborn child's father. Her journey eventually leads her within a day's wagon ride of Jefferson. There, outside of Frenchman's Bend, she walks by Armstid and Winterbottom. Both men see Lena pass, remark upon her condition, and speculate upon both her point of departure and her destination:

> "Visiting somebody back down the road, I reckon," Winterbottom said.
> "I reckon not. Or I would have heard. And it aint nobody up my way, neither. I would have heard that, too."
> "I reckon she knows where she is going," Winterbottom said. "She walks like it."
> "She'll have company, before she goes much further," Armstid said. The woman had now gone on, slowly, with her swelling and unmistakable burden. Neither of them had seen her so much as glance at them when she passed in a shapeless garment of faded blue, carrying a palm leaf fan and a small cloth bundle. "She aint come from nowhere close," Armstid said. "She's hitting that lick like she's been at it for a right smart while and had a right smart piece to go yet."
> "She must be visiting around here somewhere," Winterbottom said.
> "I reckon I would have heard about it," Armstid said. The woman went on. She had not looked back. She went out of sight up the road: swollen, slow, deliberate, unhurried and tireless as augmenting afternoon itself. She walked out of their talking too; perhaps out of their minds too (*LIA*, 9-10).

Lena is presented as a cipher to be read and interpreted and Armstid and Winterbottom do a decent job of figuring her out. She does in fact know where she is going, Jefferson, and she has not come from anywhere close, Doane's Mill, Alabama. It is critical that Armstid and Winterbottom's act of figuration occurs in language rather than in the mind. Lena is captured by their language: she is described as having "walked out of their talking" as well as their sight. She may still be in their minds, the narrator is purposefully vague on that point, but she comes to exist and then ceases to be as a result of the men's language. She is created in discourse. There is however a price for the capture: while we learn Lena "looked at the wagon and men once," the narrator tells us neither Armstid nor Winterbottom "had seen her so much as glance at them" (*LIA* 7). In looking at Lena, then, the men miss the fact that she has looked at them. How that look may have changed the men's act of interpretation is of course impossible to say, but what can be said is that the men have seen incompletely. They have, perhaps, allowed their attempt at definition obscure their vision.

The narrative stays with the men after Lena's departure from their talk, and what is disclosed has crucial bearing on *Light in August*:

> Because after a while Armstid said what he had come to say. He had already made two previous trips, coming in his wagon five miles and squatting and spitting for three hours beneath the shady wall of Winterbottom's barn with the timeless unhaste and indirection of his kind, in order to say it. It was to make Winterbottom an offer for a cultivator which Winterbottom wanted to sell. At last Armstid looked at the sun and offered the price which he had decided to offer while lying in bed three nights ago. "I know one in Jefferson I can buy at that figure," he said.
>
> "I reckon you better buy it," Winterbottom said. "It sounds like a bargain."
>
> "Sho," Armstid said. He spat. He looked again at the sun, and rose. "Well I reckon I better get on toward home"(*LIA* 10-11).

The passage is both stylistically and thematically telling. Armstid's peculiar delay in disclosing his reason for going to Winterbottom's, accomplished with the use of a lengthy subordinate clause and several indefinite pronouns, is indicative of a larger process of delay and indirection at work throughout *Light in August*. Most particularly, the emphasis on indirection is played out throughout *Light in August* as the novel moves back and forth between the lives of Joe Christmas and Lena Grove without allowing the two main characters to meet. As a consequence it is up to the reader to make the connections between the two strands that make up the text. It is relevant that the narrator tells us that Armstid twice looks at the sun because those acts of reading work in two directions. On the one hand, to look at the sun is to determine and consequently fix the time of day by reading the sun's position. On the other hand, looking at the sun means running the risk of blindness. The play between reading and interpreting correctly on the one hand and being blinded by one's acts of reading and interpretation on the other remains at hand throughout *Light in August* and culminates in Gavin Stevens's and the traveling salesman's readings and interpretations of, respectively, Joe Christmas and Lena Grove.

Eric Sundquist notes that Joanna Burden's body, with its head "cut pretty near off," seems "an intentional mirror image of Madame L'Espanaye" in Poe's "The Murders in the Rue Morgue."[9] Sundquist argues that *Light in August*'s invocation of Poe's story, because the story "should be read in part as an oblique, libidinous racial fantasy," works in concert with Faulkner's racial, misogynist thematic.[10] To invoke an intertextual connection is, as Iser indicates in his theory of fictionalizing, to transport the entire field of reference into the text. That transportation means that we have to see the whole of "The Murders in the Rue Morgue." Poe's story is most directly concerned with the act of interpretation and the role of the reader. The introductory frame of the tale is nothing short of a gloss of the fiction-making and meaning-making process. We learn that "[the analyst] derives pleasure from even the most trivial occupations bringing his talents into play. He is fond of enigmas, of conundrums, of hieroglyphics."[11] *Light in August* is at once both conundrum and hieroglyphic, both a play on and with language and a figure or group of figures to be read and interpreted. In *Mosquitoes*, Faulkner invokes Poe's "Israfel" to at once delineate and examine the novel's main characters; in *Light in August*, Faulkner invokes Poe's "The Murders in the Rue Morgue" to suggest the novel's fictive and metafictive concerns with reading, interpretation, and meaning.

Furthermore, *Light in August* links reading and interpretation with language and the rites of passage. Language's arbitrariness creates a necessary gap between signifier and signified and hence a playful indeterminacy that enables the text to reveal the fictive or empty aspect of language, the way in which a culture fills language, and the ways in

---

[9]Eric Sandquist, *William Faulkner: The House Divided* (Baltimore: Johns Hopkins University Press, 1983) 87.

[10]See, e.g., ibid.

[11]Edgar Allan Poe, *The Complete Poems and Stories of Edgar Allan Poe* (New York: Alfred A. Knopf, 1946) 650.

which fiction can disclose both. *Light in August* brings into startling relief the tensions necessarily a part of any process of figuration with the passage in which Joe Christmas faces Joanna Burden for the last time: then, "his body seemed to walk away from him" and light the bedroom lamp; in that light he sees "the shadow of it [the pistol] and of her arm and hand. . . . the shadow of both monstrous, the cocked hammer monstrous, backhooked and viciously poised like that of a snake" (*LIA* 282). Joe remains intent upon the shadows even as Joanna trips the trigger: "But he was not watching them [her eyes]. He was watching the shadowed pistol on the wall; he was watching when the cocked shadow of the hammer flicked away" (*LIA* 282-83). The scene depicts how fiction works. It shows "language as *Abbildung* (copy, portrait, figuration, representation)," and the concept of ideologies that govern language and the figurations that are produced.[12] The shadow on the bedroom wall is "on the one hand, a pure and simple *reflection*, a reflection that respects what it accepts, and refers, *de-picts*, sense as such, in its proper original colors, re-presenting it in person. . . . But on the other hand, this repro-duction imposes the blank mark of the concept."[13]

We share Christmas's focus as we read. Christmas watches the image, the shadow, and not the object itself; we read the language that is the printed, *insubstantial*, image of the object itself. *Light in August* tells us over and over again that words are empty. For instance, Byron Bunch thinks "*It was like me, and her, and all the other folks that I had to get mixed up in it, were just a lot of words that never stood for anything*" (*LIA* 401-402). At the same time, *Light in August* makes it clear that language is a tool of cognition: "It was as if with speech he were learning about women's bodies"; and language also differentiates us from the "lower" animals: "Still she [Mrs. Hines] glared at him, dumb, beastlike, as though she did not understand English" (*LIA* 196; 403). It is between the aspects of language as fundamental and as fundamentally empty that the text's metadiscourse plays. And as we have seen elsewhere, the phenomenological displacement inherent in fictions creates the space for the play which in *Light in August* focuses on rites of passage in order to illuminate identity and ideology and critique culture and community.

---

[12]Jacques Derrida, "Form and Meaning: A Note on the Phenomenology of Language," in *Margins of Philosophy*, trans. Alan Bass, 165.

[13]See, e.g., ibid.

Gail Hightower, the dispossessed Presbyterian minister, tells Byron after Lena gives birth, "'Ah yes.' Hightower's voice shakes a little, high and thin. 'Byron Bunch, the guardian of public weal and morality. The gainer, the inheritor of rewards, since it will now descend upon the morganatic wife of—Shall I say that too? Shall I read Byron there too?'" (*LIA* 364). Hightower's question explicitly points to the text's focus on reading and interpretation. The question also highlights the importance of rites of passage to identity, and our reading them as such, by suggesting that Byron's actions have been scripted and he has been determined in the same fashion as a morganatic wife is determined by a form of contracted marriage. The allusion to a rite of passage as that which determines how we read and what we interpret discloses the importance of rites of passage, and especially the rite of marriage, to Lena Grove and Joe Chistmas.

Christmas's life is summed up in the sentence that propels Mr. and Mrs. Hines on their journey to Jefferson: "'Christmas! That white nigger that did that killing up at Jefferson last week!'" (*LIA* 344). The sentence hinges on the oxymoronic subject "white nigger." Walter Slatoff argues that oxymorons are fundamental to Faulkner's craft because they suggest opposition to synthesis or resolution; further, "The oxymoron, on the one hand, achieves a kind of order, definiteness, and coherence by virtue of the clear and sharp antithesis it involves. On the other, it moves toward disorder and incoherence by virtue of its qualities of irresolution and self-contradiction."[14] Slatoff considers the oxymoron in *Light in August* a metaphor for the novel itself: the union, in suspension, of largely discrete stories. It is a union, according to Slatoff, as unresolvable as the oxymoron.

The reader needs to resolve the phrase "white nigger" if he or she is to read that phrase and therefore Joe Christmas. In addition, it behooves the reader to deal with such social contradictions as unwed mother and a minister dispossessed of his church. If we see the oxymoron in a different light, then the carefully turned unresolvable phrase can be viewed as a metaphor for the rite of passage in *Light in August*. Like the oxymoron, a rite of passage involves a looking back to a point and a looking forward to another point; at the same time the participant in the rite is held in suspension. Also like the oxymoron, the rite of passage has

---

[14]Walter J. Slatoff, "The Edge of Order: The Pattern of Faulkner's Rhetoric," *Twentieth Century Literature* (October 1957): 110.

within it qualities of disorder, incoherence, and extreme tension. The oxymoron that remains unresolved is a phrase that denies fixing or determination; as a consequence it exists for the reader between the components making up the phrase and "cannot 'happen' in words or diagrams, but only as a result of the analogic or *interpretive 'competence'* of those perceiving" it.[15] The oxymoron also stands as a carefully tooled metaphor for both Joe Christmas and Lena Grove as we receive them. The liminal space fundamental to the oxymoron is analogous to the liminal space through which both Joe Christmas and Lena Grove move as they each attempt a particular rite of passage. That necessarily social movement and its presentation in turn occasions an examination of the other questions of social determination suggested in Armstid and Winterbottom's conversation and prevalent throughout *Light in August*.

Given that *Light in August* focuses on reading and interpretation, it is appropriate that, as is the case with Lena Grove, Joe Christmas is first presented as a cipher:

> Byron Bunch knows this: It was one Friday morning three years ago. And the group of men at work in the planer shed looked up, and saw the stranger standing there, watching them. They did not know how long he had been there. He looked like a tramp, yet not like a tramp either. His shoes were dusty and his trousers were soiled too. But they were of decent serge, sharply creased, and his shirt was soiled but it was a white shirt, and he wore a tie and a stiffbrim straw hat that was quite new, cocked at an angle arrogant and baleful above his still face. He did not look like a professional hobo in his professional rags, but there was something definitely rootless about him, as though no town nor city was his, no street, no walls, no square of earth his home. And that he carried this knowledge with him always as though it were a banner, with a quality ruthless, lonely and almost proud (*LIA* 31-32).

The narrative refuses to fix Christmas, refuses to give the reader anything without in the next instant taking it away. Christmas looks like a tramp; Christmas does not look like a tramp. Christmas has a rootless quality; Christmas does not look like a hobo. It remains for the men to read

---

[15]Wagner, *Symbols That Stand for Themselves*, 51.

Christmas, both in look and in name, in order to understand the figure posed silently before them. Their acts of reading and interpretation are in turn analogous to our acts as we attempt to determine the identity of the character who materializes before the men in much the same fashion as he appears before us in what has up until then been Lena's story.

The men work on Christmas's look first, his "face darkly and contemptuously still" that bespeaks disdain, and wonder aloud if they should erase the look from Christmas's face. While Christmas is soon dismissed "from the talk" of the men, a dismissal that duplicates the relationship between Lena Grove and Armstid and Winterbottom, he returns when the men learn his name (*LIA* 32). The discussion, centering on Christmas's nationality and color ("Is he a foreigner?" and "Did you ever hear of a white man named Christmas?" are the central questions asked), leads Byron to think that "a man's name, which is supposed to be just the sound of who he is, can be somehow an augur of what he will do, if other men can only *read the meaning in time*" (*LIA* 33 emphasis added).

In order to read Christmas, his name, and the oxymoronic "white nigger," we must come to terms with Christmas's life as it is presented in what Eric Sundquist has characterized as the "long, long plunge into his [Christmas's] past that Faulkner requires seven chapters (almost exactly the middle third of the book) to negotiate."[16] Sundquist goes on to state that "the flashback of Joe's earlier life centers him 'within' a novel pervaded by frames, by memories of memories, by stories embedded within stories embedded within stories."[17] The text's problematic structure makes it difficult to get a fix on Christmas. However, if Joe is at the center, then his life and to a certain extent the text emanates from his failed relationship with Bobbie.

Joe is seventeen years old when he first meets Bobbie, a waitress by day and prostitute at night. Joe does not initially know about her nighttime activities, and he also probably does not know at first that he has fallen in love. Nevertheless, the text makes it clear that Joe is in love with Bobbie from almost the moment he meets her. The fact that he does not expect to see her again after their first chance meeting is of little consequence since, "love in the young requires as little of hope as of desire to feed upon" (*LIA* 177). The love Joe experiences enables him to

---

[16]Sundquist, *William Faulkner: The House Divided*, 77.
[17]See, e.g., ibid.

realize that Bobbie, or what she represents to him, is why he refused to have intercourse with a black woman three years earlier.

When Joe is fourteen, he and four of his friends have the opportunity to have intercourse with an apparently willing young black woman. When Joe's turn comes, however, he balks at the idea and begins to kick the surprised and frightened woman. His friends come to help her and Joe fights with them as well. It is not until Joe meets Bobbie for the first time three years later that the reader learns with Joe why he had aggressively attacked the woman in a physical, non-sexual way. Joe thinks, *"that already there is something for love to feed upon: that sleeping I know now why I struck refraining that negro girl three years ago and that she must know it too and be proud too, with waiting and pride"* (*LIA* 177). In the antebellum "American South, as in England and France, sleeping with a woman was an informal rite of virilization," but Joe refuses that informal rite.[18] He longs instead for the legitimization of love, sexual desire, and union at the heart of more formal rites. His desire finds its form in his relationship with Bobbie.

Joe acts like a young man in love. He twice experiences uneasiness, embarrassment, and shame in the restaurant where Bobbie works. On the first occasion he stands outside, looks at the "dingy doorway" and thinks *"It's terrible to be young. It's terrible. Terrible"* (*LIA* 181). On the second occasion the laughter of those in the restaurant drives him from the establishment (*LIA* 184). Nevertheless, Joe continues to court Bobbie. He buys her a "stale and fly-specked box of candy" (*LIA* 191). It is the only time that Joe gives a gift to anyone.[19] The act of giving symbolizes the bonding which Joe desires most with Bobbie. He is, as Max says, Romeo to Bobbie's Juliet. Still in that liminal state, not yet in the world represented by bonding with Bobbie yet out of the world dominated by Simon McEachern, Joe yearns to come out on the other side.

The narrative makes it clear that Joe has been in a liminal state since the beginning of his relationship with Bobbie. He is described as having "climbed from his window and dropped the ten feet to the earth" in order to make his first clandestine meeting with Bobbie (*LIA* 186). The act of

---

[18]Wyatt-Brown, *Southern Honor*, 296.

[19]For the anthropological implications of gift-giving see, for instance, Marcel Mauss, *The Gift*, trans. Ian Cunnison (New York: Norton, 1967) and Stanley Diamond, *In Search of the Primitive: A Critique of Civilization* (New Brunswick NJ: Transaction Books, 1974) 133-34.

passing through the threshold represented by the window marks Joe's entry into the world of courtship and sexual relations. Faulkner underscores the significance of the movement by using the scene of Christmas going through the window and down the rope to frame the story of the relationship between Joe and Bobbie. Like Miss Quentin in *The Sound and the Fury*, Joe opts for a threshold that denies the traditional point of transition between the familial world and the outside world. As Benjy narrates, Miss Quentin climbs down the same tree her mother climbed up to see Damuddy on her deathbed:

> "I hushed, and then Luster stopped, his head toward the window. Then he went to the window and looked out. He came back and took my arm. Here she come, he said. Be quiet, now. We went to the window and looked out. It came out of Quentin's window and climbed out across the tree. We watched the tree shaking. The shaking went down the tree, then it came out and we watched it go across the grass" (*SF* 84).

"It" is Miss Quentin, and for Benjy "it" is everyone who can cross the threshold and move into the adult world of sexual activity. Typically, passage through a window threshold signifies actions not sanctioned by the community because windows and "other openings do not have the same quality of a point of transition between the familial world and the external world" as the main door.[20] Joe Christmas's actions are no more sanctioned by his adopted father then were Miss Quentin's by her family, and, like Miss Quentin, Joe is seen; McEachern discovers Joe's attempted passage when he sees him pass by his bedroom window on his way to meet Bobbie at a country dance.

McEachern arrives at the dance, sees Joe and Bobbie dancing, yells at Bobbie, and strikes Joe. Joe retaliates by hitting his adopted father on the head with a chair. Bobbie flees after Joe strikes down McEachern, and Joe follows her after pilfering the last of Mrs. McEachern's savings. Joe's violent actions toward the McEacherns, particularly toward Simon

---

[20]Van Genep, *Rites of Passage*, 25. Miss Quentin is "it" because she is moving through the threshold to a place alien to Benjy. Faulkner's choice of the indefinite pronoun shows how far Miss Quentin is outside family when she moves through the threshold. Like her mother Caddy, whose name is not to be mentioned in the Compson household after her illegitimate pregnancy disgraces the family, Miss Quentin is unnamed. Later in this chapter we will see how and why both Joe Christmas and Doane's Mill go unnamed.

McEachern, serve to destroy all that had both represented and created the preliminal state. He gets to Max and Mame's house to find Bobbie packed to leave. Max asks Joe why he has come to the house, and Joe responds, "What did I come for? I came to get Bobbie. Do you think that I—when I went all the way home to get the money to get married—" (*LIA* 216). Knowing that Bobbie is a prostitute does not deter Joe from attempting to realize and socially sanction his love for her through the rite of marriage.

Rites of passage are important to Christmas: earlier he rejected the informal rite of virilization in favor of more formal rites; he had also conducted a ritual of purification after being told about menstruation. Joe avoids hunting with his friends for the first two Saturdays following being told. On the second Saturday he gets his gun and leaves home before his friends come for him; Faulkner makes clear however that Joe does not hunt (*LIA* 185). Rather, he finds a flock of sheep in a valley, stalks and kills one of them, and "Then he knelt, his hands in the yet warm blood of the dying beast, trembling, drymouthed, backglaring" (*LIA* 185). Joe's actions symbolize something completely different from the rite of initiation Ike McCaslin goes through in "Delta Autumn." When Ike has his face marked by the blood of the slain buck it is an act that is meant to honor the animal he has killed and insure that Ike will not shame the memory of the animal's spirit. The act bonds together hunter and slain. Joe's ritual immersion in the still warm blood of the dying sheep that he did not kill through the act of hunting is, however, a rite of immunization or protection as well as a rite of purification. Joe's rite is an attempt to symbolically establish a distinction and distance between himself and women. Therefore, the fact that the sheep is not yet dead is vitally important to Christmas, for Joe feels the need to immerse at least a part of himself in the warm blood of the still living animal that he would have symbolize the blood produced in the menstruation cycle if he is to attain the purification and protection he desires.[21]

The ritual of purification's location in the narrative, recounted in the chapter concerned with Bobbie, accentuates the importance of ritual and rites of passage to Christmas, his relationship with Bobbie, and the text as a whole. Bobbie refuses the proposed rite of marriage, however, and

---

[21]On the relationship between rites of initiation and rites of purification see, for instance, J.S. La Fontaine, *Initiation* (Manchester: Manchester University Press, 1986) esp. 117-61.

Max and another man beat up Joe. Realizing that Bobbie does not want to marry him, Joe helps to enact his own punishment. The narrative describes him as having sprung "full and of his own accord into the stranger's fist" (*LIA* 218). Having failed to make the passage he desired, Joe achieves "passage" of another sort. Beaten, bloodied, and alone, Joe steps "from the dark porch, into the moonlight, and with his bloody head and his empty stomach hot, savage, and courageous with whisky" he enters "the street which was to run for fifteen years" (*LIA* 223).

Joe Christmas accepts the perverted passage he achieved as a result of his relationship with Bobbie, a passage marked by denial, violence, and disintegration. It is precisely Christmas's acceptance of the "passage" that shapes his actions. The street takes him to a succession of oil boomtowns, small towns, and cities throughout the country. In the cities, especially, the street leads Christmas to "interchangeable section[s] . . . where beneath the dark and equivocal and symbolic archways of midnight he bedded with the women and paid them when he had the money, and when he did not have it he bedded anyway and then told them that he was a negro" (*LIA* 224). The archways of midnight symbolize the threshold or portal through which the participant must move if passage is to be achieved.[22] They are equivocal because the liminality of the rite allows for the possibility of change in the ritual and the community even as it enables the participant to change; therefore, the subjunctive nature of the rite, highlighted by Faulkner's phrasing of midnight as "dark and equivocal and symbolic archways," should work to preclude arriving at a certain, preordained outcome without interrogation by all participants. Not so for Joe Christmas, and this too makes the archways of midnight equivocal, for his actions in the liminal space muddle the symbolic import of the archways by repeatedly commodifying the female body and physical relationships and thus denying the possibility of love and emotional relationships with women. Joe forgets Bobbie's name, but not the moment he enters the road or what took place immediately prior to the beginning of his journey. Joe's identity is constantly regenerated by memory and actions that reestablish the pattern begun with Bobbie. The pattern becomes all important because for Joe Christmas it is self-defining.

Consider Joe's relationship with Joanna Burden. He goes to her house after nightfall to steal food. He chooses to crawl through the window rather than pass through the unlocked kitchen door. The repetition of his

---

[22]On portal rituals, see, for instance, van Gennep, *Rities of Passage*, esp. 19-26, 55-64.

earlier symbolic passage into liminality should compel us to see his relationship with Joanna in light of his relationship with Bobbie. The failure of the former is a direct consequence of the earlier failure.

Joanna begins to leave food out for Joe after they become lovers. Joe reciprocates through the act of sexual intercourse. However, the relationship is made problematic by the fact that Joanna does not mind that Joe believes that he is part black. Joe uses his suspected black heritage whenever he wishes a repetition of the pattern of passage achieved through his relationship with Bobbie. For instance, he believes that white women will turn him out when he tells them that he is part black. This tactic works while Joe is in the South; it fails in the North. In the North a white prostitute tells him in so many words that color does not matter. As a consequence Joe turns to violence in order to get his way. Joe acts as he does because the woman deviates from the pattern he is accustomed to seeing. Rites of passage and rituals work in predetermined, sharply defined ways. To change the ritual is to change the meaning of the ritual, to change the rite is to change the meaning of the rite, for "The rite is a structure [that] employs a certain number of fixed actions, each one of which transmits a single, more or less definite meaning. Change the actions or the order of the actions, and the rite's meaning is completely changed."[23] Joe demands that the rite proceed along predetermined lines. Like the prostitute, however, Joanna attempts to deviate from the pattern Joe has established and refuses to change.

The first deviation occurs when Joanna accepts Joe's claim of black ancestry. It does not affect her. She continues to leave Joe food even after he tells her of his suspected ancestry. She accepts his forcible attempt to "make a woman of her" and responds by setting out more food for him. Joe in turn throws the food against the wall to avoid having to offer something in return (*LIA* 236). He cannot do so because that would mean recognizing the deviation from the pattern and somehow being an active part in the new movement. Still drawn to Joanna, Joe thinks she is "some enemy upon whom he had wreaked his utmost of violence and [she] contumely stood, unscathed and unscarred" (*LIA* 237).

The second deviation from the accepted pattern occurs when Joanna begins to bring up marriage and children. She "talked about it impersonally at first, discussing children. Perhaps it was sheer and instinctive

---

[23]Roger Grainger, *The Language of the Rite* (London: Darton, 1974) x.

feminine cunning and indirection, perhaps not. Anyway, it was some time before he discovered with a kind of shock that she was discussing it as a possibility, a practical thought. He said No at once" (*LIA* 264-65). Joanna's turn to marriage and children has its underpinnings in the ideology of American kinship structures. Having turned his back on family when Bobbie turned her back on him, Joe cannot accept the offer for reintegration into community embedded in Joanna's invitation into a family structure. He avoids her for four months but returns to see her when she leaves a note for him on his cot in the cabin. She tells him that he is wasting his life and that she wants to help him to improve himself. Joe, facing yet another deviation from the accepted pattern, avoids her once again. The final deviation is Joanna's attempt to get Joe to pray with her. Joe thinks that he killed Joanna because she "started praying over me" (*LIA* 105). Praying would mean reentering the world dominated by Simon McEachern, the world of repressive Christian ideology, and Joe refuses to do that. Trapped, facing not only deviation but regression, Joe kills Joanna.

After killing Joanna, Joe Christmas becomes a fugitive from the law. During the seven days he is free, Joe loses any orderly sense of time as he moves completely outside the community that at best only allowed him harbor in the interstices (*LIA* 331-38). He recognizes that people run away from him because "there is a rule to catch me by and to capture me that way would not be like the rule says" (*LIA* 337). The notion of playing by the rules is essential to Christmas and remains a part of his life; here, however, the rules work against his desire to find peace. At the end of seven days, as he rides in a wagon toward Mottstown and certain capture, Joe knows that "he is entering it again, the street which ran for thirty years. It had been a paved street, where going should be fast. It had made a circle and he is still inside it. Though during the last seven days he has had no paved street, yet he has travelled further than in all the thirty years before. And yet he is still inside the circle" (*LIA* 339). Joe concludes what the text has already disclosed to the reader: "'But I have never got outside that circle. I have never broken out of the ring of what I have already done and cannot ever undo'" (*LIA* 339). Christmas is determined by his past actions governed by an attempt at a rite of passage. The townspeople are more correct than they can possibly know when they say that "It looked like he [Christmas] had set out to get himself caught like a man might set out to get married" (*LIA* 349). That is, having failed in his attempt to get married to Bobbie years before,

Christmas substitutes the pattern of action that ends with his decision to be captured. The capture in turn leads to the ultimate rite of passage of death.

Like Joe Christmas, Lena Grove goes through a window in order to enter the world of sexual relations. The movement through that window, "which she learned to open and close again in the dark without making a sound," into and through pregnancy, culminates in childbirth (*LIA* 5). What is lacking, however, is the rite of marriage, the social sanction of sexual activity, and Lena, knowing this, takes to the road to find and marry Lucas Burch. However, her movement, unlike Christmas's, is grounded firmly in the temporal and physical. It is difficult for the reader to be unaware or forgetful of how far Lena has come and how long the journey has taken her. The text begins with Lena thinking, "'I have come from Alabama: a fur piece. All the way from Alabama awalking. A fur piece. Thinking *although I have been not quite a month on the road I am already in Mississippi*'" (*LIA* 3). *Light in August* ends with Lena grounded firmly in her opinion of the importance of physical movement: "'My, my. A body does get around. Here we ain't been coming from Alabama but two months, and now its already Tennessee'" (*LIA* 507).

Lena's ability to "get around" is a direct result of her ability to enlist aid: "the evocation of *far* is a peaceful corridor paved with unflagging and tranquil faith and people with kind and nameless faces and voices . . . backrolling now behind her [in] a long monotonous succession of peaceful and undeviating changes from day to dark and dark to day again, through which she advanced in identical and anonymous and deliberate wagons" (*LIA* 7). Lena's ability derives directly from her use of language. Armstid imagines that Lena explains her situation without "even waiting for them [the men outside Varner's store] to ask. . . . Telling them of her own accord about that durn fellow like she never had nothing particular to either hide or tell" (*LIA* 24-25). Lena's explanation is a "prepared speech," and Lena's articulation of her story is described as a speech throughout *Light in August* (*LIA* 22). That speech is what enables her to reach Jefferson. However, it is what the language, the speech, does not say that compels people to help Lena. The men see Lena's pregnancy, read it, listen to Lena's speech, interpret it correctly by seeing that it is predicated upon a lie, and consequently fix her. Given this, the men's actions are clearly motivated by their understanding of what is false in Lena's speech.

Mrs. Armstid asks "Is your name Burch yet?" and Lena responds, "I told you false. My name is not Burch yet. It's Lena Grove"; her admission only further infuriates Mrs. Armstid (*LIA* 17, 18). Mrs. Armstid calls Lena's bluff, catches her in the figuring fiction of her lie, and the two women "look at one another, suddenly naked, watching one another" (*LIA* 17). Mrs. Armstid reads and interprets correctly and is doubly incensed. She is mad at Lena for living a fiction; she is mad at "durn men" for seeing fit to allow Lena to live that fiction. The men are perfectly content to let Lena perpetuate her lie because the duplicity enables them to fix Lena with the simplest of readings: "'Here's another gal that thought she could learn on Saturday night what her mammy waited until Sunday to ask the minister'" (*LIA* 501). Such a reading enables the men to avoid confronting the whole of Lena's story and a potentially disconcerting examination of the male's role in Lena's situation.

B. Illuminating Ideology in *Light in August*

Joe Christmas's self-definition is formally and thematically governed by repetition that is, in turn, motivated and dictated by a failed rite whose key is a failed romance. The brilliance of *Light in August* is that the issues of figuration and disfiguration so fundamental to the rite of passage and to Joe's identity as it is shaped by a failed rite occasion a turn to a critique of the ideology governing the community that inscribes Joe's death. That is, Joe Christmas's attempts at determining identity effectively culminate in the text's movement to an examination of the ideology operating upon him. Similarly, Lena Grove's self-definition is formally and thematically governed by a rite of passage and motivated by her belief in family. As is the case with Christmas, Lena's identity is bound up in community and ideology as both work to inscribe her life. Christmas is trapped by his actions and his suspected ancestry, Lena is trapped by her gender, and *Light in August* employs both formal and stylistic devices to illuminate the ideologies of both race and gender that govern and regulate the community that spawned them and construct the two protagonists of the text as other.

Althusser argues that ideology in general has no history because it is "eternal, i.e. omnipresent in its immutable form throughout history."[24] Because ideology is eternal we are, in Althusser's words always already subjects who "live in ideology, i.e. in a determinate (religious, ethical, etc.) representation of the world whose imaginary distortion depends on [our] imaginary relation to [the] conditions of existence, in other words, in the last instance, to the relations of productions and to class relations."[25] The ideology of modern industrial capitalism, for instance, creates the imaginary corresponding relation between the wage, in the form of currency, and labor in order to cover and repress the laborer's alienation from the product produced in the name of surplus value. Ideological State Apparatuses such as the Church, the educational system, the legal system, the family, etcetera, are employed by a culture to insure that the "imaginary relationship of individuals to their real conditions of existence" is maintained.[26]

Althusser asks "What is the ideology of a society or a period if it is not that society's or period's consciousness of itself, that is, an immediate material which spontaneously implies, looks for and naturally finds its forms in the image of a consciousness of self living the totality of its world in the transparency of its own myths?"[27] Ideology, which produces the consciousness that is false consciousness, "always exists in an apparatus, and its practice, or practices" that work to insure the creation and perpetuation of this deceptive "totality."[28] It is possible to employ Althusser's reading of ideology in order to understand the "strategies of containment, whether intellectual or (in the case of narrative) formal" that are employed and disclosed within the world of the literary text.[29] Althusser himself does so in his reading of Bertolazzi's *El Nost Milan* and Brecht's *Mother Courage* and *Galileo*. In "The Piccolo Teatro: Bertolazzi and Brecht," Althusser argues that classical theatre, with the exception of Shakespeare and Moliere, is an example of a cultural apparatus within which ideology is manifested as a strategy of containment without being read and critiqued as such. The "uncriticized ideo-

---

[24]Althusser, *Lenin and Philosophy*, 161-62.

[25]Ibid., 166-67.

[26]Ibid., 143; 162.

[27]Louis Althusser, *For Marx*, trans. Ben Brewster (New York: Vintage, 1970) 144.

[28]Althusser, *Lenin and Philosophy*, 166.

[29]Jameson, *The Political Unconscious*, 53.

logy" apparent in the apparatus and practice of classical theatre is "simply the 'familiar,' 'well-known,' transparent myths in which a society or an age can recognize itself (but not know itself)."[30]

However, the dual nature of ideology as illusory and allusory, for it both masks the real conditions of existence and alludes to reality, means that a proper interpretation will reveal it for what it is.[31] A critical reflection upon the ideology in/of the world of the literary text will reveal it is both "the mirror it [a society, an age, or an individual] looks into for self-recognition" and "precisely the mirror it must break if it is to know itself."[32] The strategy of containment that is narrative in *Light in August* both presents and breaks the mirror of false self-recognition through the use of "cultural agents" that relay ideological information.[33] First Gavin Stevens and then a nameless traveling salesman fill the function of cultural agent; in each case the character asserts his subjectivity and, in so doing, discloses the ideological information governing his reading and definition as interpretation of, respectively, Joe Christmas and Lena Grove. The "totality" they attempt to express manifests itself in "narrative frames or containment strategies which seek to endow their objects of representations [themselves included] with formal unity."[34] To that extent their actions are not dissimilar from the wealthy Jew's in "New Orleans." *Light in August*, however, unmasks the expressions, discloses their repressive nature, and thus objectifies the ideological structures informing the expressions. In order to best see how *Light in August* operates in this regard we must first briefly consider the omniscient narrator of *Light in August*.

Throughout the first twenty chapters of *Light in August* the narrator exhibits ample control of both the narrative and the story. Consider two examples: "From that face squinted and still behind the curling smoke from the cigarette which was not touched once with hand until it burned down and was spat out and ground beneath a heel, Joe was to acquire one of his own mannerisms. But not yet"; and the shorter and perhaps simpler, "This is not what Byron knows now" (*LIA* 178; 36). In both

---

[30]Althusser, *For Marx*, 144.

[31]Althusser, *Lenin and Philosophy*, 162.

[32]Althusser, *For Marx*, 144.

[33]Kaja Silverman, *The Subject of Semiotics* (New York: Oxford University Press, 1983) 48.

[34]Jameson, *The Political Unconscious*, 54.

instances what is suggested is that the narrator knows the complete story and takes pains to refer to what he knows—even before the characters know. Both examples suggest that the narrator possesses the story and is in control of its disclosure as narrative. The narrator is in a powerful position, and his stance can be read as an understanding of writing as currency to be alternately hoarded and spent in the aegis of discourse's power.

The narrator's control at times depotentiates critical endeavor in a fashion similar, for instance, to that employed in James's *The American*. In that work the narrator at once suggests control of the story and mastery of the narrative:

> And she took it [Newman's card] and read his name: "Christopher Newman." Then she tried to read it aloud, and laughed at her bad accent. "Your English names are so droll!"
> "Droll?" said Mr. Newman, laughing too. "Did you ever hear of Christopher Columbus?"
> "Bien sur! He invented America; a very great man. And is he your patron?"[35]

James's narrator does not allow the critical reader a chance to independently connect Newman with Columbus. The narrative solidifies the connection with Newman's affirmative response to Mlle. Noemie Nioche's last question. In much the same fashion, when Christmas thinks about Joanna just prior to meeting her for the last time the narrator tells us that "he [Christmas] believed with calm paradox that he was the volitionless servant of the fatality in which he believed that he did not believe. He was saying to himself *I had to do it* already in the past tense; *I had to do it. She said so herself*" (*LIA* 280). The narrator's intrusion upon Christmas's thoughts denies the critical reader the opportunity to independently arrive at the conclusion that Christmas is speaking of a future act as a deed already committed. Any speculation upon the narrative intrusion in turn leads the reader to an awareness of the resonances behind it, while the lack of terminal punctuation enables the import of Christmas's grammatical act of figuration to resonate throughout the text.

---

[35]Henry James, *The American*, ed. James W. Tuttleton (New York: W.W. Norton, 1978) 21.

Given the narrator's control of both the story and its disclosure as narrative it may seem odd that Gavin Stevens is allowed to take control of the story of Christmas's final flight. Stevens, the district attorney who as a young man left the South to be educated at Harvard and Heidelberg, offers his theory of why Christmas either fled to or finally arrived at Hightower's house. The narrative articulating the theory is presented to us as Stevens's *recapitulation* of the story he tells to his visiting friend from out of town: "Then the train began to move and Stevens turned and saw the professor. He began the story as they rode to town and finished it as they sat on the veranda of Stevens' home, and there recapitulated" (*LIA* 445). Because Stevens's narrative is a recapitulation of a story of the event, we would do well to see Stevens as both reader and critic of the event and his story as he extracts from both the material that comprises the interpretation we get in the form of a recapitulation. Given that, Stevens's narrative as interpretation discloses as much about the district attorney and Jefferson as it does about Joe Christmas.

He begins: "I think I know why it was, why he ran into Hightower's house for refuge at the last" (*LIA* 445). With that beginning Stevens linguistically defines himself and asserts his subjectivity, for "language puts forth 'empty' forms which each speaker in the exercise of discourse appropriates to himself and relates to his 'person'" and the "language" he has appropriated.[36] Because "I refers to the act of individual discourse in which it is pronounced, and by this it designates the speaker," the act of discourse enables the "speaker to proclaim himself as the 'subject,'" and the formalization of "I" enables the "speaker to appropriate to himself an entire language."[37] Stevens's opening articulation of his recapitulation discloses both his assertion of subjectivity and the end to which that subjectivity will be directed. The repetition of "I" draws our attention to Stevens's appropriation of language and declaration of subjectivity; the act of filling the indefinite pronoun "it" with the clause "why he ran into Hightower's house for refuge at the last" symbolizes the filling of the empty forms of language in the act of discourse. The text makes it clear that declaring oneself a speaking (or writing) subject and appropriating a language means subjecting oneself to ideology, for Stevens does nothing less than fill the empty forms of language and the figure of

---

[36]Emile Benveniste, *Problems in General Linguistics*, trans. Mary Elizabeth Meek (Coral Gables FL: University of Miami Press, 1971) 227.

[37]Ibid., 226.

Christmas in an account that defines a self that is governed by and grounded in community and culture. Given the nature of language this is understandable: the speaking subject's attempt at autonomous rule of the narrative is mitigated by language's inherent arbitrariness. The necessary inequivalancy between signifier and signified demands that speaker and audience, "I" and "you," share a sign system in order that communication be achieved. That shared sign system, however, is always culturally determined. Consequently, "every utterance must be conceived as having various levels of signification, and issuing from multiple voices. It is spoken not only by the palpable voice of a concrete speaker, writer, or cluster of mechanical apparatuses, but the anonymous voices of cultural codes which invade it in the form of connotation."[38] Reading Gavin Stevens's narrative, then, will enable us to read the other voice(s) present, the ideology that Kaja Silverman labels "cultural codes," and to see the light in which Faulkner casts Jefferson and, by extension, a culture.

Stevens's interpretation rests upon what Sundquist terms the "fantasy" of Christmas's black blood. Sundquist argues that Stevens's reading of Christmas's actions is rooted "in service of an unbearable anxiety that, because it constantly threatens to dissolve into anarchy both a social and a psychic structure, can only be contained by the simplest of theories— one that is necessarily rendered farcical by renouncing the dangerous complexities generated in the surrounding actions of the novel."[39] That anxiety moves Stevens to articulate a theory of Christmas's warring or disharmonious blood. Stevens discloses the overdeterminacy of his narrative when he tells his friend that "of course I dont know what she [Mrs. Hines] told him [Christmas]. I dont believe any man could recon-struct that scene" (*LIA* 448). Nevertheless, Stevens does precisely that. He positions himself as reader, teller, and critic as he reads and interprets the construction that is his narrative. His overdetermination is not directed so much at fixing the figure of Christmas for its own sake, however, as it is at incidentally fixing the figure of Christmas in such a fashion that Jefferson will not be indicted for its actions. Those actions begin with the townspeople's hushed speculation upon the black man the sheriff ques-tions immediately after Joanna's body is found. They want the black man to be the murderer, and they "hoped that she had been ravished too: at

[38]Silverman, *The Subject of Semiotics*, 50.
[39]Sundquist, *William Faulkner: The House Divided*, 70.

least once before her throat was cut and at least once afterward" in order
that their deepest fears and anxieties might be realized (*LIA* 288). The
actions culminate with the frenzied chase of Christmas and his castration
at the hands of Percy Grimm. Stevens falls prey to the danger
metaphorized by Armstid's look at the sun: his attempt at reading,
interpretation, and definition for the sake of social and cultural salvation
only serves as a dazzling act of self-definition and indictment.

Stevens's recapitulation, then, is nothing less than the mirror the
community of Jefferson "looks into for self-recognition." The narrative
of *Light in August* "breaks" the mirror and reveals the binding and
blinding ideology of the community by supplementing Stevens's
interpretation. *Light in August*, that is, performs what Jameson terms "the
authentic function of the cultural text" by enabling the reader to see,
through Faulkner's supplement to Stevens's reading, "the privileged form
of . . . disunity or dissonance" that brings about "the objectification of the
ideological."[40] The supplement, the narrator's own disclosure of Christmas's final flight, works contrapuntally by showing the reader how, like
a cinematic suture, the text confers subjectivity upon the reader.[41] The
subjectivity Stevens confers upon the "you" of his discourse, the visiting
college professor and the reader, is disclosed by the enjambing supplement or "interlocking shot" with which the text compels us to reread and
reinterpret Stevens's reading and interpretation. The supplement suggests
the deficiency inherent in Stevens's reading and interpretation, a deficiency initially disclosed by Stevens's admission of overdetermination.
That supplement, or re-rendering, calls Stevens's reading into question by
showing how Christmas is both individually undefined and socially
defined, determined, or—to use a term Paul Smith usefully employs in
his consideration of subjectivity—cerned. In order to see how this is so
we must realize that the final reading and rendering of Christmas is also
a reading and rendering of Percy Grimm.

The object of Grimm's desire makes him perhaps Faulkner's most
reprehensible character. Of Grimm we learn that,

> He could now see his life opening before him, uncomplex and
> inescapable as a barren corridor, completely freed now of ever again
> having to think or decide, the burden which he now assumed and

---

[40]Jameson, *The Political Unconscious*, 56.
[41]On suture see Silverman, *The Subject of Semiotics*, 194-236.

carried as bright and weightless and martial as his insignatory brass: a sublime and implicit faith in physical courage and blind obedience, and a belief that the white race is superior to any and all other races and that the American is superior to any and all other white races and that the American uniform is superior to all men, and that all that would ever be required of him in payment for this belief, this privilege, would be his own life (*LIA* 451).

Completely bounded by the ideology of white superiority, Grimm is the precursor of the modern white supremist. When Percy Grimm dresses in his captain's uniform and parades downtown on "each national holiday that had any martial flavor whatever" with an "air half belligerent and half the selfconscious pride of a boy" the result is a caricature at once ludicrous and painful to behold (*LIA* 451).

That caricature is presented to us with language as profoundly humorless as earlier passages in *Light in August* are profoundly humorous. Consider just this exchange between Grimm, his name an augur for his actions, and Sheriff Kennedy:

> "Come here, boy," the sheriff said. Grimm halted. He did not approach; the sheriff went to him. He patted Grimm's hip with a fat hand. "I told you to leave that [pistol] at home," he said. Grimm said nothing. He watched the sheriff levelly. The sheriff sighed. "Well, if you wont, I reckon I'll have to make you a special deputy. But you aint to even show that gun unless I tell you to. You hear me?"
> "Certainly not," Grimm said. "You certainly wouldn't want me to draw it if I didn't see any need to."
> "I mean, not till I tell you to."
> "Certainly," Grimm said, without heat, patiently, immediately. "That's what we both said. Dont you worry. I'll be there" (*LIA* 455-56).

Faulkner's language in this perversion of ritual oath-taking is as resolutely playful as ever, but it is a cold, tense, calculating play. The failure in communication at the pivotal "certainly not" is chilling rather than funny because Grimm uses language to assert his subjectivity and therefore his immunity from the sheriff's power. That power is grounded in language and discourse. The sheriff orders Grimm to keep the pistol holstered until he, the sheriff, tells him to do otherwise. Grimm refuses to listen to the sheriff and in so doing denies the sheriff power and mastery. Earlier, Mrs. Armstid and Lena are "suddenly naked" in the silence that follows Mrs. Armstid's awareness and articulation of Lena's lying discourse (*LIA* 17). Here, Grimm remains clothed and cloaked in language as ideologically governed as the "American uniform" he wears believing that it is "superior to *all men*" [emphasis added].

Grimm's immunity and position of dominance are grounded in his belief that "We got to preserve order," that "We must let the law take its course. The law, the nation. It is the right of no civilian to sentence a man to death" (*LIA* 451-52). Grimm conjoins law and nation, making the one synonymous with the other, and in so doing creates a connection of greater gravity than that made in *Sanctuary* between law and community. Grimm will take the law into his own hands and justify his actions by refusing to see himself as a civilian.

It is precisely Grimm's way of seeing that the text is intent on disclosing. Toward that end Joe Christmas's manacled hands flash, glint, glare, and glitter as Percy Grimm takes the law into his own hands and runs Christmas down. The narrative makes it difficult for the reader to avoid those manacled hands, bound hands that cause Grimm to reason "he cant run very fast," and that he sees "glint once like the flash of a heliograph as the sun struck the handcuffs" (*LIA* 459, 461). Those manacled hands do nothing less than signal to Grimm by reflecting the light of the sun and flashing it for and into Grimm's eyes. It is at this moment that the narrative forcefully returns to the dangers of reading and interpretation metaphorized in Armstid's look into the sun. Immediately afterward, those hands are "glinting as if they were on fire," and in Hightower's house they are "full of glare and glitter like lightning bolts" (*LIA* 461, 463).

In Derrida's "White Mythology," a brief discussion of Plato's *Republic* centers on the sun:

> In the *Republic* (VI-VII), before and after the line which presents ontology according to the analogies of proportionality, the sun appears. In order to disappear. It is there but as an invisible source of light, in a kind of insistent eclipse, more than essential, producing the essence— Being and appearing—of what is.[42]

Light in August presents the sun as more than essential as well, in as much as it produces the essence, the Being and appearing, of Joe

[42]Derrida, "White Mythology," 242.

Christmas. We do not see the sun, but its light illuminates *by reflection* the bonded figure that is Christmas. It is a figure, moreover, governed by proportion, "'I think I got some nigger blood in me'"; which creates Being, "'If I'm not [part black], damned if I haven't wasted a lot of time'"; at the expense of appearance, "'He [Christmas] don't look any more like a nigger than I do'" (*LIA* 196; 254; 349).

Christmas does not appear to be black, and yet Grimm and Jefferson resolutely hunt him down. The community sees Christmas in the light of the cuffs. We have already noted that the light reflected off the handcuffs is a signal, making the cuffs a heliograph that calls attention to the man whom Sundquist argues must be sacrificed, but the narrative implies much more about those handcuffs. "Heliograph" also suggests a type of photoengraving; it is a creative process that fixes a figure immutably. This is precisely what the cuffs do, what ideology would have, and what can happen as a result of a rite of passage; here the cuffs define Christmas for and by the community. Grimm chases after the glitter and glare. One can say that Grimm is not blinded because he is seeing what he has all along figured was there, but the narrative suggests both that Grimm is blinded by ideology and that his blindness is indicative of Jefferson's blindness. Christmas's guilt or innocence is not at issue here, any more than Lee Goodwin's guilt or innocence is at issue before the community in *Sanctuary*. We are at least to some extent back inside Plato's cave, as Grimm and Jefferson unknowingly employ the light off of the handcuffs to justify their reading of the figure of Christmas. They do not see Christmas at all; they see the figure of a subject cast as other by the governing ideological light of racism and the concomitant anxieties regarding miscegenation. Heliograph suggests both "here I am" and "here I am figured," and Faulkner's supplement to Steven's reading is unrelenting in making clear Stevens's wronging reading and interpretation by showing us the false light in which Jefferson sees, reads, and interprets the *figure* of Joe Christmas as subject.

Grimm's pursuit leads him and his followers to Hightower's house, "bringing with them into its stale and cloistral dimness something of the savage summer sunlight which they had just left" (*LIA* 463). Consequently, "It [the sunlight] was upon them, of them: its shameless savageness" (*LIA* 463). Smith points out that in Marx's writings "the metaphor which describes ideology is always a visual one" and *Light in August*'s metaphorization of the sun as ideological center discloses the light in which men see and that makes Christmas their necessary subject.[43] Christmas's race for freedom is bounded by the glinting handcuffs, bounded by the postbellum "political atmosphere of diffused terror and repression through which the propertied whites determinedly regain[ed] control of the [ideological] apparatus of state governments, creating laws and an administration of injustice" governed by the honor-shame dialectic.[44] In *Light in August* the sunlight is shameless, is without shame, because the men's savagery is sanctioned by the ideology in which they invent themselves and the world around them. The men are at once backlit by that savage sunlight and embody it in their actions. They are doing the "honorable" thing, but Faulkner's modification of the center as "savage" discloses the wrong-mindedness governing the men and sanctioning brutality and inhumanity. Hightower almost immediately recognizes the light in the men's eyes: "Gentlemen!" Hightower said. Then he said: "Men! Men!" (*LIA* 463). The minister initially couches his plea in the language of society and community, but Hightower immediately replaces his initial appellation with the more general and more humane "men." It is as though Hightower understands that his only hope is to appeal to the men's basic humanity; to appeal to their social nature is to tap into the very source of their savage and misguided actions.

Hightower's call echoes Althusser's process of hailing and interpellation by which ideology "'recruits' subjects among the individuals (it recruits them all) or 'transforms' the individuals into subjects (it transforms them all)."[45] The men refuse to recognize Hightower linguistically, blinded as they are by their own ideological light, and consequently cannot see his subjectivity and its more humane ideology. Interpellation is denied, and Hightower's discourse is cut off by Grimm.

Hightower fails, as he must if the full force of Faulkner's unsettling critique is to be attained, and Christmas dies. Although he attempts to hide behind an overturned table, he cannot hide "the bright and glittering hands . . . resting upon the upper edge" (*LIA* 464). The image is startling, as Faulkner literally presents Christmas's hands to both Grimm and the reader, there being no reason why Christmas could not pull his hands

---

[43]Paul Smith, *Discerning the Subject* (Minneapolis: University of Minnesota Press, 1988) 13.

[44]William N. Parker, "The South in the National Economy," *Southern Economic Journal* 46/4 (April 1980): 1022.

[45]Althusser, *Lenin and Philosophy*, 174.

down behind the table, so that no one might miss what so graphically symbolizes the hold ideology has on us all. But how is Christmas finally rendered? In order to answer that question we must look closely at the final scene of Christmas's life:

> Then Grimm too sprang back, flinging behind him the bloody butcher knife. "Now you'll let white women alone, even in hell," he said. But the man on the floor had not moved. He just lay there, with his eyes open and empty of everything save consciousness, and with something, a shadow, about his mouth. For a long moment he looked up at them with peaceful and unfathomable and unbearable eyes. Then his face, body, all, seemed to collapse, to fall in upon itself, and from out the slashed garments about his hips and loins the pent black blood seemed to rush like a released breath. It seemed to rush out of his pale body like the rush of sparks from a rising rocket; upon that black blast the man seemed to rise soaring into their memories forever and ever. They are not to lose it, in whatever peaceful valleys, beside whatever placid and reassuring streams of old age, in the mirroring faces of whatever children they will contemplate old disasters and newer hopes. It will be there, musing, quiet, steadfast, not fading and not particularly threatful, but of itself alone serene, of itself alone triumphant (*LIA* 464-65).

Percy Grimm is fixed in that final scene; Joe Christmas is not. Christmas leaves the text, becoming the indefinite pronoun "he" and the equally indefinite possessive "his." Because linguistically the third person "he" is "not a 'person,'" the narrative effectively does not fix Christmas.[46] Christmas is never figured in his own mind, he is never completely certain and at ease with his identity, and the text indicates this by denying him the fixing proper noun. What might be labelled Christmas's internal ideology, with which he reinvented and rediscovered himself "in the same ideological representations" by which he first knows himself, literally forces him to be a nobody, a nothing.[47] Furthermore, the text fixes Grimm and the community in the telling light of an ideology that enables neither Grimm nor Jefferson to need to identify Christmas any more specifically than "nigger murderer." At the end of chapter 19, only Grimm remains to complete the task sanctioned and required by the community. What is more, there is little to suggest that it is Christmas that rises "soaring into

---

[46]Benveniste, *Problems in General Linguistics*, 197.
[47]Silverman, *The Subject of Semiotics*, 217.

their memories forever and ever." In many ways it makes more sense that the figure of the apotheosis be Percy Grimm. After all, it is Grimm who is described as "prophetlike," and the image of Grimm standing above the man he has just castrated is undoubtedly memorable (*LIA* 453). Moreover, it is Grimm who is serene and triumphant, Grimm who is "not particularly threatful" because he is nothing more than the active cultural agent of the community. Whatever the case, it seems clear that while Grimm is quite clearly delineated, Christmas remains fundamentally unfigured by Faulkner in either spoken or written discourse. In fixing Percy Grimm, however, *Light in August* unremittingly shows what is vulgar (e.g., common and reprehensible) about the man *and* the community. Christmas's rite of passage ends, then, with both the closure of death and the narrative's disclosure of his continued enclosure in the community's race-governed voice of ideology.[48]

While the birth of Lena's child seems to celebrate life, her inability to achieve the rite of marriage taints that celebration. And while her final statement suggests some closure, "'My, my. A body does get around. Here we aint been coming from Alabama but two months, and now it's already Tennessee'" echoing "'I have come from Alabama: a fur piece,'" the narrative suggests that that closure is governed by the ideology that the traveling salesman is subject to as he recounts the story of Lena, her child, and Byron Bunch on the road in search of Lucas Burch (*LIA* 507; 3). An examination of his narrative, which accounts for nearly the entire final chapter of *Light in August*, discloses that, like Joe Christmas, Lena Grove remains mastered by ideological constraints.

The last chapter of *Light in August* begins with a prefatory paragraph that sets the stage for the traveling salesman's tale:

> There lives in the eastern part of the state a furniture repairer and dealer who recently made a trip into Tennessee to get some old pieces of furniture which he had bought by correspondence. He made the journey

---

[48]Jefferson's inscription of Christmas as subject-as-other is indicative of what Napier terms a culture's need to define the "strange," isolate it, and flee from it with the help of prevailing cultural myths in order to create and preserve self-definition; see *Foreign Bodies*, 142-54. For his suggestion of the analogous relationship between the construction of the strange and liminality see *Foreign Bodies*, 154 n16.

in his truck, carrying with him, since the truck (it had a housedin body with a door at the rear) was new and he did not intend to drive it faster than fifteen miles an hour, camping equipment to save on hotels. On his return home he told his wife of an experience which he had had on the road, which interested him at the time and which he considered amusing enough to repeat. Perhaps the reason why he found it interesting in the retelling is that he and his wife are not old either, besides his having been away from home (due to the very moderate speed which he felt it wise to restrict himself to) for more than a week. The story has to do with two people, passengers whom he picked up; he names the town, in Mississippi, before he entered Tennessee (*LIA* 494-95).

Several things are revealed in the first paragraph of chapter 21. First, the absolute break between itself and what precedes it; there is nothing in the paragraph suggesting a link between it and the previous chapters of the text. That there is a connection, revealed slowly across the next page or so but not made explicit until the last third of the chapter, is not so important as the fact that Faulkner uses the first paragraph to divorce the last chapter from the first twenty. This disruption both creates a separate and special space for the last chapter and, in a cunning rhetorical move, leads the careful reader to the realization that he or she must read and interpret the story and make the connection between it and the text as a whole. Only then will the reader understand Faulkner's marginalization of chapter 21. Second, the oral nature of the prefatory paragraph foreshadows the orality of the traveling salesman's story and begins to fix him within an established oral tradition. Third, the dramatic nature of the paragraph, with the stage direction quality of the last line—"The story has to do with two people, passengers who he picked up; he names the town, in Mississippi, before he entered Tennessee"—serves to frame the salesman's tale and hint at the salesman's role in part of the story. That is, the salesman casts himself in the role of audience as he watches the short play starring Lena Grove and Byron Bunch. The structure places the reader in the position of the salesman, which, as we shall see, is all the more unsettling given the salesman's subjectivity. The dramatic nature of the last line also serves to turn over the story to the salesman. The earlier omniscient narrator divorces himself from the ensuing tale and save for a few intrusions remains removed from the story. Faulkner's erasure of his omniscient narrator should also lead the reader to take an active role in interpreting the traveling salesman's story—as well as his reasons for telling it.

Faulkner suggests throughout his fiction that speech is cognitive, and the traveling salesman's talk is his attempt to know Lena and Byron. The salesman tells his narrative to his wife, in their bed, after intercourse. The location and timing are telling. Matthews points out that there is throughout Faulkner's fiction a correspondence "between verbal discourse and sexual intercourse" and in *Light in August* the traveling salesman's narrative can be seen as generated from the earlier act of sexual inter-course. Matthew's also states that "narratives repeatedly issue from marri-ages in Faulkner," but the traveling salesman's narrative, although generated after the act of sexual intercourse that rites of marriage sanction, does not issue from a marriage between Lena Grove and Byron Bunch.[49] The tale told in the dark, reminiscent of the pillow talk between Joe Christmas and Bobbie after they had made love, stands in juxta-position and direct contradistinction to Lena and Byron's situation; Lena and Byron do not talk in bed, in the dark, after making love. The traveling salesman's narrative carries or contains a voice of experience that is completely incongruous with Lena and Byron's situation insofar as the location is completely alien to their experience together. The salesman can term Byron one of Lena's husbands, but we know that his tale issues from separation. What we have is a tale told in a marriage bed and born after sexual intercourse that is conceived from and concerned with an episode of divorce and separation.

The traveling salesman is a character straight from humorous oral tradition in America, a stock figure who is both a part of and the brunt of a part of American humor. The man is a fine storyteller, knows how to pace a tale and manipulate an audience, is adept at wordplay, and laces his story with a healthy dose of sexual innuendo. For instance, in response to his wife's query regarding Byron's intentions toward Lena, the salesman responds, "*You wait till I come to that part. Maybe I'll show you, too*" (*LIA* 498). Shortly thereafter, he answers his wife's question of what Byron Bunch had "desperated up" to do by saying that he had "*just showed you* [his wife] *once*," and then adds, "*You ain't ready to be show-ed again, are you*" (*LIA* 499). The salesman is also a perceptive reader of other people, as evidenced by his remark that Byron Bunch looked "like a fellow that aint used to lying" and his further comment that Byron knew that his lies would not be believed (*LIA* 495). Most importantly, at

---

[49]Matthews, *The Play of Faulkner's Language*, 17.

the climatic moment of *his* role in the action of the tale he is telling, the traveling salesman falls back on oral tradition in order to make an analogy to the situation in which he finds himself. As such, the salesman comes out of and is situated in late nineteenth-century American humor.

We must, however, be careful of how we take *Light in August*'s nameless final narrator. By the 1930s his star is on the descent; both his kind of humor and his type have begun to be replaced by a different sort of humor and character.[50] Leading the rise of this new, subtler non-rural humor was *The New Yorker* magazine. Walter Blair writes that, even from its beginning in 1925, *The New Yorker* had no interest in rural and small-town readers, precisely the audience for which characters such as the narrator at the end of *Light in August* would have been created:

> *The New Yorker* [said the Prospectus] will be the magazine which is not edited for the old lady in Dubuque. It will not be concerned with what she is thinking about . . . *The New Yorker* is a magazine avowedly published for a metropolitan audience and thereby will escape an influence that hampers most national publications. It expects a considerable national circulation, but this will come from persons who have a metropolitan interest.[51]

Blair points out that the humor in *The New Yorker*, from writers such as Clarence Shepard Day and James Grover Thurber, was in direct opposition to the tradition of humor employed by characters like Faulkner's traveling salesman. Given Faulkner's interest in and concern with magazines such as *The New Yorker*, he attempted to place stories in major East Coast publications throughout his career, it seems reasonable to assume that he understood the fragility of the traveling salesman's narrative position. While it is an extreme position to argue that one should deny the legitimacy of the traveling salesman's story simply because he is something of an anachronism, one has to be careful of taking what this jokester says straight. This cautionary attitude increases when one realizes the importance of the specific folk ballad referred to during the climatic moment of the tale.

---

[50]Walter Blair, *Native American Humor* (Chicago: Chandler Publishing Co., 1937) 168.

[51]See, e.g., ibid.

Byron Bunch leaves Lena and the furniture salesman after Lena rejects his sexual advances. Lena, according to the salesman, physically removes Byron from her bed while admonishing him for his actions. Consequently, Byron is not back the next morning when the salesman and Lena break camp and start traveling on toward Tennessee. The salesman hangs "'out the seat to look back, hoping that he [Byron] would show up before we got around the curve'" (*LIA* 505). Byron does not show up before they round the curve and the traveling salesman tells his wife that he felt like "a fellow being caught in the depot with a strange baby on his hands" (*LIA* 505). With that statement the salesman draws an allusion to a cycle of thematically connected railroad ballads first heard in America in the 1860s: the folk ballads "Fooled in a Railroad Car" and "The Charming Young Widow I Met in the Train." In both ballads the theme is one of deception and robbery by an artful maid.[52] The young woman in "Fooled in a Railroad Car" charms an unsuspecting young man and then leaves him at the depot with her "baby." The young man discovers that he has been robbed and that the baby is only a dummy. The traveling salesman seems here to suggest that he assumes the role of the innocent young man while Byron assumes the role of the trickster. But Byron Bunch is no trickster; he does not use language nearly well enough. Furthermore, the traveling salesman knows that Byron is not a trickster; the salesman is well aware of Byron's inability to lie successfully. The salesman, then, perverts the allusion by both misusing it and by interpreting incorrectly.

Like Gavin Stevens's narrative, which is marked by overdetermination, the salesman's narrative includes the allusion because of his overdetermined attempt to make a connection between the woman trickster and Lena Grove.[53] The traveling salesman clearly places Lena in kinship with that sort of woman who beguiles and deceives. He tells his wife that he thinks Lena

---

[52]Norm Cohen, *Long Steel Rail: The Railroad in American Folksong* (Urbana: University of Illinois Press, 1982) 50.

[53]This argument suggests that Faulkner has his character both appropriate and pervert the folk ballad in order that the reader can see both the traveling salesman and Lena. Daniel Hoffman points out that this same strategy of appropriation and perversion is evident in Faulkner's "Was." See Hoffman, "Faulkner's 'Was' and 'Uncle Adam's Cow'," in *Faulkner and Humor*, eds. Fowler and Abadie, 57-78.

"was just travelling. I don't think she had any idea of finding whoever it was she was following. I don't think she ever aimed to, only she hadn't told him [Byron] yet. . . . I think she had just made up her mind to travel a little further and see as much as she could, since I reckon she knew that when she settled down this time, it would likely be for the rest of her life. That's what I think" (*LIA* 506).

The salesman's narrative suggests that for him sexual intercourse and language are sources of power. He holds sway over his wife by his use of both intercourse and discourse. His sexual banter does not disguise the fact that his ability to "give" his wife sexual intercourse is perceived as a source of power; similarly, his ability to give his wife the story should also be seen as a source of power. Lena is threatening to the salesman because of her denial of the power men receive from both intercourse and discourse. In the last chapter the salesman tells his wife that "I just lay there" and listened to "them talking, or him talking" and what he learns is that Lena listens to Byron without being moved by what he says (*LIA* 501). His discourse is powerless. Byron gets no power from intercourse either. It is no wonder then that the salesman considers Lena a threat. Teresa de Lauretis argues that "As social beings, women [and men] are constructed through effects of language and representation," and the traveling salesman does nothing less than construct Lena in narrative.[54] Lena and the baby are left "on" the traveling salesman's hands to be dealt with, but the salesman, because he cannot see Lena as anything save an object to control or master, can only fault, falter, and fault her.[55]

The wronged allusion suggests overdetermination and discloses the deficiency of the traveling salesman's critique. Perhaps it is best, as Matthews suggests, to see the salesman as unconsciously bounded by the cultural strictures that make him a vessel through which "a rhetoric of sexual power, domination, and objectification" speaks.[56] That is, we can read the salesman discourse as being born out of love for his wife, while at the same time understanding that Faulkner employs the wronged allusion to disclose the rhetoric of a patriarchal culture operating through-

---

[54]Teresa de Lauretis, *Alice Doesn't: Feminism, Semiotics, and Cinema* (Bloomington: Indiana University Press, 1984) 14.

[55]On "fault" in *Absalom, Absalom!*, see Matthews, *The Play of Faulkner's Language*, 15-17.

[56]John T. Matthews, personal correspondence with author.

out the narrative and bounding his final narrator. As such, the ideology of gender governing the salesman's narrative is also disclosed. The salesman's wife, we should note, also directs the reader's attention to the ideology of gender relations governing her husband's discourse. She says, *"I reckon the reason you knew you never had to worry was that you had already found out just what she would do in a case like that,"* to which he responds, *"Sho. . . . I didn't aim for you to find that out. Yes, sir. I thought I had covered my tracks this time"* (*LIA* 503). The banter does not disguise the sexual politics and conflicting claims to authority it contains. The wife attempts to turn the narrative away from Lena and to her husband's role in the story. Such a turn constitutes a shift in the mastery of the narrative enabling the reader to see how the focus shifts away from Lena and to the confrontation of the salesman's depiction of her as a sexual object to be possessed and mastered. The wife, that is, compels the sensitive reader to see the governing ideological trace even as she forces the salesman to make humorous light of it. The joke or play is on "tracks," with its sexual and narrative connotations, and Faulkner includes it to further illuminate and depotentiate the traveling salesman's discourse.

Chapter 21 suggests that coming to terms with Lena's passage in the way the traveling salesman's narrative does locks Lena into a male grid of perception so tainted that it allows for only a skewed perception. The use of that voice, what the voice says, and how it says it, suggest that Faulkner was knowingly depotentiating and delegitimizing the salesman's narrative. The other alternative to the male voice at the end of the text is the realization that Faulkner is dealing with something he cannot close properly or well. Throughout his life it seems as though Faulkner looked at the movement of women to adulthood in the same way that he looked at his daughter's movement to adolescence and womanhood: with fear and a certain lack of understanding. He would say, about his daughter's maturation, that "This is the end of it. She'll grow into a woman."[57] In *Mosquitoes,* Dawson Fairchild remarks that women get into life and become a part of it by conceiving and bearing children. Men, Fairchild states, can only look on as women make this rite of passage into life. The ending of *Light in August,* indeed the whole of Lena's portion of the text, suggests that the Dawson Fairchild voice continues to live in Faulkner's

---

[57]Quoted in Minter, *William Faulkner,* 93. Faulkner's various responses to women and womanhood are described in Minter.

fiction and in Faulkner. Therefore, Faulkner could not return, as he did in the case of Christmas's final moments, to his omniscient narrator. Faulkner's use of the traveling salesman as the closing voice, bearing in mind where that voice comes from, serves to close the book on Lena the best way that Faulkner, in 1932, is able. He leaves Lena the only way he can. She has come "a fur piece," and yet in some sense she has gone nowhere at all.

Using the traveling salesman's narrative, with its carefully embedded allusion to a revealing cycle of nineteenth-century ballads, is a stunningly crafty and craftful move on Faulkner's part. The salesman's voice allows Faulkner the luxury of sidestepping what he found most difficult to write about, and alluding to the nineteenth-century ballads reveals the prejudice of the salesman's position. The carefully calculated freeplay of that last chapter leads the readers to, as Matthews suggests, "surrender themselves to engagement, exposure, embrace, intimacy, and creation."[58] The reader engages the text and participates in its act of creation. Successfully engaging the text enables the reader to see that the traveling salesman's narrative wrongs language (the allusion to the railroad ballads), wrongs his subject (Lena), and consequently wrongs his audience (both his wife and the reader). Faulkner discloses the narrative's acts of perversion and, as was the result of the depotentiation of Gavin Stevens's narrative, lets us know that "'most of what folks tells on other folks aint true to begin with'" (*LIA* 54). Faulkner empties the strand for us, pulls back the boundedness of the salesman's narrative, so that we might better see not Lena so much as the problem of identifying her. Lena Grove's strand of the text, then, is closed without closure. She travels onward, chapter 21 suggests, but Faulkner lets us know that she travels in the closed space of male perception, interpretation, and objectification. The men in *Light in August* read and decipher Lena precisely as they wish to, fix her precisely as they must, and misread or read incompletely. We remember Lena on the road, in motion, but the telling fact is that the curtain of *Light in August* comes up on Lena "Sitting beside the road" waiting for someone, some man, to come along and take her for a ride (*LIA* 3). She is stationary at the beginning of the novel and she remains something fixed throughout *Light in August*. To again invoke Matthews, Lena's self-objectification as a "body" that "gets around" at once "replicates and

---

[58]Matthews, *The Play of Faulkner's Language*, 17.

exposes [the] social assumptions" governing her.[59] Captured in and by discourse, both her own and that of men, Lena is consequently at once readable and undecipherable. Both Lena Grove and Joe Christmas, then, are presented in such a way that we see them as "subject/individual[s] . . . *cerned*" by narrative strategies of containment that Faulkner both uses and exposes.[60] That exposure denies the legitimacy of the controlling ideologies at work.

In *Orality and Literacy* Walter Ong argues that

> The fact that oral peoples commonly and in all likelihood universally consider words to have magical potency is clearly tied in, at least unconsciously, with their sense of the word as necessarily spoken, sounded, and hence power-driven. Deeply typographic folk forget to think of words as primarily oral, as events, and hence as necessarily powered: for them, words tend rather to be assimilated to things, "out there" on a flat surface. Such "things" are not so readily associated with magic for they are not actions, but are in a radical sense dead, though subject to dynamic resurrection.[61]

Faulkner's incorporation of orality in the form of the spoken discourse of Stevens and the traveling salesman subtly turns the text away from the fixing and consequently killing powers of written discourse. That orality allows us to see that *Light in August* is at once an articulation of Joe Christmas's and Lena Grove's individual self-determining rites of passage and the community's determination of both individuals as subjects. We see that both Joe and Lena are appropriated by the community as currency to be spent, exhausted as signs as it were, in the service of the ideologies ruling Jefferson and by extension the South. Faulkner also employs the narrative strategies of Gavin Stevens and of the salesman to show us that their discourse is currency. Faulkner understands and discloses language's role as the link between ideology and subject, and the disclosure serves to suggest how speech's magical powers can be perverted when tainted by the modern world.

---

[59]John T. Matthews, personal correspondence with the author.
[60]Smith, *Discerning the Subject*, 23.
[61]Walter J. Ong, *Orality and Literacy* (London: Methuen Books, 1982) 33.

C. The Burden of Joanna's Body

Both *As I Lay Dying* and *Light in August* make it clear that the issue of personal identity is bound up with the issue of cultural identity, and that both come together in the figure of the rite of passage and its liminal phase. The conflicts between opposing systems of order and between the individual and a system of order are played out within the liminal stage of the rite of passage and within the subjunctive space of the fictional text that results from fiction's essential indeterminacy. The Bundrens' effort, if we discount Darl's, runs contrary to the traditional meaning and meaning-making process encoded in rituals and rites of interment. What amounts to the family's commodification of the body is directly attributable to the encroaching capitalist ideology which *As I Lay Dying* informs the reader threatens to empty the rite of passage of significance and disenfranchise a culture.

While *As I Lay Dying* is an examination and disclosure of the effects of an encroaching ideology on a traditional system of signification, *Light in August* is an examination and disclosure of the dangers of the traditional honor-shame ideology the South was attempting to hold onto throughout the time Faulkner was composing his high modern works. We have seen how the narrative of *Light in August* makes clear the ways in which ideology impinges upon the individual and transforms him or her into a subject. The text also discloses how ideology impinges upon rites of passage and, in particular, the rite of interment. It is to that latter act of disclosure that we turn now in order to understand the relationship the text posits between the traditional honor-shame ideology and the encroaching modern ideology.

A crowd quickly forms as Joanna Burden's house burns. The burning house immediately takes on the character of an event as neighbors, families, countrymen on their way to town, and townspeople having come in "racing and blatting cars" gather to "look down at the body [of Joanna] on the sheet with the static and childlike amaze with which adults contemplate their own inescapable portraits" (*LIA* 287-88). That event is read in the light of the honor-shame ideology which stresses protection of women and fear of the black man. There are those in the crowd who "believe aloud that it was an anonymous negro crime committed not by a negro but by Negro and who knew, believed, and hoped that she had been ravished too: at least once before her throat was cut and at least once afterward"; some of the men who had arrived aboard the fire truck nearly immediately begin searching for "someone to crucify" in the name of Womanhood (*LIA* 288). The crowd is transformed when the sheriff has one of his deputies bring him a black man for questioning regarding the inhabitants of the cabin behind Joanna's house. Their faces are "identical one with another" as they become one subject of the ideology that speaks "filling the air though not louder than the voices and much more un-sourceless *By God, if that's him, what are we doing, standing around here? Murdering a white woman the black son of a* " (*LIA* 291).

The people objectify the body of Joanna Burden by placing a value on it in the service of the traditional ideology. Ironically, it is precisely that ideology that dictated that "None of them [enter] the house" while she was alive, that their wives not "call on her," and that as children they called "after her on the street, 'Nigger lover! Nigger lover!'" (*LIA* 291-92). Reading the body as symbol is so important that they become bewildered when the sheriff has it removed and strive *unsuccessfully* to fix the place it had lain before it was taken away. When they cannot see the body, well after they give up trying to point out where it had lain, they turn first to the fire and then to the sheriff. The act of staring at the fire takes on the characteristic of ritualized action and is broken only when the sheriff prepares to leave. The crowd leaves when the sheriff does and, as a consequence, "when the caravan reached town it had something of that arrogant decorum of a procession behind a catafalque" (*LIA* 294). While processions are vitally important to traditional societies and, for instance, were also an important form of ritual in late medieval Christianity, the fact that the procession in *Light in August* is a perversion of the rite of interment is driven home by the fact that the body is not at its head: Joanna's corpse had been taken to town much earlier.[62] However, the narrative's transformation of the caravan into this peculiar "procession behind a catafalque" serves to remind the reader of the extent

---

[62]See Cliford C. Flannigan, "Liminality, Carnival, and Social Structure: The Case of Medieval Biblical Drama," in *Victor Turner and the Construction of Cultural Criticism*, 42-63, and "The Roman Rite and the Origins of the Liturgical Drama," in *University of Toronto Quarterly* xliii/3 (Spring 1974): 263-84. Faulkner includes a parody of the rite of interment in *Sanctuary* (1931). The hearse carrying the body of Red, the man Popeye enlisted to be Temple's lover while he watched, is followed by six hired Packards empty save for their drivers. Behind the Packards are a string of cabs and private cars, all of which leave the procession before the hearse reaches the cemetery. The narrative informs us that "at last only the hearse and the six Packards were left, each carrying no occupant save the liveried driver" before it too cuts away from the scene (263).

to which rites of passage are employed to transform the individual into a subject of and in service of an ideology. The presence or absence of the body does not matter; what matters is that the people have something to focus on and believe in. It is most apt that Lena's arrival in Jefferson momentarily halts the procession, because by bringing her story and Joanna's into conjunction the narrative prepares the reader to see to what extent Lena's determination by men is analogous to the community's determination of Joanna.

The townspeople believe that womanhood must be protected and that the primary threat to it is the black man.[63] That belief prohibits them from letting Joanna "be dead in peace and quiet" (*LIA* 289). They hold their belief that "the body . . . cried out for vengeance" because it

> made nice believing. Better than the shelves and the counters filled with longfamiliar objects bought, not because the owner desired them or admired them, could take any pleasure in the owning of them, but in order to cajole or trick other men into buying them at a profit; and who must now and then contemplate both the objects which had not yet sold and the men who could buy them but had not yet done so, with anger and maybe outrage and maybe despair too. Better than the musty offices where the lawyers waited lurking among ghosts of old lusts and lies, or where the doctors waited with sharp knives and sharp drugs, telling man, believing that he should believe, without resorting to printed admonishments, that they labored for that end whose ultimate attainment would leave them with nothing whatever to do (*LIA* 289).

The text makes clear that objectifying the body in the service of the traditional ideology is necessary because it helps repress the reality of the desire for profit (which undermines human relations) and the empty end of labor in modern (and postmodern) culture. Joanna's body is tellingly likened to economic objects used in an exchange for the acquisition of surplus value. There is no concern for the individual in the men's

---

[63]George Fitzhugh wrote in 1854 that "So long as she is nervous, fickle, capricious, delicate, diffident, and dependent, man will continue to worship and adore her. . . . in truth, woman, like children, has but one right and that is the right of protection." On women's status in the South see also Degler, *At Odds: Women and the Family in America from the Revolution to the Present* (Oxford: Oxford University Press, 1980), 26-65; Anne Firor Scott, *The Southern Lady: From Pedestal to Politics* (Chicago: University of Chicago Press, 1970), 3-45; and Wyatt-Brown, *Southern Honor*, 117-253.

objectification of the body, and that enables the reader to see a telling determination. That is, Joanna's disfigured body becomes currency transporting the men's anxieties into the text. Their need to objectify Joanna is neatly described as a circumvention of emptiness when the narrative discloses that their interpretation is "Better than the musty offices . . . where the doctors waited . . . telling man, believing that he should believe, without resorting to printed admonishments, that they labored for the end whose ultimate attainment would leave them with nothing whatever to do." The empty end of labor that is the pursuit of the fetish of the coin must be managed by the transformation of Joanna's body into currency to be spent in the support of a culture that perpetuates the traditional ideological fictions of womanhood and race in order to repress any understanding of an encroaching ideology and its fiction of labor's relation to the fetish.

The effect of that encroaching ideology is made all too clear when Faulkner describes the town of Doane's Mill in the first chapter of *Light in August*. While it is easy to forget that "little less-than-village" that is only briefly before the reader in what is one of Faulkner's longest novels, it must be confronted if one is to understand the range of Faulkner's cultural critique in *Light in August*:

> All the men in the village worked in the mill or for it. It was cutting pine. It had been there for seven years and in seven years more it would destroy all the timber within its reach. Then some of the machinery and most of the men who ran it and existed because of and for it would be loaded onto freight cars and moved away. But some of the machinery would be left, since new pieces could always be bought on the installment plan—gaunt, staring, motionless wheels rising from mounds of brick rubble and ragged weeds with a quality profoundly astonishing, and gutted boilers lifting their rusting and unsmoking stacks with an air stubborn, baffled and bemused upon a stumppocked scene of profound and peaceful desolation, unplowed, untilled, gutting slowly into red and choked ravines beneath the long quiet rains of autumn and the galloping fury of vernal equinoxes (*LIA* 4-5).

Faulkner includes the damning description of Doane's Mill to disclose the ultimate production of the capitalist/industrial ideology even as it was at work in his region and the nation. Everything is laid to waste by the mill, and there is nothing either attractive or humorous in the portrayal. Nor is there anything liberating. The town of Doane's Mill is predicated upon the production of a fetish, money, which binds and blinds as it acts as a substitute for the objects produced by the labor of the workforce. The workforce is alienated from the product of its labor, they do not use the wood, and the coin doubles the alienation by acting as a substitute for the labor. It is an unequal substitution, however, because the coin hides the fact of surplus value. Money attempts to naturalize labor's erosion of the body and in so doing creates the situation where the workers "existed because of and for it" [both the mill and modern industrial capitalism] (*LIA* 4). To exist because of and for the mill is to have a false sense of identity, to have fallen into the trap of alienation and reification so central to "industrial capitalism [that] struggled to give some natural credibility to its products and the conditions of their manufacture."[64]

In the face of this disquieting picture the culture of Jefferson turns to the traditional honor-shame ideology. *Light in August* makes clear that the turn is both a repression and a turn to a ideology so racist and sexist that it is no less disquieting. All that is left are misreadings born of blindness. The text implicates both the men of Jefferson and the predominant culture of the South with an unwillingness or inability to see both Doane's Mill and Lena Grove as locations of production. Neither wishes to reflect upon the implications of either those locations of production or their role in them. Consequently, they turn away from the mill after "destroy[ing] all the timber within its reach" and fix Lena with the simplest of readings. What remain are a perverse monument to industrial capitalism, the "gaunt, staring, motionless wheels . . . and gutted boilers," and the practice of a rhetoric of domination. *Light in August* shows the reader precisely the extent which the culture of the South is trapped. It cannot go ahead—to do so is to move to the disturbing picture of Doane's Mill. It cannot go back—to do so is to move to repression, racism, and sexism. It is small wonder, then, that the car carrying Mollie Worsham Beauchamp and Miss Worsham drives away from Jefferson at the conclusion of *Go Down, Moses* rapidly "as though in flight."

---

[64]John Carlos Rowe, "Modern Art and the Invention of Postmodern Capital," *American Quarterly* 39/1 (Spring 1987): 156.

Afterword

"Listen, Stranger;
This was myself; this was I"

"The writing I am currently executing and the reading you are currently performing are also in this respect rituals of ideological recognition, including the 'obviousness' with which the 'truth' or 'error' of my reflections may impose itself on you."

—*Louis Althusser*

William Faulkner completed *Light in August* in February of 1932; it would be nearly three years before he finished his next novel, *Pylon*, in December of 1934. What remained after the completion of *Light in August* was the effort to achieve what Shreve and Quentin strive for long into the cold of a New England winter night: "a happy marriage of speaking and hearing" (*AA* 316). And so for us. For like Shreve and Quentin, we need to engage in an act of overpassing in order to bridge or join together author and audience in a happy marriage of speaking and hearing that stands against the background of the failed rites as a successful rite of passage. To do so, it behooves us to turn to considerations of Faulkner's articulations of the identity of the writer and that of the reader. For the former we need to return to *Mosquitoes*. Faulkner's literary career has been nicely drawn by Joseph Blotner, David Minter, Judith Sensibar, and Judith Wittenberg, and it is not my intention to retrace the ground they have already covered. Rather, I want to examine Faulkner's fictionalization of himself in *Mosquitoes* in order to suggest his early and acute awareness of the nature of his art and the identity of the writer. To examine the identity of the reader we shall turn first to Narcissa Benbow in *Flags in the Dust* and then to *Requiem for a Nun*.

Faulkner's personification of "Elmer" in a September 1925 letter to his mother, "I have *him* half done, and I have put *him* away to begin a new one," suggests the importance of identity of and in the fictional text.[1] That he would draw his self-portrait on the reverse of a manuscript page in turn points to the importance of the text to Faulkner's conception of

---

[1] *Selected Letters of William Faulkner*, ed. Joseph Blotner (New York: Random House, 1978) 24-25 emphasis added.

his own identity. We give people pictures so that we can somehow remain before them and they can remember us as we were at the time the picture was made or taken. Faulkner's gift to his mother of self-portraiture on a manuscript page that is part of a work in progress breaks the work *and* fixes him at a moment in time. It is to say "This is who I am/was at the time I turned away from this text," and to imply "This is who I am/was before I turned to the new text that I've begun working on." We can conceive of the self-portrait as fixing for his mother who he was while he worked on and failed to complete "Elmer." Who Faulkner becomes, his emerging identity as a writer of fiction, is articulated in the text to which he next turned: *Mosquitoes*.

Near the end of the second day aboard the *Nausikaa* Faulkner enters the text within the course of a conversation between Jenny and Pat concerning what Pat had overheard Jenny exclaim to Mr. Talliaferro when he tried to awaken her with a kiss. Pat's fascination with the utterance occasions Jenny's story of how she came into its possession. That story, however, digresses almost immediately to light upon "a funny man . . . awful sunburned and kind of shabby dressed" who flirted with Jenny during the evening when she first heard the statement. The man's name, Jenny remembers after some thought, is Faulkner, and she remarks to Pat that he was crazy. She also tells Pat that Faulkner said "he was a liar by profession" (*MOS* 144-45). The text's digression upon the figure of Faulkner serves to disclose Faulkner's awareness of his identity as a writer. To write is to lie. The idea that writers lie dates to Plato. More recently, Wolfgang Iser has stressed the importance of the transgressive nature of the fiction writer's lies, as he or she employs the fictionalizing acts of selection and combination in order to subjectively re-order reality.[2]

In stressing the connection between fictionalizing and lying, Faulkner places himself within and against the tradition of Southwestern humor in general and that practiced by Mark Twain in particular. Like Faulkner, Twain plays with the nature of lying in essays such as "My First Lie and How I Got Out of It" and "On the Decay of the Art of Lying." While Twain focuses in the latter on the "lie of silent assertion," Faulkner stresses, in *Mosquitoes* at least, his role as a liar. Twain holds that a silent

---

[2]See, Iser, "Feigning in Fiction" and "Fictionalizing: The Anthropological Dimension of Literary Fictions," *New Literary History* 21/4 (Autumn 1990): 939-56.

lie is "the deception which one conveys by simply keeping still and concealing the truth." Laurence Holland argues that Twain himself practices the silent lie in *Adventures of Huckleberry Finn*. Faulkner, on the other hand, tells lies that, as we have seen, reveal the truth. That is, Faulkner is a liar bent upon exposing that which underlies and underpins reality.[3]

The writer is crazy in the same way that Darl is crazy; like Darl, Faulkner crosses the boundaries of (bourgeois) order to articulate its unseen and/or unacknowledged reality. In his "Introduction" to *The Sound and the Fury*, Faulkner makes clear that he sees and understands both the role of bourgeois order in the lives of individuals and the space and function of art:

> It [art] is a part of the glitter or shabbiness of the streets. The arrowing buildings rise out of it and because of it, to be torn down and arrow again. There will be people leading small bourgoise [sic] lives (those countless and almost invisible bones of its articulation, lacking anyone of which the whole skeleton might collapse) whose bread will derive from it—[4]

Still, Faulkner is well-aware that articulating the unseen and un-acknowledged reality is no easy task; the narrator of *Flags in the Dust* remarks of Horace Benbow in the act of writing that, "The pen ceased, and still poised, he sought the words that so rarely eluded him, realizing as he did so that, though one can lie about others with ready and extemporaneous promptitude, to lie about oneself requires deliberation and a careful choice of expression" (*Flags* 399). Throughout his career, and indeed his adult life, Faulkner carefully and deliberately "lied" about his life and work in order to, at least in part, destabilize his audience and, if we are astute enough to realize it, direct our attention to the role of the lie in his fictions.

---

[3]On lies and Southwestern humor see, for instance, Schmitz, *Of Huck and Alice: Humorous Writing and American Literature* (Minneapolis: University of Minnesota Press, 1983) and "Tall Tales, Tall Talk: Pursuing the Lie in Jacksonian Literature," *American Literature* xlvii/4 (January 1977) 474-91. For the silent lie in *Adventures of Huckleberry Finn* see Holland, "A 'Raft of Trouble': Word and Deed in *Huckleberry Finn*" in *American Realism*, ed. Sundquist, 66-81.

[4]"Introduction," *MQ* 410.

The ludic spirit motivating Faulkner's self-fictionalization is fundamental to the cultural critique Faulkner creates through the use of the rites
of passage to tell the story of man and his/her environment.[5] The reflexivity necessary for such a creation is predicated upon the self-reflexivity
disclosed in *Mosquitoes*, for "the ability to differentiate or abstract oneself, to turn around on one's own performance and, so to speak, see
oneself" is vital to the "antic" spirit essential to the act of writing fiction.[6]
Just as Faulkner's texts have a philosophical identity grounded in the
thinking of Husserl, Vaihinger, and, to a lesser extent, Kant, there is a
philosophical dimension to his own identity as a writer which is grounded
in Hegel. Hegelian "Consciousness is intentionality or consciousness of,"
which Davis shows is fundamental to the subject's determination of
difference and a necessary prerequisite to the dialectical life.[7] Iser's
theorizing on fictions and fictionalizing leads him to argue that fictions
are intentional acts of transgression.[8] This can only be so if the writer is
fully conscious in Hegelian terms. Faulkner's self-fictionalizing discloses,
then, his "intentionality [and] consciousness" of himself and, by extension, that he is conscious of the structures determining subjectivity in his
culture. For to be conscious that he is a liar is to be conscious that his
transgressions produce the difference fundamental to an understanding of
identity and subjectivity. At the same time, the act of (w)riting is directed
inward and Faulkner is transformed.[9] What is more, Faulkner's reflexivity
compels the reader to see the reflexive nature of a literary fiction and to
engage in reflexive acts himself/herself.

Faulkner's texts articulate and examine the instability of culture by
focusing on the cultural construct that attempts to maintain cultural stability by determining identity—the rite of passage. The fragmentary nature

---

[5]James B. Meriwether and Michael Milgate, eds., *Lion in the Garden* (New York:
Random House, 1968) 177.

[6]Jerome S. Bruner, "Nature and Uses of Immaturity," *American Psychologist* 27
(1972): 5.

[7]Davis, *Inwardness and Existence*, 358.

[8]Iser, *"Feigning in Fiction,"* 208-223.

[9] Faulkner's self-reflexivity and transformation during the fiction-writing process most
likely contributed to the difficulties he had whenever he finished a novel, left Yoknapatawpha, and returned to the real world. (See Blotner, *William Faulkner*, passim—
especially 719-721; Minter, *William Faulkner*, passim—especially 133-135, 150-152,
168). For a brief example of how the act of literary creation is ritually transformative see
McIntyre, "Drama as Rite: R. J. Sorge's Odysseus," *German Quarterly* 50:32-37.

of texts like *As I Lay Dying* and, to a lesser extent, *Light in August* and the deconstruction of the social language of the rites of passage within them suggest that Faulkner is acutely aware of the instability of his culture as he transforms and inscribes it in his fiction. Apparently knowing culture's role in "controlling meaning," Faulkner represents his culture in order to disclose ideology's role in that control.[10]

This is not to say, however, that Faulkner was immune to the effects of ideology upon the determination of identity. One need only recognize the importance in his fiction of the dialectic between nature and culture to see that he was not free of cultural paradigms. Consider the importance of the nature/culture dialectic in *As I Lay Dying*. We have already noted that Addie embeds her theory of signification in the story of her life. That life, an unending series of denials and frustrations, is marked by her awareness of the gap between herself and the natural order. She begins her narrative by telling the reader that she would go down to the spring where she could be quiet and hate the children she teaches, and that "It would be quiet there then, with the water bubbling up and away and the sun slanting quiet in the trees and the quiet smelling of damp and rotting leaves and new earth; especially in the early spring, for it was worst then" (*AILD* 155). Addie longs for quiet, in the form of the absence of language, because she understands both the gap between signifier and signified and that that gap is analogous to and constitutive of the gap between the natural order and culture. Addie can at best just bear what the wild geese tell her as they return north every spring: that there is a rhythm to the natural world and that she is not part of it. Instead, culture can at best only translate that rhythm into the constructs necessary to give life meaning. That translation creates a gap that can never be closed. One can argue, then, that the structure of the rite of passage as Faulkner uses it articulates a double bind. The conventional that is the construct of the rite of passage encloses the natural, the liminal and its fundamental indeterminacy, in order to repress it, but at the same time the natural is incorporated in the rite because of our longing for what we hesitantly think must be repressed.

Faulkner suggests that Addie taps into the natural rhythm by giving birth. Although the birth is tainted by Anse's need to displace the rhythm into language, and hence into culture, Addie still considers Cash and Darl

---

[10]Stephen Foster, "Symbolism and the Problematics of Postmodern Representation," in *Victor Turner and the Construction of Cultural Criticism*, ed. Ashley, 130.

"of me alone, of the wild blood boiling along the earth, of me and of all that lived; of none and of all" (*AILD* 162). Later births are tainted by Addie's need to "replace" Jewel, but at least at one point in her life Addie both heard the land and had its voiceless speech running through her. Karl Zender's consideration of the nature and power of sound in Faulkner suggests that the "natural" sound Addie hears fades in Faulkner's later fiction as other "images of sound begin to exemplify the growing power of the nation as a whole to destroy the individuality of its members."[11] Zender further argues that the preponderance of these new "modern" sounds in the later fiction is linked to Faulkner's sense of his own diminishing creativity as a writer.

Before it can fade, however, the natural sound must be heard; Faulkner must come to terms with his creativity as a writer of fiction. In order to do so he must move beyond the telling point where the largely autobiographical "Elmer" breaks down: when Elmer confronts his screaming illegitimate child "watching him with the blankness of a carven idol." Idols are worshipped because they help a culture determine meaning and value. An idol is also, archaically, something that is visible without having substance. Elmer's child is inscrutable in its blankness; it remains for Faulkner to carve his texts in a manner that will enable them to be visible and meaningful without substance, as is the nature of fictions, in order that they will be truly valuable. Faulkner only begins to tolerate the unnatural sound of his fictional texts, his offspring, when he employs the rites of passage in them, for then the liminality of the rite enables him to commemorate the natural world while displacing that world—its order and rhythm—into the constructs of language and fiction. What is more, just as his fictionalizing acts constitute a destabilization of culture, his self-fictionalization in *Mosquitoes* is a complicated act of disclosure that frees him to "lie" while destabilizing the trope of the author as a master-figure controlling meaning and directing the reader's gaze and interpretive acts to "author-figures" creating meaning in the service of various ideologies. The reader, then, is ready for the various "authors" of *As I Lay Dying* and for Gavin Stevens's and the traveling salesman's acts of authorship in *Light in August*.

---

[11]Karl F. Zender, "Faulkner and the Power of Sound," 97.

For Grainger, as for van Gennep, Turner, Wagner, and others, rites of passage are a means of encounter. Through them the initiate "learns the truth about society and social organisation" which, again according to Grainger, "actively promotes his [and her] personal health and happiness."[12] The thrust of our discussion, however, has been to show how Faulkner's texts employ rites of passage that promote in his initiates neither personal health nor happiness. Unhappiness rather than happiness is the issue for his characters; the same should be true for his readers. Yet, as Wadlington points out, we run the risk of diminishing Faulkner's achievement if we grant him canonization in a fashion that "cosmetically obscur[es] the real intimations of outrageousness which are among the conditions of his power to stir the 'immortal brief intransigent blood' of a reading posterity."[13] We must, that is, read well.

To put it another way, we must not read as Narcissa does. In *Flags in the Dust* (1927), William Faulkner's first book to be set in Yoknapatawpha County, Narcissa Benbow resorts to a novel because she is unwilling to deal with the disconcerting image of young Bayard Sartoris atop the runaway horse in town. She turns the "pages restively under her unseeing eyes," only to have "the thunderous climacteric of the afternoon's moment"—the sight of Bayard as he fights for control of the stallion—recur after she puts the book down and attempts to play the piano (*Flags* 160). That evening Narcissa undresses and takes her book to bed with her, "where again she held her consciousness deliberately submerged as you hold a puppy under water until its body ceases to resist. And after a time her mind surrendered wholly to the book and she read on, pausing to think warmly of sleep, reading a page more" (*Flags* 162). Here reading is both an act of substitution and an act of violent suppression. Narcissa takes a book to bed with her as the substitute for

---

[12]Grainger, *The Language of the Rite*, 164.

[13]Wadlington, *Reading Faulknerian Tragedy*, 59-60. Something like this appeared, alas, to be happening at the University of Mississippi's annual Faulkner and Yoknapatawpha conference I attended in 1987. The apparent eagerness of a number of the audience to embrace the memory of Faulkner without, again apparently, embracing his texts was for me at least a bit unsettling. For some of the audience, if I read them correctly, the event was like a primitive ritual gone awry; instead of the "reduction and cultural use of anxiety," the Conference was dedicated to the obliteration of anxiety (Diamond, *In Search of the Primitive*, 152). I hasten to add (and perhaps give voice to my own anxiety) that I have nothing but respect for the conference and its organizers, and think it an essential forum for the consideration of Faulkner's work and life.

taking young Bayard to bed. Reading enables her to suppress her sexual desire by deliberately drowning her consciousness, by submerging herself in the book. Enthralled by the illusory desire "To be . . . [her] own ideal once more, in regard to sexual no less than other trends, as . . . [she was] in childhood," Narcissa reads so that she might be "lost from [the] lesser and inconstant things" that would and do threaten her ideal (*Flags* 185).[14]

Later Narcissa acts as companion and nursemaid to a bedridden Bayard recovering from broken ribs suffered in an automobile accident. Narcissa is never completely comfortable when alone in the room with Bayard and her uneasiness deepens when her aunt, in whose house Bayard is convalescing, is away. Thus at that time Narcissa momentarily hesitates outside the bedroom, hoping Bayard is asleep so she will not have to confront him, her emotions, and her desire. She crosses into the room, finds Bayard awake, and immediately turns to the new book she has brought to read when he asks her how she feels about keeping him company. She tells him, "I've brought a new book," and the narrator remarks that her comment is evasive (*Flags* 271). The narrative disclosure tells us what we can see for ourselves: for Narcissa the act of turning to a book and reading is often evasive. Reading serves as protection for Narcissa; she reads swiftly to Bayard that afternoon, "as though she were crouching behind the screen of words her voice raised between them" (*Flags* 272). Reading also enables Narcissa to attain a position of mastery. She is in control of the book and as a result she is also in control of the situation. Her need for control and mastery leads her to experience "ludicrous and friendly bewilderment" while trying to find the page she was reading when Bayard fell asleep earlier that afternoon (*Flags* 277). Bayard tells her to "just read anywhere," but Narcissa must find the right place so that she can remain in control.

Although Narcissa eventually will become comfortable enough with young Bayard to occasionally discard the book in favor of talking with him, she returns to the book when Faulkner conjoins a discussion of marriage with the act of reading. In reply to Narcissa's query for advice regarding marriage Miss Jenny says, "I wouldn't advise anybody to marry. You wont be happy, but women haven't got civilized enough yet

---

[14]Freud, *Standard Edition* xiv, 100. Freud writes, "The condition of sleep, [which Narcissa desires and will drown her consciousness to obtain] too resembles illness in implying a narcissistic withdrawal of the positions of the libido on to the subject's own self, or, more precisely, on to the single wish to sleep" (*Standard Edition* xiv, 83).

to be happy unmarried, so you might as well try it. We can stand any-thing, anyway. And change is good for folks. They say it is, that is" (*Flags* 287). We next read:

> But Narcissa didn't believe that. I shall never marry, she told herself. Men . . . that was where unhappiness lay. And if I couldn't keep Horace, loving him as I did . . . Bayard slept. She picked up the book and read on to herself, about antic people in an antic world where things happened as they should. The shadows lengthened eastward. She read on, lost from mutable things (*Flags* 288, ellipses are Faulkner's).

When Narcissa turns away from a consideration of marriage rites and to the novel and the act of reading she discloses that she seeks refuge in literature; for her the book is a sanctuary. In love with her brother Horace, Narcissa laments the fact that her love was not strong enough to keep him from turning to Belle; simultaneously, Narcissa is outraged at the affront to order that is Horace's affair with a married woman. To take another man's wife, and to be taken by her, is to make a mockery of mar-riage, to unbound one of the cultural constructs upon which community is based. In love with young Bayard Sartoris, Narcissa struggles to repress that love because the desire motivating it represents a loss of control. Bayard also represents a rage against order. It is Bayard's exercise of a will to disorder, a disorder that ultimately leads to the violent closure of death, from which Narcissa flees. Narcissa does not believe that change is "good for folks" so she turns to the novel, a place of order where "things happened as they should." When Narcissa reads, then, as length-ening shadows mark the beginning of dusk's descent and the approach of the most liminal time of the day, she is, ironically, "lost from mutable things."

Having vowed never to marry, Narcissa attempts to substitute the happy marriage of speaking and hearing, or more precisely writing and hearing, born of reading the sort of literature she favors. The passage forges a connection between reading fictions and the rites of passage, which in turn suggests a connection between reading and identity. What is more, the very language of the passage suggests that Faulkner would have us be aware of the connection. Consider the following sentence: "She picked up the book and read on to herself, about antic people in an antic world where things happened as they should" (*Flags* 288). What is the phrase "to herself" doing in the sentence? What does it contribute to our understanding? At once nothing, and everything. On the one hand the phrase "to herself" is superfluous: it need not be there for the sentence to make grammatical sense; nor is it necessary for us to understand, at the most basic level, the passage in which the sentence is located. Yet on the other hand the ironic use of the reflexive pronoun "herself," ironic insofar as Narcissa reads in order to avoid reflecting on either self or self-consciousness, stresses both identity and reflection while "to" takes the form of the copula to further articulate the relationship between reading and identity.

Narcissa's desire for immutability is analogous to the reader's desire for consistency that some texts oppose. If the reader is annoyed by the indeterminacy created by such texts, by the gaps that force one into various acts of interpretation, then he or she "obviously expects literature to present us with a world that has been cleared of contradictions."[15] So it is with Narcissa Benbow, whose desire for what might be termed textual consistency, a smooth read if you will, is in no small measure due to the contradictions, uncertainty, and anxiety threatening to, like Bayard atop the runaway stallion, disrupt the veneer that she would have be her life-world.

Faulkner will not let Narcissa so easily off the hook however. Beyond her attraction to the at least in part obscene and hence destabilizing letters Byron Snopes writes her, the last of which she reads, finally, with her requisite "tranquil detachment" the day before her wedding, there is an act of reading that leads to the appearance of anxiety in Narcissa:

> She put the afternoon from her mind deliberately, and for a while and with a sort of detachment she watched her other self sink further and further into the book, until at last the book absorbed her attention. But then the vacuum of her relaxed will roused her again, and although she read deliberately on, a minor part of her consciousness probed ceaselessly, seeking the reason, until with a stabbing rush like a touched nerve it filled her mind again—the bronze fury of them, the child become an intent and voiceless automaton of fear, Bayard's bleeding head chiselled and calm and cold (*Flags* 161).

Faulkner, then, does not allow Narcissa to completely appropriate reading as a sanctuary. This is not the same, however, as an immersion in the reading act that leads to the possibility of change. One might argue that

---

[15]Iser, *Prospecting*, 27.

Narcissa is able to avoid change, is able to thrust Bayard "without her bastions again" and reattain the position of reading as "tranquil detachment," precisely because the text and her reading act are not intimately connected to the production of anxiety that might lead to transformation (*Flags* 161, 333).

For Davis anxiety is fundamental to any self-awareness and determination of subjectivity. While Narcissa tries to do without anxiety and hence avoid both psychic and social conflict, Davis argues that we must "live anxiety" if are to achieve the dialectical life necessary to understand our conflicted self, our conflicted world, and our identity as subjects. Davis writes, "all anxiety is ultimately anxiety before oneself and over oneself; it is anxiety over the core conflicts that make a given situation one's own situation." That is, anxiety fuels identity, and vice-versa.[16] Subjects are positioned in relation to and by acts, and Narcissa "fails" as a reading subject because her identity as a reader is neither psychologically nor socially agonistic. Rather, her actions, and for the purposes of the present discussion especially her actions as a reader, are directed at avoiding the conflicts and anxiety that Faulkner most wishes to expose and explore.

Narcissa's "interpretation" of literature, her act of reading with its reliance on things happening as they should, denies change, violent or otherwise, but much of Faulkner's work—with its fragmentary structure, dizzying temporal complexity, radical elision, play with language and characterization, and experimentation with form—is predicated upon disjunction for rhetorical effect. As Warwick Wadlington argues, while working from the premise that Faulkner strove to determine the efficacy of tragedy in the modern world and for the modern reader,

> Faulkner's evident rhetorical instinct was to tempt outrage. . . . Not only the challenging techniques but the subject matter prominent in Faulkner's major phase (the now-familiar inventory of incest, rape, fratricide, idiocy, castration, bodily corruption, and tragic miscegenation which can

---

[16]Davis, *Inwardness and Existence*, 270. Freud's fullest treatment of anxiety, in which he abandons his earlier notion that anxiety is simply transformed libido, can be found in *Inhibitions, Symptoms and Anxiety, Standard Edition* xx, 87-172. We shall see that Faulkner offers in *Requiem for a Nun* a view of the reading act as producing at least a modicum of anxiety and being transformative.

still unsettle the new or unjaded reader of Faulkner) make affront a constant possibility.[17]

While for Narcissa reading is a chance to attain mastery and control and
experience order, the violent disjunctive nature of many of Faulkner's
texts, coupled with the violence involved in reading them, dictates that
the sensitive reader relinquish the sense of control that comes when a text
hews to traditional literary guidelines and accepted literary conventions
of form, content, and taste. The outrageous nature of the Faulknerian text,
its transgression of those boundaries determined by convention, helps the
reader to see that, as Maurice Blanchot has remarked while considering
transgressive literature in general, "the book alone is important, as it is,
far from genres, outside rubrics—prose, poetry, the novel, the first-
person-account—under which it refuses to be arranged and to which it
denies the power to fix its place and determine its form."[18]

Assuming we do not put them down unfinished, Faulkner's texts lead
us into what I will term the rites of reading, and as a direct consequence
help us to recover the mutable nature of ourselves and our lives.
Although Victor Turner would in all likelihood have had difficulty with
my phrasing of the rites of reading, given that he held rites and rituals to
be of a religious or magico-sacred nature, I think that the phrase is apt
when applied to the texts we have before us. Turner, moreover, argued
that liminality "produces in men their highest pitch of self-consciousness," which I suggest is also true of the act of reading Faulkner's fictions, and near the end of his career went so far as to suggest that in the
contemporary moment "*narrative* and cultural drama may have the task
of poesis, that is, of remaking cultural sense, even when they seem to be
dismantling ancient edifices of meaning that can no longer redress our
modern [and postmodern] 'dramas of living'—now evermore on a global
and species-threatening scale."[19] Roger Grainger is among the numerous
critics and theorists stressing the analogous relationship between art and
rites, arguing that "ritual exists in the artistic relation of content and form,

---

[17]Wadlington, *Reading Faulknerian Tragedy*, 60-61.

[18]Quoted in Adena Rosmarin, *The Power of Genre* (Minneapolis: University of
Minnesota Press, 1985) 7-8.

[19]Turner, *Dramas*, 255; "Social Dramas" 164 emphasis added). For Turner's
distinction between the liminal and liminoid see "Variations of a Theme of Liminality,"
in *Secular Ritual*, 36-52.

in which what is familiar, ordinary, domestic, responds to the challenge of what is new, strange, alien, just as self-hood responds to otherness. . . . In its true identity . . . [the rite] is a means of encounter."[20]

Literature too is a means of encounter, one which "draws life from tensions with and impacts on the cultural context from which it has emerged. It intervenes in its real environment and establishes its uniqueness not least by highlighting its otherness in relation to the situations that have conditioned it."[21] The highlighted "otherness" of Faulkner's texts makes culture visible by "culture shock" and enables us to see how that culture determines the identity of Faulkner's characters and, by extension, his readers.[22] The "otherness" of Faulkner's text must destabilize the reader if culture is to be made visible. Thus, as Davis argues is true with reading Nietzsche and Marx for instance, one has not begun to truly read Faulkner "until one is 'profoundly wounded' by everything he says."[23] In reading Faulkner one becomes profoundly wounded with the realization, first, that much of the experimentation and concomitant shock is related to the rites of passage in his texts, and, second, that the rites of passage play a profound role in producing our identity and our consciousness. Narcissa Benbow reads in order to kill her consciousness, and her self-consciousness; it is my contention that the role played by rites of passage in Faulkner's early fiction helps make the reader conscious of the structures that define the person and the community.

The exposure and exploration that are necessarily the province of literature and what Turner terms social drama must be matched by exposure of and exploration by the reader if literature is to interpret, interrogate, and elicit change. What Iser terms a literary anthropology can only elucidate a "chronic process of self-reflection [that] enables us to see through the attitudes offered us, if not imposed on us, by our everyday world" if we accept the unsettling and destablizing nature of the act of reading.[24] This difficult but necessary acceptance corresponds to the acceptance of participants in the social drama. Turner defines social drama as a processual unit used by cultures when essential conflicts occur. Without acceptance there is no hope of getting to the crucial third

---

[20]Grainger, *The Language of the Rite*, 161.

[21]Iser, *Prospecting*, 282.

[22]Wagner, *The Invention of Culture*, 9.

[23]Davis, *Inwardness and Existence*, 188.

[24]Iser, *Prospecting*, 281.

phase, redressive action, whose liminal nature is marked by the sub-junctive mood enabling individuals and cultures to "break the cake of custom and enfranchise speculation."[25] While both Turner's final phase, reintegration or recognition of the schism that necessitated the social drama, and van Gennep's postliminal phase mark a move back to the indicative and determinant, the subjunctive mood of the liminal can bring about "a transformative self-immolation of order as presently constituted [and] even sometimes a voluntary sparagmos or self-dismemberment of order."[26]

If exposure and exploration on the part of the reader lead to trans-formation and self-dismemberment of order, then they do so because of the reading act's connection with the subjunctive and the social drama, for as Wadlington points out, "reading is grounded . . . in the necessity that cultures create persons by empowering them in a dialogue of per-formances."[27] Wadlington's reading of reading Faulknerian tragedy (and writing Faulknerian tragedy) is compelling. My own approach to the reader in Faulkner differs in three ways, the first of which can be deter-mined by using a quotation from *Reading Faulknerian Tragedy* as a point of departure: "We will need, that is, to classify writing, reading, and genre conversions with the creating and consummating of the formative scripts of culture itself."[28] The thrust of my argument is that the rites of passage are the essential formative scripts of the culture Faulkner interrogates, and that as narrative strategy and stratagem they determine the form of the texts examined. Second, because of the fundamental role of rites of passage in Faulkner's fictions my turn to Turner, van Gennep,

---

[25]Turner, *The Forest of Symbols*, 106.

[26]Turner, *"Social Dramas,"* 160. For Turner on the connection between drama, ritual, rite, and liminality, in addition to those works already cited, as well as on the necessity for an ethnodramatics, see, "Frame, Flow, and Reflection: Ritual and Drama as Public Liminality," in *Performance in Postmodern Culture;* "Dramatic Ritual/Ritual Drama: Per-formative and Reflexive Anthropology," *Kenyon Review* 1 (1979): 80-93; and "Liminality and the Performative Genres" in *Rite, Drama, Festival, Spectacle*, ed. MacAloon, 19-41. For a reading of the connection between Turner's redressive phase of the social drama and art see Raybin, "Aesthetics, Romance, and Turner," in *Victor Turner and the Construction of Cultural Criticism*, 21-41. For an attempt to theorize the relationship and difference between ritual and literature see Morgan, "Borges's 'Immortal': Metaritual, Metaliterature, and Metaperformance," in *Rite, Drama, Festival, Spectacle*, 79-101.

[27]Wadlington, *Reading Faulknerian Tragedy*, 50.

[28]Ibid., 14.

Geertz, anthropology in general, and literary anthropology in particular is both different and more involved than Wadlington's use of Geertz and Turner. Third, I am interested in the "Afterword" in probing Faulkner's construction of the reader in "The Jail" section of *Requiem for a Nun* in order to suggest what I take to be Faulkner's understanding of the rites of reading. With "The Jail," the final prose section of *Requiem for a Nun*, Faulkner articulates an awareness of the dramatic and performative natures of "successful" reading (as opposed to Narcissa's "failed" readings) that parallels and compliments his awareness of the identity of the literary text, his fictional world, and his characters. That act of reading, moreover, brings about change, and hence offers us a model for the reading of Faulkner's texts and at least some sense of the efficacy of a literary anthropology.

In response to a student's question regarding the form of *Requiem for a Nun* Faulkner said that he felt the story he was trying to tell was best served by the combination of drama and prose. He said that "The longer—I don't know what you would call those interludes, the prefaces, the preambles, whatever they are—was necessary to give it the contrapuntal effect which comes in orchestration, that the hard give-and-take of the dialogue was played against something that was a little mystical, made it sharper, more effective in my opinion."[29] Richard Moreland's reading of the text demystifies the prose sections: they serve as "extended stage directions" that "accommodate not the mere costumes, lighting, and layout of the stage but the larger social contexts and longer historical backgrounds" that he argues are more and more necessary if we are to understand the crises enacted.[30]

Those crises issue from two acts of violence and violation: the violence done to nature by the townspeople in order to realize "a vision of their historical destiny in which the wilderness, with its wild animals and 'wild men' (along with the old white men who would recognize and regret the passing of these 'wild men') would all be 'obsolescent' obstructions cast silently out of the way of progress" and the jailbreak that tacitly questions the vision of destiny and threatens to reveal its "violence and costs to others as well as themselves."[31] The curious nature

---

[29]*Faulkner in the University*, eds, Gwynn and Blotner, 122.
[30]Richard Moreland, *Faulkner and Modernism: Rereading and Rewriting* (Madison WI: University of Wisconsin Press, 1990) 195.
[31]Ibid., 204.

of the jailbreak, the bandits remove one wall of the building in order to escape, creates an image of "the jail open to the world like a stage" (*REQ* 14). It is fitting that upon that stage the drama of Jefferson, Yoknapatawpha, and the country is played out, for the act of violence that creates the stage, two-fold violence when we consider that the act of fictionalizing is a violent one, corresponds to the violence of drama conceived as "both the *representation* and the intense present reenactment (redoing) of sociohistorical violence."[32] In dramatic terms the prose sections of *Requiem* link the text to both nineteenth-century drama and the epic.[33] Both are necessary if Faulkner is to ground his text in order that he might critique his culture. Moreland argues that by "figuring the stage as the site of a frightening jailbreak," which marks the breech of the culture's power to contain what it must if order is to be preserved and the dominant ideology is to survive, "*Requiem* effectively reopens a marginal space in the public discourse—also a transitional time in the historical discourse, and the psychic space of a 'boundary state' in the psychological discourse."[34] The marginal space is analogous to that opened by the liminality of the social drama and akin to the "historicizing" tendency of nineteenth-century drama. Historicization is accomplished by a space opened "in which the play evokes otherwise unnamed realms of tension in a manner that initiates a debate not only about the status of the characters' claims regarding the world, but also the social and ideological codes that the play must propose—according to its own rules—as a means of resolving the contradictions that emerge between these characters."[35]

While Faulkner's need to give his text a contrapuntal quality so that he might articulate and critique his culture is solved by the prose sections, their epic rather than modern quality creates a problem of its own. That is, while *Requiem for a Nun*, "contrary to a certain modernist line," is

---

[32]Iser, "Feigning in Fiction," 208. Jonathan V. Crewe, "The Violence of Drama: Towards a Reading of the Senecan Phaedra," *Boundary* 2 17/3 (1990): 107 emphasis added.

[33]On the nineteenth-century drama as social drama see Gilman, *The Making of Modern Drama* (New York: Farrar, Straus and Giroux, 1974); on the relationship between social drama and epic see Szondi, *Theory of the Modern Drama*, trans. Michael Hays (Minneapolis: University of Minnesota Press, 1987) 35-41.

[34]Moreland, *Faulkner and Modernism*, 200.

[35]Michael Hays, "Declassified Documents: Fragmentations in the Modern Drama," *Boundary* 2 17/3 (Summer 1990): 113.

"not unresponsive to the complexities of social existence," its reliance on nineteenth-century dramatic form in particular and the epic in general implicates it in the crisis Peter Szondi saw being experienced in drama in the second half of the nineteenth century.[36] That crisis "can be traced to the forces that drove people out of interpersonal relations and into isolation."[37] Because the meaning of the rite is "specifically inter-personal" Faulkner was compelled to devise a rhetorical and narrative strategy that might move the reader out of isolation and into some sense of community, however fleeting, in order to articulate what I have termed the rites of reading.[38] We have seen how Faulkner appropriates nineteenth-century humorous style and form in *Light in August* in order to articulate the dominant ideologies of his culture; in *Requiem for a Nun* he appropriates the form of nineteenth-century drama to articulate the sociohistorical violence of his region and the country and adapts the form in "The Jail" to achieve the interpersonal and dramatic quality necessary for the transformation of the reader.

The adaptation is made possible by the dual nature of the jail as stage. It is both the site of violence and a space where that violence can be articulated for the reader. The townspeople, after all, lock the bandits in the jail not to protect themselves, "but to protect the bandits from the settlement" (*REQ* 12). While the act of protection guarantees the abdication of the fledgling settlement to the larger authority of the State, and hence marks the jail as the stage for the articulation of the conflict and violence already mentioned, metafictively it also articulates the stage and drama as locations where, as is the case with social dramas and rites of passage, conflict is played out and transformation is made possible.

Ibsen was fond of remarking that theater in Greek means "a place for seeing" and the theater that is the jail and "The Jail" is precisely that.[39] The penultimate chapter of *Light in August*, a text in which seeing and interpretation are paramount and which can easily be read dramatically, opens with a telling image and scene which inscribes a path to "The Jail" as a place of seeing: "Now the final copper light of afternoon fades; now the street beyond the low maples and the signboard is prepared and empty, framed by the study window like a stage" (*LIA* 466). That sign,

---

[36]See, e.g., ibid.

[37]Szondi, *Theory of the Modern Drama*, 57-58.

[38]Grainger, *The Language of the Rite*, 164.

[39]Quoted in Gilman, *The Making of Modern Drama*, 46.

on stage, prepared by Hightower to advertise his availability as *artist and teacher* after he leaves the pulpit, is, like the street, empty for two reasons. First because it "is even less to him than it is to the town; he is no longer conscious of it as a sign, a message" (*LIA* 60). Hightower's "reading" of the sign discloses what can happen to language, ritual, and rites of passage. Faulkner, we have seen, is bent upon revitalizing language and the rites of passage in order to revitalize literature and critique culture. For the critique and revitalization to be fully realized, however, there must be active participation on the part of the reader, and the sign is prepared *but* empty precisely insofar as it wants a reader to engage in the act of interpretation.

For our purposes in seeing Faulkner's awareness and articulation of the identity of the reader it is instructive that *Light in August* informs us that the dramatic path to seeing is accomplished and the sign filled by "a stranger happening along the quiet and remote and unpaved and littleused street" who, after pausing to read the sign, would "now and then . . . mention the sign to some acquaintance in the town" and receive the story of Hightower, his wife, and her suicide (*LIA* 59). While the stranger's turn to an acquaintance to get the story suggests a move out of isolation and toward interpersonal relations, it lacks any notion of either the anxiety or the transformation necessary for an act of interpretation that would constitute a rite of reading. The stranger's turn to an acquaintance to learn the story of Hightower and his wife prefigures the "storytelling episode" between Gavin Stevens and the college professor much later in the text. It is worth remarking both the similarities and the differences. Neither case leads to either the production of anxiety or transformation; indeed, Stevens's version of Joe Christmas's final flight is fueled by a subconscious attempt to allay anxiety. The primary difference between the two episodes is that while we get no sense that Stevens's visiting friend cared to learn the story, the stranger early on in *Light in August* cares to know and thus seeks out the story from his acquaintance.

It is worth noting that the location of the sign the stranger reads in *Light in August* suggests Faulkner's awareness of how difficult it is to find the sort of reader his texts demand. The sign is beside a "quiet and remote and unpaved and littleused street," and the succession of adjectives culminating in "littleused" marks, metaphorically, the location of his literary texts in relation to the reading public. With the stranger's return in *Requiem for a Nun* Faulkner makes one last, albeit romantic, attempt as artist and teacher to educate us in the reading act so that we might turn to and truly read his fictions.

When Faulkner returns to the figure of the stranger in "The Jail" the act of reading inscribed is nothing short of modern, interpersonal, and transformative. Like the existential dramatist who "does not set people in their 'normal' surroundings (as the naturalist set them in their milieu) . . . [but] removes them to a new context," Faulkner makes his stranger "an outlander say from the East or the North or the Far West" either passing through town by accident or there because of a desire to understand why a "cousin or friend or acquaintance" had elected to live there (*REQ* 217).[40] In existential drama this type of displacement "repeats the metaphysical 'throw' as an experiment, [and] allows the existentialia, that is 'Dasein's character of Being' (Heidegger), to appear in estranged form as the situationally determined experience of the dramatis personae."[41] Faulkner estranges the reader from himself/herself, an act of estrangement vital to the act of reading, by using the second person pronoun to address the stranger (*REQ* 217). "You" is the reader, then, and as a member of the dramatis personae, we enter the space of the stage.

It is this act of transforming the reader into a character that moves the drama that is *Requiem for a Nun* away from solely the sociohistorical and epic and enables Faulkner to inscribe a successful rite of reading. Faulkner throws us into essential strangeness in "The Jail" and as a result compels us to confront our own existence. That confrontation is necessitated by and the product of the act of reading "Cecilia Farmer April 16th 1861" scratched faintly in a pane of glass in the jail. Zender is quite correct in noting that the name and the date serve "as the text for a transformative act of reading" that, Faulkner shows us, hinges upon the engagement of the reader.[42]

It is of no small importance that we must engage in the act of reading a name. If we trace the names of Januarius Jones in *Soldiers' Pay* and Tommy in *Sanctuary* we can better see how reading the name of Cecilia Farmer leads to acts of interrogation that reveal identity. Jones is an orphan "born of whom he knew and cared not, becoming Jones alphabetically, January through a conjunction of calendar and biology, Januarius through the perverse conjunction of his own star and the com-

---

[40]Szondi, *Theory of the Modern Drama*, 61.
[41]See, e.g., ibid.
[42]Zender, *"Faulkner and the Power of Sound,"* 99.

pulsion of food and clothing."[43] Jones's name, that is, is determined by chance, and his identity, as inscribed in and by his name, looks, Janus-like in two directions: back to the arbitrariness of language and the phoneme that captures his birth and existence and forward to the acts that determine his identity. As Robert Creeley suggests in his poem for January, "The Door," the month (like Janus) "faces two ways / but goes only one." The only way is forward, of course, for to go backward into the abyss of language from which we emerge is, as Quentin Compson makes painfully clear, deadly.

To go forward is to bring into conjunction identity and subjectivity, for names determine our existence in a community and as we have seen subject us to ideology. They are strategies of containment. Faulkner makes this clear when in *Sanctuary* the body of Tommy is brought to town to "lay on a wooden table, barefoot, in overalls, the sun-bleached curls on the back of his head matted with dried blood and singed with powder, while the coroner sat over him, trying to ascertain his last name."[44] None in the town know it, however, and their inability to fix Tommy with his complete name is indicative of the ambivalent status he and the other moonshiners have in the community. To be fully named, then, is to have an identity as subject in a community, and to read Cecilia Farmer (historicized by the date so that Faulkner might also push forward his cultural critique) is to confront that fact.

We, the stranger(s), are unsettled, shocked, and annoyed by passage into the "private quarters of a strange woman engaged in something as intimate as cooking a meal" that symbolizes passage through the threshold and into the liminality of the reading act (*REQ* 219; 218). Once immersed in that liminal space, we *must* participate in acts of interrogation in order to arrive at interpretation. Faulkner writes that "you ask questions, not only which are expected of you, but whose answers you *must have* if you are to get back into your car and fumble with any attention and concentration among the road signs and filling stations, to get on to wherever it is you had started" (*REQ* 220 emphasis added). The reading act inscribed in "The Jail" amounts to the sort of possession characteristic in ritual whereby one is "startled in a meaningful way; one may be encouraged to experience a transformation that has social mean-

---

[43]William Faulkner, *Soldiers' Pay* (Chatto & Windus: London, 1957) 50.
[44]William Faulkner, *Sanctuary* The Corrected Text (Vintage: New York, 1987) 117.

ing."[45] What is moved to in "The Jail" and played out in the last scene of *Requiem for a Nun* is the possibility of dialogue as a way to achieve interpersonal relations and meaning and, as a result, "rescue" both the drama and the individual.[46] If we are to find our way, in both the text and the world, what must be arrived at through this dialogue that stresses interpersonal relations and community is an understanding and awareness of identity and subjectivity: who is Cecilia Farmer? who are we? who am I? With and in "The Jail," then, Faulkner discloses that the act of reading is one of interrogation that illuminates identity and is transformative.

In the case of the stranger in "The Jail" the transformative reading act marks a return to what he once knew (*REQ* 225). The stranger engages in the three "interpretations of interpretation" that Davis defines as "the attempt to identify aporias that can never be sublated; the attempt to generate a content by liberating the truth one finds in some privileged abstraction; and the effort to probe those tragic situations a subject must mediate in order to maximize its existence."[47] The final line of "The Jail" would have us realize that the act of inscribing one's name brings with it a mediation of opposites characteristic of the interpersonal relation of drama striving toward a sublation that is achieved in our hearing (and reading) "'*Listen, stranger; this was myself: this was I*'" (*REQ* 225).[48]

Because we must remove ourselves from the liminal, must stumble "outside again . . . to unfumble among the road signs and filling stations to get back onto a highway you know, back into the United States," we cannot maintain the vision we have attained (*REQ* 225). Instead, Faulkner makes us dramaturgically aware of "Cecilia Farmer," "'This was I'," if only as romantic possibility, so that we might better understand, when back in not Jefferson nor Yoknapatawpha but the United States, our mediated and unmediated selves. Hence, "As in drama, where the opposed motives and desires of vitally connected characters produce a

---

[45]Napier, *Foreign Bodies*, 158.

[46]On the importance of dialogue in drama see, for instance, Kennedy, *Dramatic Dialogue: The Duologue of Personal Encounter* (Cambridge: Cambridge University Press, 1983), and Szondi, *Theory of the Modern Drama*, 52-54; on the drama of the subject and subjectivity see Davis, *Inwardness and Existence*, 232-366; on performance and the evocation of meaning in postmodern ethnography see Tyler, "Post-Modern Ethnography: From Document of the Occult to Occult Document," in *Writing Culture*, eds. Clifford and Marcus, 122-40.

[47]Davis, *Inwardness and Existence*, 348-49.

[48]Szondi, *Theory of the Modern Drama*, 55.

progressive development of conflict toward an irreversible outcome," the "genuine dialectic" that Faulkner articulates and would have the reader experience leaves both the figures of mediated and unmediated subject intact for us as we emerge from the liminality of the reading act.[49] We are left, then, with Faulkner's disclosure that the act of reading is more than inviting; it is compelling. For we must read if we are to find ourselves and in the process find our way.

---

[49]Davis, *Inwardness and Existence*, 326.

Bibliography

Althusser, Louis. *Lenin and Philosophy*. Translated by Ben Brewster. London: Monthly Review Press, 1971.

——. *For Marx*. Translated by Ben Brewster. New York: Vintage, 1970.

Anderson, Sherwood. *Letters of Sherwood Anderson*. Edited by Charles E. Modlin. Knoxville: University of Tennessee Press, 1984.

Bailey, Beth L. *From Front Porch to Back Seat: Courtship in Twentieth-Century America*. Baltimore: Johns Hopkins University Press, 1988.

Bell, Millicent. "Narrative Gaps/Narrative Meaning." *Raritan* 1 (Summer 1986): 84-102.

Belmont, Nicole. *Arnold van Gennep: The Creator of French Ethnography*. Translated by Derek Coltman. Chicago: University of Chicago Press, 1979.

Benveniste, Emile. *Problems in General Linguistics*. Translated by Mary Elizabeth Meek. Coral Gables FL: University of Miami Press, 1971.

Betz, Albrecht. "Commodity and Modernity in Heine and Benjamin." *New German Critique* 33 (Fall 1984): 179-88.

Blair, Walter. *Native American Humor*. Chicago: Chandler Publishing Co., 1937.

Bleikasten, Andre. *Faulkner's As I Lay Dying*. Translated by Roger Little. Bloomington: Indiana University Press, 1973.

Blotner, Joseph. *William Faulkner: A Biography*. 2 vols. New York: Random House, 1974.

Boles, John B. and Evelyn Thomas Nolan, editors. *Interpreting Southern History*. Baton Rouge: Louisiana State University Press, 1964.

Bowers, Alfred W. *Mandan Social and Ceremonial Organization*. Chicago: University of Chicago Press, 1950.

Braudel, Fernand. *Afterthoughts on Material Civilization and Capitalism*. Translated by Patricia M. Ranun. Baltimore: Johns Hopkins University Press, 1977.

——. *Capitalism and Material Life 1400-1800*. Translated by Miriam Kochan. New York: Harper & Row, 1973.

Brooks, Cleanth. *Toward Yoknapatawpha and Beyond*. New Haven CT: Yale University Press, 1978.

Burke, Carolyn. "Getting Spliced: Modernism and Sexual Difference." *American Quarterly* 39/1 (Spring 1987): 98-121.

Bruner, Jerome S. "Nature and Uses of Immaturity." *American Psychologist* 27 (1972): 1-22.

Carrithers, Michael, Steven Collins, and Steven Lukes, editors. *The Category of the Person: Anthropology, Philosophy, History*. Cambridge: Cambridge University Press, 1985.

Catlin, George. *O-kee-pa*. Edited by John C. Ewers. New Haven CT: Yale University Press, 1967.

Clifford, James. "Introduction: Partial Truths." In *Writing Culture: The Poetics and Politics of Ethnography*, edited by James Clifford and George E. Marcus, 1-27. Berkeley: University of California Press, 1986.

Clifford, James and George E. Marcus, editors. *Writing Culture: The Poetics and Politics of Ethnography*. Berkeley: University of California Press, 1986.

Cohen, Norm. *Long Steel Rail: The Railroad in American Folksong*. Urbana: University of Illinois Press, 1982.

Cowley, Malcolm, editor. *The Faulkner-Cowley File: Letters and Memories, 1944–1962*. New York: Viking Press, 1966.

Crewe, Jonathan V. "The Violence of Drama: Towards a Reading of the Senecan *Phaedra*." *Boundary 2* 17/3 (1990): 95-115.

Davis, Richard B., C. Hugh Holman, and Louis D. Rubin, Jr. editors. *Southern Writing 1585-1920*. New York: Odyssey Press, 1970.

Davis, Walter A. *The Act of Interpretation: A Critique of Literary Reason*. Chicago: University of Chicago Press, 1978.

—. *Inwardness and Existence: Subjectivity in/and Hegel, Heidegger, Marx, and Freud*. Madison: University of Wisconsin Press, 1989.

Degler, Carl N. *At Odds: Women and the Family in America from the Revolution to the Present*. Oxford: Oxford University Press, 1980.

deLauretis, Teresa. *Alice Doesn't: Feminism, Semiotics, Cinema*. Bloomington: Indiana University Press, 1984.

Derrida, Jacques. "Form and Meaning: A Note on the Phenomenology of Language." In *Margins of Philosophy*, translated by Alan Bass, 155-74. Chicago: University of Chicago Press, 1982.

—. "The Law of Genre." *Glyph* 7 (1980): 176-201.

—. "The Supplement of Copula: Philosophy Before Linguistics." In *Textual Strategies*, edited by Josue V. Harari, 82-120. Ithaca: Cornell University Press, 1979.

—. "White Mythology: Metaphor in the Text of Philosophy." In *Margins of Philosophy*. Translated by Alan Bass, 207-72. Chicago: University of Chicago Press, 1982.

Diamond, Stanley. *In Search of the Primitive: A Critique of Civilization*. New Brunswick: Transaction Books, 1974.

Dwyer, Kevin. "The Dialogic of Anthropology." *Dialectical Anthropology* 2 (1977): 143-51.

—. *Morroccan Dialogues*. Baltimore: Johns Hopkins University Press, 1982.

Falkner, Murray C. *The Falkner's of Mississippi: A Memoir*. Baton Rouge: Louisiana State University Press, 1967.

Fass, Paula. *The Damned and the Beautiful: American Youth in the 1920s*. New York: Oxford University Press, 1977.

Faulkner, Jim. *Across the Creek: Faulkner Family Stories*. Jackson: University Press of Mississippi, 1986.

Faulkner, John. *My Brother Bill: An Affectionate Reminiscence*. New York: Trident Press, 1963.

Faulkner, William. *Absalom, Absalom!*. Modern Library Edition. New York: Random House, [n.d.].

—. *As I Lay Dying*. The Corrected Text. New York: Vintage Books, 1987.

—. "Elmer." Edited by James B. Meriwether. *Mississippi Quarterly* 36 (Summer 1983): 343-447.

—. *Essays, Speeches and Public Letters*. Edited by James B. Meriwether. New York: Random House, 1966.

—. *Faulkner in the University*. Edited by Fredrick Gwynn and Joseph Blotner. Charlottesville: University of Virginia Press, 1959.

—. *Flags in the Dust*. New York: Vintage Books, 1974.

—. *Go Down, Moses*. New York: Vintage Books, 1973.

—. "Introduction to *The Sound and the Fury*." Edited by James B. Meriwether, *Mississippi Quarterly* 26 (Summer 1973): 410-15.

—. "Introduction to *The Sound and the Fury*." Edited by James B. Meriwether, *Southern Review* 8/4 (Autumn 1972): 705-10.

—. *Light in August*. The Corrected Text. New York: Vintage International Edition, 1990.

—. *Mosquitoes*. New York: Liveright, 1927.

—. "New Orleans." In *New Orleans Sketches*, edited by Carvel Collins. New Brunswick NJ: Rutgers University Press, 1958.

—. *Requiem for a Nun*. New York: Vintage Books, 1975.

—. *Sanctuary*. The Corrected Text. New York: Vintage Books, 1987.

—. *Selected Letters of William Faulkner*. Edited by Joseph Blotner. New York: Random House, 1978.

—. *Soldiers' Pay*. London: Chatto & Windus, 1957.

—. *The Sound and the Fury*. The Corrected Text. New York: Vintage Books, 1987.

—. *Uncollected Stories of William Faulkner*. Edited by Joseph Blotner. New York: Vintage Books, 1981.

Faust, Drew Gilpin. "The Rhetoric and Ritual of Agriculture in Antebellum South Carolina." *Journal of Southern History* 45 (1979): 541-68.

Fitzhugh, George. *Sociology of the South*. Richmond: Morris, 1854.

Flannigan, C. Clifford. "Liminality, Carnival, and Social Structure: The Case of Late Medieval Biblical Drama." In *Victor Turner and the Construction of Cultural Criticism*, edited by Kathleen M. Ashley, 42-63. Bloomington: Indiana University Press, 1990.

—. "The Roman Rite and the Origins of the Liturgical Drama." *University of Toronto Quarterly* 43/3 (Spring 1974): 263-84.

Flowers, Linda. *Throwed Away: Failures of Progress in Eastern North Carolina*. Knoxville: University of Tennessee Press, 1990.

Foster, Stephen William. "Symbolism and the Problematics of Postmodern Representation." In *Victor Turner and the Construction of Cultural Criticism*, edited by Kathleen M. Ashley, 117-37. Bloomington: University of Indiana Press, 1990.

Foucault, Michel. *Madness and Civilization*. Translated by Richard Howard. New York: Random House, 1965.

Fowler, Doreen and Ann Abadie, editors. *Faulkner and the Craft of Fiction*. Faulkner and Yoknapatawpha 1987. Jackson: University Press of Mississippi, 1989.

Freud, Sigmund. *The Standard Edition of the Complete Psychological Works of Sigmund Freud*, 24 vols. Edited by James Strachey. London: Hogarth Press, 1966–1974.

Gautier, Theophile. *Mademoiselle de Maupin*. Translated by Paul Selver. London: H. Hamilton, 1948.

Geertz, Clifford. *The Interpretation of Cultures*. New York: Basic Books, 1973.

—. *Works and Lives: The Anthropologist as Author*. Stanford: Stanford University Press, 1988.

Genette, Gerard. *Narrative Discourse*. Translated by Jane E. Lewin. Ithaca: Cornell University Press, 1980.

Gill, Sam. "The Trees Stood Deep Rooted." In *I Become Part of It*, edited by D. M. Dooling and Paul Jordan-Smith. New York: Parabola Books, 1989.

Gilman, Richard. *The Making of Modern Drama*. New York: Farrar, Straus and Giroux, 1974.

Girard, Rene. *Violence and the Sacred*. Baltimore: Johns Hopkins University Press, 1972.

Glaser, Barney G. and Anselm L. Strauss, editors. *Status Passage*. Chicago: Aldine Atherton, Inc., 1971.

Grainger, Roger. *The Language of the Rite*. London: Darton, Longman & Todd, 1974.

Grantham, Dewey W. *Southern Progressivism: The Reconcilation of Tradition and Progress*. Knoxville: University of Tennessee Press, 1983.

Graves, Robert. *The Greek Myths*. New York: G. Braziller, 1957.

Gresset, Michel."Introduction: Faulkner Between the Texts." In *Intertextuality in Faulkner*, edited by Gresset and Noel Polk. Jackson: University Press of Mississippi, 1985.

Hall, Robert L. and Carol B. Stack, editors. *Holding on to the Land and the Lord: Kinship, Ritual, Land Tenure, and Social Policy in the Rural South*. Athens: University of Georgia Press, 1982.

Hanneborg, Knut. *Anthropological Circles: Observations on the Nature of Views of Man in Science*. New York: Humanities Press, 1962.

Hardin, Richard F. "'Ritual' in Recent Criticism: The Elusive Sense of Community." *PMLA* 98/5 (October 1983): 846-60.

Hays, Michael. "Declassified Documents: Fragmentations in the Modern Drama." *Boundary 2* 17/2 (Summer 1990): 102-28.

Hepburn, Kenneth Wm. "Faulkner's *Mosquitoes*: A Poetic Turning Point." *Twentieth Century Literature* 17/1 (1971): 19-28.

Herrnstein-Smith, Barbara. "Narrative Versions, Narrative Theories." *Critical Inquiry* 7/1 (1980): 213-36.

Hoffman, Daniel. "Faulkner's 'Was' and 'Uncle Adam's Cow'," In *Faulkner and Humor*, edited by Doreen Fowler and Ann J. Abadie. Jackson: University of Mississippi Press, 1986.

Holland, Laurence. "A 'Raft of Trouble': Word and Deed in *Huckleberry Finn*." In *American Realism*, edited by Eric Sundquist, 66-81. Baltimore: Johns Hopkins University Press, 1982.

Husserl, Edmund. *Ideas*. Translated by W. R. Boyce Gibson. New York: Colliers, 1962.

Irwin, John T. *Doubling and Incest/Repetition and Revenge*. Baltimore: Johns Hopkins University Press, 1975.

Iser, Wolfgang. "Feigning in Fiction." In *Identity of the Literary Text*, edited by Mario J. Valdes and Owen Miller, 204-228. Toronto: University of Toronto Press, 1985.

—. "Fictionalizing: The Anthropological Dimension of Literary Fictions." *New Literary History* 21/4 (Autumn 1990): 939-56.

—. *Prospecting: From Reader Response to Literary Anthropology*. Baltimore: Johns Hopkins University Press, 1989.

James, Henry. *The American*. Edited by James W. Tuttleton. New York: W. W. Norton, 1978.

Jameson, Fredric. *The Political Unconscious*. Ithaca: Cornell University Press, 1981.

Jehlen, Myra. *Class and Character in Faulkner's South*. Secaucus: Citadel Press, 1978.

Kant, Immanual. *Critique of Judgment*. Translated by J. H. Bernard. New York: Hafner Publishing Co., 1951.

Kartiganer, Donald M. *The Fragile Thread: The Meaning of Form in Faulkner's Novels*. Amherst: University of Massachusetts Press, 1979.

Kawin, Bruce. "The Montage Element in Faulkner's Fiction." In *Faulkner, Modernism, and Film*, edited by Evans Harrington and Doreen Fowler, 103-26. Jackson: University of Mississippi Press, 1979.

Kennedy, Andrew K. *Dramatic Dialogue: The Duologue of Personal Encounter*. Cambridge: Cambridge University Press, 1983.

Kermode, Frank. *The Sense of an Ending: Studies in the Theory of Fiction*. New York: Oxford University Press, 1967.

Kinney, Arthur F. "Faulkner and the Possibilities of Heroism." *Southern Review* 6 (Autumn 1970): 1110-25.

Lacan, Jacques. *Ecrits: A Selection*. Translated by Alan Sheridan. New York: W. W. Norton & Co., 1977.

La Fontaine, J. S. *Initiation*. Manchester: Manchester University Press, 1986.

—. "Person and Individual: Some Anthropological Reflections." In *The Category of the Person*, edited by Michael Carrithers, et.al., 123-40. Cambridge: Cambridge University Press, 1985.

Lenz, Guenter H. "'Ethnographies': American Culture Studies and Postmodern Anthropology." *Prospects: An Annual of American Cultural Studies* 16 (1991): 1-40.

Lipsitz, George. "Listening to Learn and Learning to Listen: Popular Culture, Cultural Theory, and American Studies." *American Quarterly* 42/4 (December 1990): 615-36.

Lyotard, Jean-Francois. *The Differend: Phrases in Dispute.* Translated by Georges Van Den Abbeele. Minneapolis: University of Minnesota Press, 1988.

Matthews, John T. "The Elliptical Nature of *Sanctuary.*" *Novel* 17/3 (1984): 246-65.

——. *The Play of Faulkner's Language.* Ithaca: Cornell University Press, 1982.

Mauss, Marcel. *The Gift.* Translated by Ian Cunnison. New York: W. W. Norton, 1967.

McIntyre, Allan J. "Drama as Rite: R. J. Sorge's *Odysseus.*" *German Quarterly* 50: 32-37.

Meriwether, James B. and Michael Milgate, editors. *Lion in the Garden.* New York: Random House, 1968.

Messenger, Christian. *Sport and the Spirit of Play in Contemporary American Fiction.* New York: Columbia University Press, 1990.

Minter, David. *William Faulkner: His Life and Work.* Baltimore: Johns Hopkins University Press, 1980.

Moore, Sally Falk and Barbara Myerhoff, editors. *Secular Ritual.* Leyden: Van Gorcum, 1977.

Moore, Winfred B. Jr., Joseph F. Tripp, and Lyon G. Tyler, Jr., editors. *Developing Dixie: Modernization in a Traditional Society.* Contributions in American History 127. New York: Greenwood Press, 1988.

Moreland, Richard C. "Compulsive and Revisionary Repetition: Faulkner's 'Barn Burning' and the Craft of Writing Difference." In *Faulkner and the Craft of Fiction*, edited by Doreen Fowler and Ann Abadie, 48-70. Faulkner and Yoknapatawpha 1987. Jackson: University of Mississippi Press, 1989.

——. *Faulkner and Modernism: Rereading and Rewriting.* Madison: University of Wisconsin Press, 1990.

Morgan, Sophia S. "Borges's 'Immortal': Metaritual, Metaliterature, Metaperformance." In *Rite, Drama, Festival, Spectacle*, edited by John J. MacAloon, 79-101. Philadelphia: Institute for the Study of Human Issues, 1984.

Napier, A. David. *Foreign Bodies: Performance, Art, and Symbolic Anthropology.* Berkeley: University of California Press, 1992.

—. *Masks, Transformation, and Paradox*. Berkeley: University of California Press, 1986.

Ong, Walter J. *Interfaces of the Word: Studies in the Evolution of Consciousness and Culture*. Ithaca: Cornell University Press, 1977.

—. *Orality and Literacy*. London: Methuen Books, 1982.

Opie, Iona and Peter. *The Classic Fairy Tales*. London: Oxford University Press, 1974.

O'Connor, William. *The Tangled Fire of William Faulkner*. Minneapolis: University of Minnesota Press, 1954.

Parker, William N. "The South in the National Economy, 1865-1970." *Southern Economic Journal* 46/4 (April 1980): 1019-48.

Pavel, Thomas G. "Incomplete Worlds, Ritual Emotions." *Philosophy and Literature* 7 (1983): 48-58.

Poe, Edgar Allen. *The Complete Poems and Stories of Edgar Allen Poe*. New York: A. A. Knopf, 1946.

Raybin, David. "Aesthetics, Romance, and Turner." In *Victor Turner and the Construction of Cultural Criticism*, edited by Kathleen M. Ashley, 21-41. Bloomington: Indiana University Press, 1990.

Ricoeur, Paul. "The Text as Dynamic Identity." In *Identity of the Literary Text*, edited by Mario J. Valdes and Owen Miller, 175-86. Toronto: University of Toronto Press, 1985.

Riffaterre, Michael. "Generating Lautremont's Text." In *Textual Strategies*, edited by Josue V. Harari, 404-20. Ithaca: Cornell University Press, 1979.

Rimmon-Kenan, Shlomith. "How the Model Neglects the Medium: Linguistics, Language, and the Crisis of Narratology." *Journal of Narrative Technique* 19/1 (Winter 1989): 157-66.

Rosenblatt, Paul C., R. Patricia Walsh, and Douglas A. Jackson, editors. *Grief and Mourning in Cross Cultural Perspective*. New Haven: HRAF Press, 1976.

Rosmarin, Adena. *The Power of Genre*. Minneapolis: University of Minnesota Press, 1985.

Ross, Stephen W. "Rev. Shegog's Powerful Voice." *Faulkner Journal* 1/1 (Fall 1985): 8-16.

Rothman, Ellen K. *Hands and Hearts: A History of Courtship in America*. New York: Basic Books, 1984.

Rowe, John Carlos. "Modern Art and the Invention of Postmodern Capital." *American Quarterly* 39/1 (Spring 1987): 155-73.

Ruby, Jay, editor. *A Crack in the Mirror: Reflexive Perspectives in Anthropology*. Philadelphia: University of Pennsylvania Press, 1982.

Schmitz, Neil. *Of Huck and Alice: Humorous Writing in American Literature*. Minneapolis: University of Minnesota Press, 1983.

—. "Tall Tale, Tall Talk: Pursuing the Lie in Jacksonian Literature." *American Literature* 48/4 (January 1977): 471-91.

Schneider, David M. *American Kinship: A Cultural Account*. Second Edition. Chicago: University of Chicago Press, 1980.

Scott, Anne Firor. *The Southern Lady: From Pedestal to Politics 1830-1930*. Chicago: University of Chicago Press, 1970.

Sensibar, Judith. *The Origins of Faulkner's Art*. Austin: University of Texas Press, 1984.

Shell, Marc. *Money, Language, and Thought*. Berkeley: University of California Press, 1982.

Silko, Leslie Marmon. *Ceremony*. New York: Penguin Books, 1977.

Silverman, Kaja. *The Subject of Semiotics*. New York: Oxford University Press, 1983.

Slatoff, Walter J. "The Edge of Order: The Pattern of Faulkner's Rhetoric." *Twentieth Century Literature* (October 1957): 107-27.

Smith, Paul. *Discerning the Subject*. Minneapolis: University of Minnesota Press, 1988.

Stowe, Steven M. *Intimacy and Power in the Old South: Ritual in the Lives of the Planters*. Baltimore: Johns Hopkins University Press, 1987.

Sundquist, Eric. *William Faulkner: The House Divided*. Baltimore: Johns Hopkins University Press, 1983.

Szondi, Peter. *Theory of the Modern Drama*. Translated by Michael Hays. Theory and History of Literature, Vol. 29. Minneapolis: University of Minnesota Press, 1987.

Tedlock, Dennis. "The Analogical Tradition and the Emergence of Dialogical Anthropology." *Journal of Anthropological Research* 35 (1979): 387-400.

—. *The Spoken Word and the Work of Interpretation*. Philadelphia: University of Pennsylvania Press, 1983.

Tindall, George Brown. *The Emergence of the New South 1913-1945*. Baton Rouge: Louisiana State University Press, 1957.

Toles, George. "The Space Between: A Study of Faulkner's *Sanctuary*." *Texas Studies in Literature and Language* 22/1 (Spring 1980): 22-47.

Turner, Victor. *Dramas, Fields, and Metaphors*. Ithaca: Cornell University Press, 1974.

—. "Dramatic Ritual/Ritual Drama: Performative and Reflexive Anthropology." *Kenyon Review* 1 (1979): 80-93.

—. "Frame, Flow, and Reflection: Ritual and Drama as Public Liminality." In *Performance in Postmodern Culture*, edited by Michel Benamou and Charles Caramello. Madison: University of Wisconsin Press, 1977.

—. "Liminality and the Performative Genres." In *Rite, Drama, Festival, Spectacle*, edited by John J. MacAloon, 19-41. Philadelphia: ISHI, 1984.

—. *On the Edge of the Bush: Anthropology as Experience*. Edited by Edith L. B. Turner. Tuscon: University of Arizona Press, 1985.

—. "Social Dramas and Stories About Them." In *On Narrative*, edited by W. J. T. Mitchell, 137-64. Chicago: University of Chicago Press, 1981.

—. *The Forest of Symbols*. Ithaca: Cornell University Press, 1967.

—. "Variations on a Theme of Liminality." In *Secular Ritual*, edited by Sally Moore and Barbara Myerhoff, 36-52. Leyden: Van Gorcum, 1977.

Tyler, Stephen A. "Post-Modern Ethnography: From Document of the Occult to Occult Document." In *Writing Culture: The Poetics and Politics of Ethnography*, edited by James Clifford and George E. Marcus, 122-40. Berkeley: University of California Press, 1986.

Vaihinger, Hans. *The Philosophy of 'As If'*. Translated by C. K. Ogden. London: Lund Humphries, 1924.

Van Gennep, Arnold. *The Rites of Passage*. Translated by Monika Vizedom and Gabrielle Caffe. Chicago: University of Chicago Press, 1960.

Vickery, Olga. *The Novels of William Faulkner*. Baton Rouge: Louisiana State University Press, 1964.

Wadlington, Warwick. *Reading Faulknerian Tragedy*. Ithaca: Cornell University Press, 1987.

Wagner, Roy. *The Invention of Culture*. Revised and Expanded Edition. Chicago: University of Chicago Press, 1981.

—. *Symbols that Stand for Themselves*. Chicago: University of Chicago Press, 1986.

Warner, W. L. *The Living and the Dead*. New Haven: Yale University Press, 1959.

Watson, James, G. "Faulkner: Short Story Structures and Reflexive Forms." *Mosaic* 4 (1978): 127-37.

—. "New Orleans, *The Double Dealer*, and 'New Orleans'." *American Literature* 56/2 (May 1984): 214-26.

Webb, James W. and A. Wigfall Green, editors. *William Faulkner of Oxford*. Baton Rouge: Louisiana State University Press, 1965.

Williams, Jack Kenny. *Dueling in the Old South: Vignettes of Social History*. College Station TX: Texas A&M Press, 1980.

Wittenberg, Judith. *William Faulkner: The Transfiguration of Biography*. Lincoln: University of Nebraska Press, 1979.

Woodman, Harold D. "Economic Reconstruction and the Rise of the New South, 1865-1900." In *Interpreting Southern History*, edited by John B. Boles and Evelyn Thomas Nolan, 254-307. Baton Rouge: Louisiana State University Press, 1964.

Wyatt-Brown, Bertram. *Southern Honor: Ethics and Behavior in the Old South*. New York: Oxford University Press, 1982.

Yates, Gayle Graham. *Mississippi Mind: A Personal Cultural History of an American State*. Knoxville: University of Tennessee Press, 1990.

Zender, Karl F. "Faulkner and the Power of Sound." *PMLA* 99 (January 1984): 89-108.

Index

About the author

CHRISTOPHER A. LALONDE received his bachelor's degree from Cornell College of Iowa and both his master's and doctorate degrees from the State University of New York at Buffalo. LaLonde has published a number of articles on Faulkner and is currently an associate professor of English at North Carolina Wesleyan College in Rocky Mount.

William Faulkner and the Rites of Passage
 by Christopher A. LaLonde

Mercer University Press, Macon, Georgia 31210-3960.
ISBN 0-86554-482-4. Catalog and wh pick number MUP/H378.
Text and interior design, composition, and layout by Jon Parrish Peede.
Front cover photograph by arrangement with Eyd Charles Kazery.
Camera-copy pages composed on a Magnavox 486 via Wordperfect
    5.1/5.2 and printed on HP Laserjet 4/4M.
Text font: TimesNewRoman Postscript 11/10/9-point.
Printed in the United States of America.